Refining Milestone Mass Communications Theories for the 21st Century

The 'Milestones' essays in *Mass Communication and Society* are reflective and analytical articles by the most notable scholars in the field. These classic essays address 21st century issues from the pioneers of media and communication studies, including Elihu Katz on new media and social movements, George Gerbner on cultivation analysis, and Dietram Scheufele on political communication. As technologies evolve and mass communication becomes mobile and democratized – more individual and also more social – these landmark scholars provide ideas about how established theories may be applied in new ways, and how future research can expand our understanding of mass communication as its reach and effects grow ever more complex. This book will be essential reading for both students and researchers of mass communications research.

This book was originally published as various issues of *Mass Communication and Society*.

Ran Wei is the Gonzales Brothers Professor of Journalism at the University of South Carolina, USA, and current Editor-in-Chief of *Mass Communication and Society*. His research focuses on mobile communication, new media, and the processes and effects of media messages in various contexts (political, social, promotional, health, and risk) that involve a wide range of media channels and devices, both traditional and emerging. He is a pioneering scholar in mobile communication research, and currently serves on the editorial board of *Mobile Media & Communication*.

Refining Milestone Mass Communications Theories for the 21st Century

Edited by
Ran Wei

LONDON AND NEW YORK

First published 2016
by Routledge
2 Park Square, Milton Park, Abingdon, Oxon, OX14 4RN, UK

and by Routledge
711 Third Avenue, New York, NY 10017, USA

Routledge is an imprint of the Taylor & Francis Group, an informa business

© 2016 Mass Communication & Society Division of the Association for Education in Journalism and Mass Communication

All rights reserved. No part of this book may be reprinted or reproduced or utilised in any form or by any electronic, mechanical, or other means, now known or hereafter invented, including photocopying and recording, or in any information storage or retrieval system, without permission in writing from the publishers.

Trademark notice: Product or corporate names may be trademarks or registered trademarks, and are used only for identification and explanation without intent to infringe.

British Library Cataloguing in Publication Data
A catalogue record for this book is available from the British Library

ISBN 13: 978-1-138-93215-9

Typeset in Times New Roman
by RefineCatch Limited, Bungay, Suffolk

Publisher's Note
The publisher accepts responsibility for any inconsistencies that may have arisen during the conversion of this book from journal articles to book chapters, namely the possible inclusion of journal terminology.

Disclaimer
Every effort has been made to contact copyright holders for their permission to reprint material in this book. The publishers would be grateful to hear from any copyright holder who is not here acknowledged and will undertake to rectify any errors or omissions in future editions of this book.

Contents

Citation Information vii
Notes on Contributors xi

1. Introduction: Milestone Studies Define the Field 1
   Ran Wei

Part I: Classic Theories for the 21st Century

2. Back to the Street: When Media and Opinion Leave Home 6
   Elihu Katz

3. Cultivation Analysis: An Overview 16
   George Gerbner

4. Uses and Gratifications Theory in the 21st Century 36
   Thomas E. Ruggiero

5. Agenda-Setting, Priming, and Framing Revisited: Another Look at Cognitive Effects of Political Communication 71
   Dietram A. Scheufele

Part II: Enduring Research Streams

6. George Gallup and Ralph Nafziger: Pioneers of Audience Research 91
   Steven H. Chaffee

7. The Politics of Studying Media Violence: Reflections 30 Years After The Violence Commission 102
   Sandra J. Ball-Rokeach

8. Children and Media: On Growth and Gaps 118
   Ellen Wartella

CONTENTS

Part III: Reflections and Future Directions

9. Where Have All the Milestones Gone? The Decline of Significant Research on the Process and Effects of Mass Communication   126
   Melvin L. DeFleur

10. The End of Mass Communication?   140
    Steven H. Chaffee and Miriam J. Metzger

11. Reevaluating "The End of Mass Communication?"   155
    Gabriel Weimann, Nirit Weiss-Blatt, Germaw Mengistu, Maya Mazor Tregerman, and Ravid Oren

12. Shifting Paradigms: Decentering the Discourse of Mass Communication Research   182
    Hanno Hardt

Index   191

Citation Information

The chapters in this book were originally published in various issues of *Mass Communication and Society*. When citing this material, please use the original page numbering for each article, as follows:

Chapter 2
Back to the Street: When Media and Opinion Leave Home
Elihu Katz
Mass Communication and Society, volume 17, issue 4 (July–August 2014) pp. 454–463

Chapter 3
Cultivation Analysis: An Overview
George Gerbner
Mass Communication and Society, volume 1, issues 3–4 (Summer–Fall 1998) pp. 175–194

Chapter 4
Uses and Gratifications Theory in the 21st Century
Thomas E. Ruggiero
Mass Communication and Society, volume 3, issue 1 (Winter 2000) pp. 3–37

Chapter 5
Agenda-Setting, Priming, and Framing Revisited: Another Look at Cognitive Effects of Political Communication
Dietram A. Scheufele
Mass Communication and Society, volume 3, issues 2–3 (Spring–Summer 2000) pp. 297–316

CITATION INFORMATION

Chapter 6
George Gallup and Ralph Nafziger: Pioneers of Audience Research
Steven H. Chaffee
Mass Communication and Society, volume 3, issues 2–3 (Spring–Summer 2000) pp. 317–327

Chapter 7
The Politics of Studying Media Violence: Reflections 30 Years After The Violence Commission
Sandra J. Ball-Rokeach
Mass Communication and Society, volume 4, issue 1 (Winter 2001) pp. 3–18

Chapter 8
Children and Media: On Growth and Gaps
Ellen Wartella
Mass Communication and Society, volume 2, issues 1–2 (Winter–Spring 1999) pp. 81–88

Chapter 9
Where Have All the Milestones Gone? The Decline of Significant Research on the Process and Effects of Mass Communication
Melvin L. DeFleur
Mass Communication and Society, volume 1, issues 1–2 (Winter–Spring 1998) pp. 85–98

Chapter 10
The End of Mass Communication?
Steven H. Chaffee and Miriam J. Metzger
Mass Communication and Society, volume 4, issue 4 (Fall 2001) pp. 365–379

Chapter 11
Reevaluating "The End of Mass Communication?"
Gabriel Weimann, Nirit Weiss-Blatt, Germaw Mengistu, Maya Mazor Tregerman, and Ravid Oren
Mass Communication and Society, volume 17, issue 6 (November–December 2014) pp. 803–829

CITATION INFORMATION

Chapter 12
Shifting Paradigms: Decentering the Discourse of Mass Communication Research
Hanno Hardt
Mass Communication and Society, volume 2, issues 3–4 (Summer–Fall 1999) pp. 175–183

For any permission-related enquiries please visit:
http://www.tandfonline.com/page/help/permissions

Notes on Contributors

Sandra J. Ball-Rokeach is a Professor of Communication in the Annenberg School for Communication at the University of Southern California, Los Angeles, CA, USA. She is also a principal investigator with the Southern California Injury Prevention Research Center, located in the School of Public Health at UCLA, Los Angeles, CA, USA.

Steven H. Chaffee was a highly regarded communication scholar and Janet M. Peck Professor Emeritus of International Communication at Stanford University, California, USA. He co-edited the popular graduate text, *Handbook of Communication Science*; edited *Communication Research*, a scholarly journal, for many years; and served as president of the International Communication Association.

Melvin L. DeFleur is a professor and renowned scholar in the field of Communications. He has taught at several universities in the United States, and is currently a Professor of Communication at Louisiana State University, LA, USA. He is on the Executive Board of the Center for Global Media Studies at Washington State University, Pullman, WA, USA, an organization whose motto, 'Global Media Cover the World . . . We Cover Global Media', connects with the focus of his recent work studying the accuracy of audience recall of news media in a cross-cultural vein.

George Gerbner was a Professor of Communication and the founder of Cultivation Theory. He taught at Temple University, Villanova University, and the University of Pennsylvania, Philadelphia, PA, USA. In 1990, he founded the Cultural Environment movement, an advocacy group promoting greater diversity in electronic media.

Hanno Hardt was Professor Emeritus in the School of Journalism and Mass Communication at the University of Iowa, Iowa City, IA, USA. His work addressed a wide range of issues in communication and media studies, from critical theory to class politics in the newsroom to visual rhetorics. He published

NOTES ON CONTRIBUTORS

nine books and numerous journal articles that garnered him international renown.

Elihu Katz is Distinguished Trustee Professor of Communication in the Annenberg School for Communication at the University of Pennsylvania, Philadelphia, PA, USA. He is a sociologist who has spent most of his lifetime in research on communication.

Maya Mazor Tregerman is a Ph.D. candidate in the Department of Communication at the University of Haifa, Israel. Her research interests include popular culture, the book publishing industry, and strategic communication.

Germaw Mengistu is a Ph.D. candidate in the Department of Communication at the University of Haifa, Israel. His research interests include media representation of minorities and immigration, journalism and nationalism.

Miriam J. Metzger is Associate Professor in the Department of Communication at the University of California–Santa Barbara, CA, USA. Her research interests lie at the intersection of media, information technology, and trust, centering on how information technology alters our understandings of credibility, privacy, and the processes of media effects.

Ravid Oren is a Ph.D. candidate in the Department of Communication at the University of Haifa, Israel. His research interests include journalism and culture, media discourse, popular culture, and strategic communication.

Thomas E. Ruggiero is Associate Professor of Communication, and Designer and Co-ordinator of the Multimedia Journalism Program at the University of Texas–El Paso, TX, USA. As a researcher, his interests include 'New Media' communication, media ethics, and intercultural media effects.

Dietram A. Scheufele is the John E. Ross Professor in Science Communication, and Vilas Distinguished Achievement Professor at the University of Wisconsin, Madison, WI, USA. He has published extensively in the areas of public and expert attitudes toward emerging technologies, including nanotechnology, synthetic biology, nuclear energy, and fracking. His most recent research examines the role of social media and other emerging modes of communication in society.

Ellen Wartella is Sheik Hamad bin Khalifa Al-Thani Professor of Communication, Professor of Psychology and Professor of Human Development and Social Policy at Northwestern University, Chicago, Illinois, USA. She researches the effects of media on children and adolescents, and the impact of food marketing in the childhood obesity crisis.

Ran Wei is the Gonzales Brothers Professor of Journalism at the University of South Carolina, USA, and current Editor-in-Chief of *Mass Communication* *and Society*. His research focuses on mobile communication, new media, and the processes and effects of media messages in various contexts (political, social, promotional, health, and risk) that involve a wide range of media channels and devices, both traditional and emerging. He is a pioneering scholar in mobile communication research, and currently serves on the editorial board of *Mobile Media & Communication*.

Gabriel Weimann is a former professor in the Department of Communication at the University of Haifa, Israel, and a former Senior Fellow at the Woodrow Wilson Center in Washington, DC, USA. His research interests include media effects, political campaigns, persuasion, and terrorism and the media.

Nirit Weiss-Blatt is a Ph.D. candidate in the Department of Communication at the University of Haifa, Israel. Her research interests include journalism and new media, blogs, big data, and information flow.

Introduction:
Milestones Studies Define the Field

Ran Wei
School of Journalism & Mass Communications
University of South Carolina

"To give faculty and students easy access to the latest ideas and thoughts of the top scholars in our field," wrote David Demers (1998, p.3), editor of *Mass Communication and Society* from 1998 to 2000, who introduced the Scholarly Milestones Essay in 1998. Highlighting established scholars writing about the current state of research in the field, the journal published two essays that year, from Melvin DeFleur (1998) and George Gerbner (1998), two prominent scholars and theorists.

According to my count, the feature has resulted in eight Milestones essays, including contributions from Ellen Wartella (1999), Sandra Ball-Rokeach (2001), and the late Steve Chaffee (2000), among others. These stand-alone essays crafted by the leading scholars in the field are thought-provoking; they served as a source of inspiration for young scholars as well as a valuable resource in graduate seminars across the country. The citations and downloads confirm those achievements.

Any discipline, whether it is hard sciences, economics, management, psychology, sociology or another area in social sciences, is built on the bedrock of fundamental theories and classic studies, i.e., "milestone" studies. One example from physics would be Galileo's experiment with falling objects at the Leaning Tower of Pisa. Landmark researchers who are associated with a theory, a model, or a study have lasting influence because their work explains an important aspect of the field and provides a foundation on which other researchers can build (Lowery & DeFleur, 1995). Sigmund Freud comes to mind for psychology; Max Weber and Robert E. Park are good examples in sociology. The Milestones essays stopped appearing in *Mass Communication and Society* during the early 2000s, but I resurrected the feature in 2014 when I became the journal's fifth editor.

Milestones are markers of the field; they offer a historic referent point, and I believe the feature "Scholarly Milestones Essay" is now a legacy of the journal. These essays define our field in terms of research focus, topical streams, and theoretical lenses to make sense of the communication phenomena in society. Even at a time when some forms of mass media are in decline, Milestone studies will continue to influence research for generations. My aspirational goal as editor of *Mass Communication and Society* is to publish work from inspiring authors and top scholars in the field to help other scholars draw on that work. I want the journal to serve as a forum for us to discuss the state of research and explore emerging trends to advance cutting-edge theory and further empirical research.

Some scholars have wondered whether 20th century mass communication theories can be applied in the emerging age of new communication technologies, global reach, and cultural revolutions in the digital 21st century. Teasing out the common issues and mastering the long-lasting theoretical constructs, which can apply to today's new realities and guide our current research, are a challenge for communication scholars. In responding to these challenges, this book presents a compilation of essays that show how the foundational theories remain relevant and vital to understanding the implications of digital media and social networking sites. Milestones essays have encompassed agenda-setting, framing, cultivation and uses and gratifications theories, among many others, and this book contains the seminal works from which researchers continue to build new extensions for the 21st century.

More recent contributions to the Milestones essays include the 2014 work by Elihu Katz, co-author with Paul Lazarsfeld of the 1955 classic on two-step flow theory, *Personal Influence: The Part Played by People in the Flow of Mass Communications*. In his "second retirement" from academic life, this Distinguished Trustee Professor of Communication continues to contribute to mass communications research and inspires scholars around the world. Katz's Milestones essay reflects on the effects of political communication, extending his research into the age of evolving new media and how this is enhancing deliberative democracy. Katz's essay is one example of how the classic theories of the 20th century remain as foundations for the digital age in the 21st century. "New" media always coincide with social change: print, radio, television, Internet, smartphones, streaming, and mobile technology. In the case of the fascinating and sometimes confusing effects of social media, the Katz essay provides a timely perspective to make sense of the evolution of new media in fostering and enhancing deliberative democracy. Both the long-range view essay and empirical studies of ongoing political events, I believe, contribute to the theorization of media effects in the digital age.

Melvin DeFleur's 1998 essay, "Where Have All the Milestones Gone? The Decline of Significant Research on the Process and Effects of Mass Communication" reminded us that mass communication research has been known to draw the best researchers and scholars into high-paying professions and away from the academy. We now know that with the transformation of traditional print media and the emergence of mobile media, academia is once again afforded new golden opportunities for teaching and research, which we haven't seen in decades. Steven Chaffee and Miriam Metzger (2001) touched on "The End of Mass Communication?" in their 2001 essay, which I include in this volume with another essay published in 2014 titled "Reevaluating 'The End of Mass Communication?'" by Gabriel Weimann, Nirit Weiss-Blatt, Germaw Mengistu, Maya Mazor Tregerman, and Ravid Oren (2014). The newer essay describes the development of several communications theories in the age of new media, such as agenda setting, audience effects, and the digital divide. The authors concluded that "old communication theories never die; they just readjust" (p. 174).

Other essays in this compilation comprise three general areas. The first is the overview or elaboration of a particular theory, such as George Gerbner's 1998 essay, "Cultivation Analysis: An Overview." This Milestones essay discusses how television viewing and cultural indicators will continue into the 21st century, and we have seen these effects evolve from Internet streaming, binge viewing, and on-demand television.

Thomas Ruggiero's synthesizing 2000 contribution, "Uses and Gratifications Theory in the 21st Century," is a foundational work that has been cited 289 times just since our journal went digital in 2009. Dietram Scheufele's 2000 essay on "Agenda-Setting, Priming, and Framing Revisited: Another Look at Cognitive Effects of Political Communication" created a new analytical model for these media effects theories, and has been cited 140 times in a short period of six years. Both Ruggiero and Scheufele provide insights into how research from the past confirms the application of such theories for future innovations. Essays such as these provide a head start for present-day researchers who focus on the effects of social and interactive media, as well as smartphones that provide instant access to television viewing and social networks for civic engagement and political mobilization.

The second area of this collection includes Milestones essays that define a particular research stream, such as Sandra Ball-Rokeach's 2001 contribution, "The Politics of Studying Media Violence: Reflections 30 Years After The Violence Commission." Ball-Rokeach addresses here the political forces that might intrude on new media research, as they did with her own work. She points out that violence in media still has an influence on audiences, and we have seen in the intervening years that media violence has only grown in availability of content and new platforms. Ellen Wartella's 1999 essay "Children and Media: On Growth and Gaps," reminds us how little research is performed on media programming for young people and she presents a useful developmental research model to aid in such research. In the age of infants' smartphone use and learning to read on tablets, this work provides a much needed foundation for addressing the gap between research, content production, and policy.

This book also contains reflections and critiques of the field, its research paradigms and its roots, such as Steven Chaffee's "George Gallup and Ralph Nafziger:

Pioneers of Audience Research," about the non-academic creators of research methods who showed us that opinions in numbers were "facts that carried their own messages" (p. 99). Hanno Hardt's 1999 essay, "Shifting Paradigms: Decentering the Discourse of Mass Communication Research," addresses the alternative discourses that challenge dominant ideology and media systems, returning communication to a participatory—even emancipatory—practice that embraces culture as well as the public. Furthering this line of argument, Elihu Katz's 2014 essay, "Back to the Street: When Media and Opinion Leave Home" addresses how 20th century mass media—newspapers, radio, and television—drove people inside their homes to consume them, while 21st century social media has served to mobilize audiences and to bring them "outside" again.

In the era of digital media, the field of mass communication faces a greater threat of further fragmentation (Weaver, 1988, 2000) due to emerging specialized subfields such as internet studies, political entertainment, and mobile communication, to name a few. I believe such a trend heightens the need for Milestone essays in mass communication research, which help us tease out common issues and focus on new insights based on the enduring theoretical constructs. Jeffres and his colleagues (2008) observed that in previous decades, mass communication scholars were "more adventuresome in advancing 'new' theories and less hesitant to 'create' theory." They noted that the 1970s in particular "bore witness to the emergence of several such theories—from the knowledge gap and agenda-setting to cultivation." The continued and fast-paced growth in the media industry provides us now with more, not less, opportunity to revive the "adventuresome" spirit in developing general media and social theories.

Milestones are not just markers of progress; they also point out new directions for travelers with a long journey ahead. The relatively young field of communication research has a long way to go to become a respectable discipline in social sciences. The Milestones essays included in this book enhance and extend valued theories that continue to prove their relevance and validity with ever-evolving digital and mobile media access. These essays represent expansive contributions to the field, and define topical areas for innovative systematic research in mass communications, whether in new media agendas, production, multi-screen media effects, cultural or social identity. These are the classics that not only stand the test of time, but continue to serve as foundations for research, technology, and civic engagements yet to come. It is my goal that readers will learn and be inspired to help us reach new milestones, which we will then publish in future issues of *Mass Communication and Society.*

Last, but not the least, I would thank Ms. Emily Ross, Editor, Routledge Special Issues as Books, who has been supportive of this edited volume. She acted promptly on the proposal and provided professional guidance on preparing the manuscripts. My editorial assistant at the University of South Carolina, Ms. Jane O'Boyle, has worked tirelessly with me on this book project from conception to production. The wisdom and experience in book publishing she brought to this book are exhibited in the pages of this volume. My thanks go to both.

REFERENCES

Ball-Rokeach, S. J. (2001). The politics of studying media violence: Reflections 30 years after the violence commission. *Mass Communication and Society,* 4(1), 3–18.

Chaffee, S. H. (2000). George Gallup and Ralph Nafziger: Pioneers of audience research. *Mass Communication and Society,* 3(2–3), 317–327.

Chaffee, S. H., & Metzger, M. J. (2001) The end of mass communication? *Mass Communication and Society,* 4(4), 365–379.

DeFleur, M. L. (1998). Where have all the milestones gone? The decline of significant research on the process and effects of mass communication. *Mass Communication and Society,* 1(1–2), 85–98.

Demers, D. (1998). Inaugural essay. *Mass Communication and Society,* 1(1–2), 1–4.

Ewan, S. (2000). Memoirs of a commodity fetishist. *Mass Communication and Society,* 3(4), 439–452.

Gerbner, G. (1998). Cultivation analysis: An overview. *Mass Communication and Society,* 1(3–4), 175–194.

Hardt, H. (1999). Shifting paradigms: Decentering the discourse of mass communication research. *Mass Communication and Society,* 2(3–4), 175–183.

Jeffres, L., Neuendorf, K., & Bracken, C. C. (2008). Integrating theoretical traditions in media effects: Using third-person effects to link agenda-setting and cultivation. *Mass Communication and Society,* 11, 470–491.

Katz, E. (2014). Back to the street: When media and opinion leave home. *Mass Communication and Society,* 4(1), 1–8.

Lowery, S. A., & DeFleur, M. L. (1995). *Milestones in mass communication research: Media effects. (3rd edition).* White Plains, NY: Longman.

Wartella, E. (1999). Children and media: On growth and gaps. *Mass Communication and Society,* 2(1–2), 81–88.

Weaver, D. H. (1988). Mass communication research: Problems and promises. In Nancy W. Sharp (Ed.), *Communications Research* (pp. 21–38). Syracuse, NY: Syracuse University Press.

Weaver, D. H. (2000). *Mass communication research at the end of the 20th century: Looking back and ahead.* Paper presented to the International Conference of School of Journalism and Communication, Chinese University of Hong Kong, Hong Kong.

Weimann, G., Weiss-Blatt, N., Mengisto, G., Tregerman, M. M., & Oren, R. (2104). Reevaluating 'The end of mass communication?' *Mass Communication and Society,* 17(6), 803–829.

Back to the Street: When Media and Opinion Leave Home

Elihu Katz
*The Annenberg School for Communication
University of Pennsylvania*

To achieve "deliberative democracy," Gabriel Tarde's formula not only demands the press hold a nation together, but also offers an agenda of issues that serves as a kind of menu for discussions in cafés and salons, which leads, in turn, to more considered opinions, and thus provides the consensual valuations that inform political, economic and aesthetic actions. The elements of the formula consist of press, conversation, opinion, and action. I argue that the long-run effect of the mainstream media—the newspaper, but even more the radio and television— moved politics off the street and into the home, hence the concern over "the narcotizing dysfunction" of the news media. In the era of the Internet, I argue that media—old or new, mass or social—are far from being the whole of the story. It is some combination of these media, plus word of mouth, plus some rather well-known elements of social-movement theory, plus the social psychology of collective behavior that help to explain. But let us not lose sight of the different functions served by the different media. If the mass media—newspapers, radio, and television—may be said to have moved people "inside," the social media, so called, serve to mobilize, and may bring them "outside," again.

Writing in Paris in 1898, in the wake of the Dreyfus Affair, Gabriel Tarde proposed that "publics" might be defined as "dispersed crowds" brought together by the newspaper. Tarde's writings on crowds, publics and other forms of "collective behavior" made a major contribution to early theorizing on communication by the Chicago School of sociology. Anticipating contemporary concern with so-called "deliberative democracy" some one hundred years later, Tarde outlined a formula whereby the press not only holds a nation together, but offers an agenda of issues that serves as a kind of menu for discussions in cafés and salons, which leads, in turn, to more considered opinions, and thus provides the kind of consensual valuations that inform political, economic and aesthetic actions. The elements of the formula consist of press, conversation, opinion, and action (Clark, 2011; Tarde, 1898).

The best part of Tarde's deliberative formula is that it is systemic; it connects the parts rather than treating them separately or in pairs. And, ecologically speaking, it follows people as they move in and out and around their natural habitats. Thus, Tarde's public moves people off the street and into their homes to read the newspaper. It moves them out again—to the café, the salon, the park, to deliberate; it moves them again to the ballot box or the marketplace. They are sometimes alone (as in reading the newspaper) and sometimes together (as in the café). Unfortunately, Tarde does not detail how opinion moves, as he assumes, from café and club to parliament or cabinet, but at least he shows us how public opinion is manufactured, how effective it is at the societal level, and, at the individual level, how it is acted upon. He argues, for example, that the newspaper has no influence unless it is talked about, and continues from there, rather than stopping short.

If I had to sum up the long-run effect of the mainstream media—the newspaper, but even more, the radio and television—I would argue that they moved politics off the street and into the home. Politics was conducted outside not only in the direct democracy of ancient Greece, but also in the demonstrations of 19th century America, according to Schudson (1998) and Brewin (2008). Putnam (1995), too, has reminded us of Tocqueville's discovery that the key to the practice of democracy in America was informal political conversation in presumably public places, and that this had all but disappeared in the era of media that keep people "inside." Echoing Habermas, Putnam's lament over the decline of deliberation in public is built, in part, on Gerbner (1976, 1998) who maintained that the perceptions of "reality" by viewers of television has displaced real reality, because viewers no longer go "outside" to see it and breathe it.

In their classic paper, Lazarsfeld and Merton (1948) named this phenomenon the "narcotizing dysfunction." They meant that even devotees of the news, not to speak of more casual audiences, deluded themselves into thinking that they were good citizens in their up-to-dateness. But the truth implicit in Lazarsfeld and Merton, is that people came home, had dinner, listened to the evening news, drank some beer, and went to sleep. Their attentiveness, and ostensible participation, failed to enter the policy-making process. Their presumed participation did not feed back into real political activity.

Ironically, the same thing may be said of so-called "deliberative democracy." These are much-studied focus groups who debate current events often with enthusiasm, but like the narcotized audiences of Lazarsfeld and Merton, their deliberations, however informed and participatory, do not make their way into the political system—not to political parties, not to parliament, not to government. They find their place in PhD dissertations in political science and communication, but that's not politics. Only opinion polling offers them voice.

There are exceptions, of course, if you believe them. Hallin and Mancini (1984), for example, tell us that things are different in Italy. Italians, they say, view the nightly news, get up from their TV sets, often irately, put on their overcoats and go the piazza to talk over what they have seen. From there, we are told, they make their way to the trade-union or to the local branch of their political party to demand political action. James Fishkin (2003) also claims that his "deliberative polls" produce change and that politicians listen. Herbst (1993) and Peters (1995) are not so sure.

Here again, we see Tarde's wisdom at work. It is not enough to be a faithful reader of the newspaper, or a persuasive discussant in a focus group. These elements of the system have to be connected to each other, and to make the ongoing connections to political action and policy making.

This is the place to suggest that if the mainstream media moved politics inside and kept them there, thus largely neutralizing opinion, perhaps the new media are moving politics outside again. Unlike the living-room media which isolate people in domesticity, the new media seem to energize their users. Like portable radio, the new media are mobile, but unlike portable radio—which plays the role of virtual companion—the new media, in all their variety, create networks of actual companionship. And, not least, these networks have cut themselves free, at least ostensibly, from control by establishments.

It is no surprise, therefore, that so many social scientists are rushing to consider whether to attribute the current uprisings—in the Arab world and elsewhere—to the diffusion of these new media. Jeffrey Alexander (2011) and Gadi Wolfsfeld et al. (2011) are prominent examples. Since I can hardly resist this temptation myself, I would like to try my hand by calling on the work of Dayan and Katz (1992) and on the idea I am developing here, of "inside" and "outside." Stated otherwise, I will try to connect the popular uprisings of the present to the argument that the effect of a medium might derive not only from knowledge of who owns it, or from its content, or from its technology (Katz, 2011) but from the way it "situates" its users, that is, where it contacts them (Freidson, 1953).

It is easy to agree that the new media—cell phone, internet, Facebook, Twitter, etc.—are *not* the place to begin. The starting point, obviously, is on the ground, in societies enduring combinations of economic deprivation and authoritarian rule. Calling this double deprivation into consciousness may well be attributable to the "window shopping" (Katz, 2010) afforded by the mainstream media, as they become more global and circumvent national control. The best example of this process at work is, of course, East Germany, which could not prevent peeking in on West German television with its display of material and political resources (Robinson, 1995). This sense of relative deprivation may be a starting point, but social movement theory (Gamson, 1993) suggests that two other ingredients are necessary before a movement takes off or an uprising explodes. One of these is the overcoming of so-called pluralistic ignorance, the other is a perception that change is achievable.

Pluralistic ignorance (Allport, 1924) describes a situation where each individual thinks that he is alone in his seemingly deviant perceptions. He is afraid to say what he thinks, until something happens to make him aware that many others think as he does. The Emperor's New Clothes wants to teach us that only the uninhibited child could proclaim the Emperor's nakedness, releasing the rest from their fears and misperceptions. The famous Asch experiment (1952; also see Katz, 1981) makes much the same point. This sudden revelation might apply just as well to episodes as varied as the mass "outing" of homosexuals following the Kinsey Report, or the standing-up to the Communist governments of Eastern Europeans. Outrageous examples of police brutality against an innocent protester—as was the case at the beginning of the Czechoslovakian uprising in 1989 (cf. Prevratil, 1995) and the Tunisian uprising in 2011—constitute "trigger events" of this kind. All of the media, not least word of mouth, seem to have a share in the diffusion of news of such outrages.

But even if the new media may also make an appearance at this point, they are not yet responsible for the mass mobilizations that follow. Theorists of social-movements posit that mass protest and expressive acting-out do not begin until an opportunity to achieve change is perceived to be available. Sometimes, this follows from what looks like contagion, that is, that it worked elsewhere—as happened in the spread of protest in Eastern Europe as the Soviets loosened their hold (Garton Ash, 1990; Jakubowicz, 1995). And it was true of the epidemic of rioting in U.S. cities in the '60s around issues of race and Vietnam (Soule, 2004). And the same thing seems to be true for the spread of protest in the Arab countries. The mainstream media probably were still the likely transmitters in these cases, but so were a cadre of leaders of relatively organized groups who saw their chance. These agents of change (Alexander calls them "carrier groups") were "internet-savvy young political organizers" who charted the places and the placards that defined the revolution. Ironically, Alexander suggests that these leaders disclaimed leadership for fear that the populist claim of "leaderlessness" might be discredited thereby.

Wolfsfeld et al. (2012) accept the likelihood that these agents of change deployed the new media, while showing, at the same time, that there is an inverse correlation between the *extent* to which the new media had penetrated in the different Arab countries and the intensity of the uprising. In other words, Wolfsfeld et al. are arguing that although the new media were not widely available at the onset of the uprisings they may well have been available to the ostensibly leaderless minority. Ironically, says Wolfsfeld, the more extensive the penetration of the new media in the 20 or so Arab states, the *less* the likelihood of an extremist uprising.

In short, we are arrived at a "stage (or phase) theory" of social movements, which posits a sequence of stages. To recapitulate, the first stage refers to the **objective** deprivation that prevails—often for a very long time. Stage two describes the self-conscious **realization** by individuals that they are deprived economically and politically; the global media do their work here. Stage three, also produced by the global media, is the discovery that many **others have similar thoughts.** Via word of mouth—usually in the wake of some act of brutality, sometimes self-inflicted—**dissident talk** is suddenly unleashed. The **resolution to act** can be attributed, once more, to the mainstream news and the pictures that show rebellion making headway elsewhere. This contagion—portraying riots or protests nearby or in similar places—proceeding from state to state or nation to nation—promises the possibility of success. The urban riots of the '60s in the U.S. can be shown to have diffused, by imitation, from city to city. Similarly, the uprisings in Eastern Europe in the late '80s can be attributed to the news that Soviets were losing their grip, and that there were incipient uprisings in country after country in the Soviet orbit. This also applies to the diffusion of protest such as the Occupy events. The next stage is the cabals of the young, intellectual leadership who employed the new media to concoct strategies for the **demonstrations**, in choosing symbolic locales (such as Tiananmen, Wenceslas, and Tahrir Squares) and strategic placements of people and placards and first-aid. This is the point at which the double meaning of "stage" becomes useful, in Dayan's idea of spectacle or in Alexander's sense of near-theatrical performance.

Mobilizing the masses to leave home and occupy the streets is the next stage, and it seems, again, that much of this was accomplished by word of mouth. In Lohmann's (1994) analysis of the demonstrations of East Germans in Leipzig in 1989-1991—what she calls "an information cascade"—she demonstrates, empirically, how people went into the streets not to follow radical extremists but only after recognizing that moderate activists like themselves were joining in.

The final stages are altogether unwritten, of course. Whether these uprisings have "somewhere to go" or not cannot easily be predicted. Following Garton Ash (1990) and the New York Times, Dayan and Katz (1992) point to the difference between the uprising in Czechoslovakia and Rumania. When the masses rallied in Wenceslas Square, they were met by establishment leaders—in the Square itself—who were prepared for debate, for compromise, for change. It is said that they harked back to the democratic tradition of the Czech republic prior to the Communist takeover. The Romanians, by contrast, rallied in the Square to heckle their erstwhile leader, Ceausescu, to drag him off the stage, to hold a kangaroo court against him and his wife, and to execute them. Unlike the Czechs, the Rumanian opposition was itself a military junta that commandeered the broadcasting station, shut off any real dialogue, and succeeded to authoritarian rule, at least for a while. There is no need even to mention the confrontation in Tiananmen Square. I hope it is obvious that we are not expert in these matters, not now, not then, but that it makes for a good comparative story—and a series of speculative hypotheses.

If accurate, this phase theory makes clear that media—old or new, mass or social—are far from being the whole of the story. It is some combination of these media, plus word of mouth, plus some rather well-known elements of social-movement theory, plus the social psychology of collective behavior that help to explain. But let us not lose sight of the different functions served by the different media. To repeat, we are suggesting that the social media—more than the mass media—may well contribute to the mobilization of protest outside the home. Stated otherwise, if the mass media—newspapers, radio and television—may be said to have moved people "inside," the social media, so called, may mobilize their users and bring them "outside," again. They can do this, we suspect, because of their "portability" and their person-to-person channels. Mobile telephones and even transistor radios belong in this group. The contrast between "portable" and "fixed" media is reminiscent of Innis (1951, 2008) "media of space" and "media of time," although it is ironic to analogize cellphones to papyrus, and television sets to pyramids!

Several obvious questions arise, in conclusion: (1) How to explain the revolutions that preceded the social media, and even the mainstream media?

(2) What role shall we attribute to the new media in these recent uprisings? (3) How did use of the media—new and mainstream—differ in the Western "uprisings"—which, after all, were atypical for living-room based societies? (4) And, finally, with all our intuitive admiration—true of many, or most, of us—are these uprisings something we want to see more of? Are we pleased that, finally, people are getting up from their TV sets and saying, "We're mad, and won't take this anymore" (Schorr, 1976).

The answer to the first question is easy. Long before there were social media, even before there was radio, there was Christianity (Stark, 2008), and there was Islam. These spread like wildfire by word of mouth, diffusing through social networks, abetted by preachers and armies. A much more recent example is the Khomeini revolution of 1979 in which a mix of leaflets, audio cassettes and a network of mosques and bazaars contributed to the overthrow of the Shah (Sreberny-Mohammadi & Mohammadi, 1994). Present-day interest in diffusion is, in part, a product of the ability of computers to deal with such networks of connections among very large numbers of peoples and places. Diffusion in modern societies may not be so different except for the wiring.

The answer to question two calls on the rather different arguments of Alexander and Wolfsfeld. The most explosive protests in the Arab world took place in countries that had very low penetration of new media. That the leaderless leadership of these movements had mastered these new media, and their revolutionary potential, seems clear. But the mass mobilization to join the protesters in the streets seems to have relied more on word of mouth than on new or old media, as Lohman's (1994) detailed analysis of the Leipzig demonstrations makes vivid. And, as has already been said, the initial steps that led from objective deprivation to consciousness of deprivation, and the liberation from pluralistic ignorance, are probably not attributable to the new media.

On the other hand, with reference to question three, in countries such as the U.S., Korea, and Israel—the proliferation of new media seem to have played a major role in mobilization, in recruiting masses to join, and even, as in the long Korean protest, to produce and broadcast material from the streets back into the homes.

Finally, with respect to question four, the easy answer is "No, I would not like to substitute crowds for publics." Of course, one would like to see publics participate in the making of enlightened policies. But the easy answer is not so easy if we recall the passivity of the public and the narcotizing dysfunction of the news media. One cannot call for more deliberative democracy without providing for "somewhere to go" (Katz, 2012). Otherwise, we are left with the old adage that the news is what elites say and what non-elites do. Enlightened democracies make room for "doings" such as getting up from the TV and declaring a strike (Rothenbuhler, 1990) or for other participatory demonstrations. Sometimes, as we have seen recently, ruling elites may even pay attention. But, on the whole, non-elite sayings (and even doings) are largely discounted. And there are only very few examples of irate viewers leaving home to "do" something. This is all very paradoxical since the mainstream media—certainly the publicly owned media—wish to situate their viewers as "citizens," while the social media situate their users as "friends" or "comrades." It is too early to tell, but the reverse may turn out to be more true, i.e., the mainstream media, following the commercial model, may ultimately situate us as "consumers," and the social media may yet mobilize us as "citizens."

For crowds rising against authoritarian regimes, one can only have sympathy. But here, there is even less of somewhere to go. Revolutions fade away without accomplishing real change, because their object is to overthrow. Crowds cannot create the institutional infrastructure of a stable society.

So, staying in won't accomplish much. Neither will going out. Together there might be progress, but only if there is somewhere further to go, some more established connection between informed public opinion and policy making.

NOTE

This paper is one of a set of three related papers: The others are Katz (2010) "Window Shopping" and Katz (2011) "Ownership, Content, Technology and Context in the Continuing Search for Media Effects."

ACKNOWLEDGEMENT

An earlier version of this paper was presented in 2011 at a conference in Sofia honoring Professor Daniel Dayan, and again at a conference in Beersheba honoring Professor Dan Caspi. It was originally published, together with other papers from the Dayan Conference, in *Divinatio* 35, Spring/Summer 2012 (Bulgaria). We are grateful to the Editor, Dr. Ivajlo Znepolski, and the publisher, for their permission.

REFERENCES

Alexander, J. (2011). *Performative revolution in Egypt: An essay in cultural power*. London, UK: Bloomsbury.

Allport, F. H. (1924). The group fallacy in relation to social science. *The Journal of Abnormal Psychology and Social Psychology, 19*(1), 60.

Asch, S. (1952). Effect of group pressure upon modification and distortion of judgments. In G. Swanson, T. Newcomb, & E. Hartley (Eds.), *Readings in social psychology*. New York, NY: Henry Holt.
Brewin, M. (2008). *Celebrating democracy: The mass-mediated ritual of election day*. New York, NY: Peter Lang.
Clark, T. (Ed.). (1969). *Gabriel Tarde on communication and social influence*. Chicago, IL: University of Chicago Press.
Dayan, D., & Katz, E. (1992). *Media events: The live broadcasting of history*. Cambridge, MA: Harvard University Press.
Fishkin, J., & Laslett, P. (2003). *Debating deliberative democracy*. Cambridge, UK: Blackwell.
Freidson, E. (1953). Relation of the social situation of contact to the media in mass communication. *Public Opinion Quarterly, 17*, 230–238.
Gamson, W., & Wolfsfeld, G. (1993). Movements and media as interacting systems. *Annals of the American Academy of Political and Social Science, 528*, 114–125.
Garton Ash, T. (1990). *The magic lantern: The revolutions of 1989 witnessed in Warsaw, Budapest, Berlin and Prague*. New York, NY: Random House.
Gerbner, G. (1998). Cultivation analysis: An overview. *Mass Communication and Society, 1*(3–4), 175–194.
Gerbner, G., & Gross, L. P. (1976). Living with television: The violence profile. *Journal of Communication, 26*(2), 173–199.
Hallin, D., & Mancini, P. (1984). Political structure and representational form in United States and Italian TV news. *Theory and Society, 13*(6), 829–859.
Herbst, S. (1993). *Numbered voices: How opinion polling has shaped American politics*. Chicago, IL: University of Chicago Press.
Innis, H. (1951, 2008). *The bias of communication*. Toronto, Canada: University of Toronto Press.
Jakubowicz, K. (1995). Media as agents of change. In D. Paletz, K. Jakubowicz, & P. Novosel (Eds.), *Glasnost and after: Media and change in Central and Eastern Europe* (pp. 19–48). Cresskill, NJ: Hampton Press.
Katz, E. (1981). Publicity and pluralistic ignorance: Notes on the spiral of silence. In Baier et al. (Eds.), *Public Opinion and Social Change*. Opladen, Germany: Westdeutscher Verlag.
Katz, E. (2011). Ownership, content, technology and context in the continuing search for media effects. In C. Salmon (Ed.), *Communication Yearbook 35*. Newbury Park, CA: Sage.
Katz, E. (in press). Nowhere to go: Some dilemmas of deliberative democracy. In K. H. Jamieson & K. Kenski (Eds.), *Oxford handbook of political communication*. New York, NY: Oxford University Press.
Katz, E. (in press). Window shopping. In C.C. Lee (Ed.), *Internationalizing International Communication*. Ann Arbor, MI: University of Michigan Press.
Lazarsfeld, P. F., & Merton, R. K. (1948). Mass communication, popular taste and organized social action. In L. Bryson (Ed.), *The communication of ideas*. New York, NY: Harper.
Lohmann, S. (1994). The dynamics of informational cascades: The Monday demonstrations in Leipzig, East Germany, 1989–1991. *World Politics, 47*(1), 42–101.
Peters, J. D. (1995). Historical tensions in the concept of public opinion. In T. L. Glasser & C. T. Salmon (Eds.), *Public opinion and the communication of consent*. New York, NY: The Guilford Press.
Prevratil, R. (1995). Czechoslovakia. In D. Paletz, K. Jakubowicz, & P. Novosel (Eds.), *Glasnost and after: Media and change in Central and Eastern Europe*. Cresskill, NJ: Hampton Press.
Putnam, R. (1995). Tuning in, tuning out: The strange disappearance of social capital in America. *PS: Political Science and Politics, 28*(4), 664–683.
Robinson, G. (1995). East Germany. In D. Paletz, K. Jakubowicz, & P. Novosel (Eds.), *Glasnost and after: Media and change in Central and Eastern Europe*. Cresskill, NJ: Hampton Press.

Rothenbuhler, E. (1990). "The liminal fight: Mass strikes as ritual and interpretation." In J. C. Alexander (Ed.), *Durkheimian sociology*. Cambridge, UK: Cambridge University Press.

Schorr, D. (1976, December 16). Review of film "Network." *Rolling Stone*.

Schudson, M. (1998). *The good citizen: A history of American civil life*. New York, NY: Free Press.

Soule, S. A. (2004). Diffusion processes within and across movements. In Snow, D. A., Soule, S. A. & H. Kriesi (Eds.), *The Blackwell companion to social movements* (pp. 294–310). Hoboken, NJ: John Wiley & Sons.

Sreberny-Mohammadi, A., & Mohammadi, A. (1994). *Small media, big revolution*. Minneapolis, MN: University of Minnesota Press.

Stark, R. (2008). *The rise of Christianity: How the obscure, marginal Jesus Movement became the dominant force in Western civilization*. Princeton, NJ: Princeton University Press.

Tarde, G. (1898/1989). L'opinion et la foule. Paris, France: Presses Universitaires de France. Excerpted in English in Clark, T. (1969/2011). *Gabriel Tarde on communication and social influence*. Chicago, IL: University of Chicago Press.

Wolfsfeld, G., Segev, E., & Shaeffer, T. (2012, August). *Role of the social media in the Arab Spring: Politics always comes first*. Paper presented at annual meeting of American Political Science Association, New Orleans, LA.

Cultivation Analysis: An Overview

George Gerbner
Bell Atlantic Professor of Telecommunications Temple University

If future historians wanted to know about the common cultural environment of stories and images into which a child was born in the second half of the 20th century, where would they turn? How would they describe its action structure, thematic content, and representation of people? How would they trace the ebb and flow of its currents? Pathetic to say, they would find no other source than our own Cultural Indicators database and reports.

Humans are the only species that lives in a world erected by the stories they tell. The storytelling process used to be handcrafted, homemade, and community inspired. Now it is the end result of a complex manufacturing and marketing process. The situation calls for a new diagnosis and a new prescription. That is what the Cultural Indicators and Cultivation research projects attempted to do.[1]

For the first time in human history, children are born into homes where mass-produced stories can reach them on the average of more than 7 hours a day. Most

---

[1] The Cultural Indicators Project began in 1967–1968 with a study for the National Commission on the Causes and Prevention of Violence. It continued under the sponsorships of the U.S. Surgeon General's Scientific Advisory Committee on Television and Social Behavior, the National Institute of Mental Health, The White House Office of Telecommunications Policy, the American Medical Association, the U.S. Administration on Aging, and the National Science Foundation. Cross-cultural comparative extensions of this work, involving long-planned international research coordination and co-operation, began in 1987 under a grant by the W. Alton Jones Foundation, and has continued with the support of the International Research and Exchanges Board, the Carter Center of Emory University, the Hoso Bunka Foundation of Japan, the Finnish Broadcasting Company, the Hungarian Institute for Public Opinion Research, Moscow State University, the National Center for Public Opinion Research of the USSR, the University of Pennsylvania, the University of Massachusetts, and the University of Delaware.

waking hours, and often dreams, are filled with these stories. The stories do not come from their families, schools, churches, neighborhoods, and often not even from their native countries, or, in fact, from anyone with anything relevant to tell. They come from a small group of distant conglomerates with something to sell.

The cultural environment in which we live becomes the byproduct of marketing. The historic nexus of state and church is replaced by the new symbiotic relationship of state and television. The "state" itself is the twin institution of elected public government and selected private corporate government, ruling in economic domains. Media, its cultural arm, are dominated by the private establishment, despite use of the public airways.

Giant industries discharge their messages into the mainstream of common consciousness. Channels proliferate and new technologies pervade home and office while mergers and bottom-line pressures shrink creative alternatives and reduce diversity of content.

Broadcasting is the most concentrated, homogenized, and globalized medium. The top 100 U.S. advertisers pay for two thirds of all network television. Four networks, allied to giant transnational corporations—our private "Ministry of Culture"—control the bulk of production and distribution and shape the cultural mainstream. Other interests, religious or educational, minority views, and the potential of any challenge to dominant perspectives, lose ground with every merger.

Formula-driven, assembly-line-produced programs increasingly dominate the airwaves. The formulas themselves reflect the structure of power that produces them and function to preserve and enhance that structure of power.

For the longest time in human history, stories were told only face to face. A community was defined by the rituals, mythologies, and imageries held in common. All useful knowledge was encapsulated in aphorisms and legends, proverbs and tales, and incantations and ceremonies. Writing was rare and holy, forbidden for slaves. Laboriously inscribed manuscripts conferred sacred power to their interpreters, the priests and ministers. State and church ruled in a symbiotic relationship of mutual dependence and tension. State, composed of feudal nobles, was the economic, military, and political order; church its cultural arm.

The industrial revolution changed all that. One of the first machines stamping out standardized artifacts was the printing press. Its product, the book, was a prerequisite for all the other upheavals to come. Printing began the industrialization of storytelling, arguably the most profound transformation in the humanization process.

When the printing press was hooked up to the steam engine, the industrialization of story-telling shifted into high gear. Rapid publication and mass transport created a new form of consciousness: modern mass publics. Publics are loose aggregations of people who share some common consciousness of how things work, what things are, and what ought to be done—but never meet face to face. That was never before possible.

Stories could be sent—often smuggled—across hitherto impenetrable or closely guarded boundaries of time, space, and status. The book lifts people from their traditional moorings as the industrial revolution uproots them from their local communities and cultures. They can now get off the land and go to work in far-away ports, factories, and continents, and have with them a packet of common consciousness—the book or journal, and later the motion picture (silent at first)—wherever they go.

Publics, created by such publication, are necessary for the formation of individual and group identities in the new urban environment, as the different classes and regional, religious, and ethnic groups try to maintain some sense of distinct integrity and also to live together with some degree of cooperation with other groups.

Publics are the basic units of self-government, originally called res-publica or rule by publics, a republic. They make it possible to elect or select representatives to an assembly trying to reconcile diverse interests. Most of our assumptions about human development and political plurality and choice are rooted in the print era.

The second great transformation, the electronic revolution, ushers in the telecommunications era. Its mainstream, television, is superimposed upon and reorganizes print-based culture. Unlike the industrial revolution, the new upheaval does not uproot people from their homes but transports them *in* their homes.

Television is the source of the most broadly-shared images and messages in history. It is the mainstream of the common symbolic environment into which our children are born and in which we all live out our lives. While channels proliferate, their contents concentrate. For most viewers, new types of delivery systems such as cable, satellite, and the Internet mean even deeper penetration and integration of the dominant patterns of images and messages into everyday life.

Our research project called Cultural Indicators, has tracked the central streams of television's dramatic content since 1967, and has explored the consequences of growing up and living with television since 1974.

TELEVISION IN SOCIETY

Television is a centralized system of story-telling. Its drama, commercials, news, and other programs bring a relatively coherent system of images and messages into every home. That system cultivates from infancy the predispositions and preferences that used to be acquired from other "primary" sources and that are so important in research on other media.

Transcending historic barriers of literacy and mobility, television has become the primary common source of socialization and everyday information (mostly in the form of entertainment) of otherwise heterogeneous populations. Many of those who now live with television have never before been part of a shared national culture. Television provides, perhaps for the first time since preindustrial religion, a daily ritual that elites share with many other publics. The heart of the analogy of television and religion, and the similarity of their social functions, lies in the continual repetition of patterns (myths, ideologies, "facts," relationships, etc.) which serve to define the world and legitimize the social order.

Television is different from other media also in its centralized mass-production of a coherent set of images and messages produced for total populations, and in its relatively non-selective, almost ritualistic, use by most viewers. Exposure to the total pattern rather than only to specific genres or programs is what accounts for the historically new and distinct consequences of living with television: the cultivation of shared conceptions of reality among otherwise diverse publics.

Compared to other media, television provides a relatively restricted set of choices for a virtually unrestricted variety of interests and publics. Most of its programs are by commercial necessity designed to be watched by large and heterogeneous audiences in a relatively nonselective fashion. Surveys show that the general amount of viewing follows the style of life of the viewer. The audience is always the group available at a certain time of the day, the week, and the season. Viewing decisions depend more on the clock than on the program. The number and variety of choices available to view when most viewers are available to watch is also limited by the fact that many programs designed for the same broad audience tend to be similar in their basic make-up and appeal.

In the typical U.S. home the television set is in use for more than seven hours a day. Actual viewing by persons over two years old averages more than three hours a day. And the more people watch the less selective they can be. Therefore, the most frequently recurring features of television that cut across all types of programming are inescapable for the regular viewer.

Various technological developments such as cable, VCR, and the Internet have contributed to a significant erosion in audience share (and revenue) for the major broadcasting networks and have altered the marketing and distribution of movies. However, there is no evidence that proliferation of channels has led to substantially greater diversity of content. On the contrary, rapid concentration and vertical integration in the media industries, the absorption of most publishing houses by electronic conglomerates, the growing practice of producing the same material for several media markets, and the habit of time-shifting by VCR users (recording favorite network programs to play back more often and at more convenient times), suggest that the diversity of what is actually viewed may even have decreased.

Given the tight links among the various industries involved in the production and distribution of electronic media content, and the fact that most of them are trying to attract the largest and most heterogeneous audience, the most popular program materials present consistent and complementary messages, often reproducing what has already proven to be profitable. Most of the variety we observe comes from novelty effects of styles, stars, and plots rather than from changes in program structure and perspective.

What is most likely to cultivate stable and common conceptions of reality is, therefore, the overall pattern of programming to which total communities are regularly exposed over long periods of time. That is the pattern of settings, casting, social typing, actions, and related outcomes that cuts across program types and viewing modes and defines the world of television. And that is also the pattern observed, coded, and recorded in the Cultural Indicators project.

Cultural Indicators is historically grounded, theoretically guided, and empirically supported (Gerbner, 1969, 1970, 1972a). Although most early efforts focused primarily on the nature and functions of television violence, the Cultural Indicators project was broadly conceived from the outset and took into account a wider range of topics, issues, and concerns. We have investigated the extent to which television viewing contributes to audience conceptions and actions in areas such as gender, minority and age-role stereotypes, health, science, the family, educational achievement and aspirations, politics, religion, and other topics.

The Cultural Indicators approach involves a three-pronged research strategy. (For a more detailed description, see Gerbner, 1973.) The first prong, called institutional process analysis, is designed to investigate the formation of policies directing the massive flow of media messages. (For some examples, see Gerbner, 1972b, 1988). More directly relevant to our present focus are the other two prongs we call message system analysis and cultivation analysis. Both relate to—and help develop—theories about the most subtle and widespread impacts of television.

In the second prong, we have since 1967 recorded annual week-long samples of U.S. network television drama (and samples in other cooperating countries, whenever possible) and subjected these systems of messages to content analysis in order to reliably delineate selected features and trends in the world television presents to its viewers.[2] We believe that the most pervasive patterns common to many different types of programs but characteristic of the system of programming hold the potential lessons television cultivates. We use these overarching patterns of content as a source of questions for the third prong, cultivation analysis.

In the third prong, we examine the responses given to questions about social reality among those with varying amounts of exposure to the world of television. (Non-viewers are too few and demographically too scattered for serious research purposes; Jackson-Beeck, 1977.) We want to determine whether those who spend more time with television are more likely to answer these

---

[2] The message system database accumulated detailed coded observations of over 26,000 characters and over 2,200 programs during the first two decades of its existence.

questions in ways that reflect the potential lessons of the television world (give the "television answer") than are those who watch less television but are otherwise comparable (in terms of important demographic characteristics) to the heavy viewers.

We have used the concept of "cultivation" to describe the independent contributions television viewing makes to viewer conceptions of social reality. The "cultivation differential" is the margin of difference in conceptions of reality between light and heavy viewers in the same demographic subgroups.

Our use of the term "cultivation" for television's contribution to conceptions of social reality is not just another word for "effects." Nor does it necessarily imply a one-way, monolithic process. The influences of a pervasive medium upon the composition and structure of the symbolic environment are subtle, complex, and intermingled with other influences. This perspective, therefore, assumes an interaction between the medium and its publics.

Thus, television neither simply "creates" nor "reflects" images, opinions, and beliefs. Rather, it is an integral aspect of a dynamic process. Institutional needs and objectives influence the creation and distribution of mass-produced messages which create, fit into, exploit, and sustain the needs, values, and ideologies of mass publics. These publics, in turn, acquire distinct identities as publics partly through exposure to the ongoing flow of messages.

The question of "which comes first" is misleading and irrelevant. People are born into a symbolic environment with television as its mainstream. Children begin viewing several years before they begin reading and well before they can even talk. Television viewing both shapes and is a stable part of lifestyles and outlooks. It links the individual to a larger if synthetic world, a world of television's own making.

When we talk about the "independent contribution" of television viewing, we mean that the development (in some) and maintenance (in others) of some set of outlooks or beliefs can be traced to steady, cumulative exposure to the world of television. Our longitudinal studies of adolescents (Gerbner, Gross, Morgan, & Signorielli, 1980; Morgan, 1982, 1987; Morgan, Alexander, Shanahan, & Harris, 1990) show that television can exert an independent influence on attitudes and behaviors over time, but that belief structures and concrete practices of daily life can also influence subsequent viewing.

The point is that cultivation is not conceived as a unidirectional but rather more like a gravitational process. The angle and direction of the "pull" depends on where groups of viewers and their styles of life are with reference to the line of gravity, or the "mainstream" of the world of television. Each group may strain in a different direction, but all groups are affected by the same central current. Cultivation is thus part of a continual, dynamic, ongoing process of interaction among messages and contexts. This holds even though (and in a sense because) the hallmark of the process, once television is established as the main cultural arm of a stable society, is either relative stability or only slow change. A radical change in social relations may, of course, lead to a change in the system of messages and consequently to the cultivation of new and different perspectives.

As successive generations grow up with television's version of the world, the former and more traditional distinctions established before the coming of television, and still maintained to some extent among light viewers, become blurred. Cultivation implies the steady entrenchment of mainstream orientations for most viewers. That process of apparent convergence of outlooks we call "mainstreaming."

METHODS OF CULTIVATION ANALYSIS

Cultivation analysis begins with message system analysis identifying the most recurrent, stable, and overarching patterns of television content. These are the consistent images, portrayals, and values that cut across most types of programs and are virtually inescapable for regular (and especially the heavy) viewers. They are the aggregate messages embedded in television as a system rather than in specific programs, types, or genres.

We must emphasize again that testing "cultivation" on the basis of program preferences, short-run exposures, or claims of program changes or diversity (all of which have been tried as "replications") may illuminate some media effects but does not address fundamental assumptions of cultivation theory. That is that only repetitive, long-range, and consistent exposure to patterns common to most programming, such as casting, social typing, and the "fate" of different social types, can be expected to cultivate stable and widely-shared images of life and society.

There are many critical discrepancies between the real world and the "world as portrayed on television." Findings from systematic analyses of television's message systems are used to formulate questions about the potential "lessons" of viewing concerning people's conceptions of social reality. Some of the questions are semi-projective, some use a forced-error format and others simply measure beliefs, opinions, attitudes, or behaviors. (None asks respondents' views about television itself.)

Using standard techniques of survey methodology, the questions are posed to samples (national probability, regional, convenience) of adults, adolescents, or children. Secondary analyses of large scale national surveys (for example, the National Opinion Research Center's General Social Surveys; NORC GSS) have often been used when they include questions that relate to potential "lessons" of the television world and viewing data are available for the respondents.

Television viewing is usually assessed by multiple indicators of the amount of time respondents watch television on an "average day." Since the amount of viewing is used in relative terms, the determination of what constitutes "light," "medium," and "heavy" viewing is made on a sample-by-sample basis, using as close to an even three-way split of hours of daily television viewing as possible. What is important is that there should be significant relative differences in viewing levels, not the actual or specific amount of viewing. The heaviest viewers of any sample of respondents form the population on which cultivation can be tested.[3]

The observable evidence of cultivation is likely to be modest in terms of absolute size. Even light viewers may be watching several hours of television a day and of course live in the same general culture as heavy viewers. Therefore, the discovery of a systematic pattern of even small but pervasive differences between light and heavy viewers may be of far-reaching consequence. It takes but a few degrees shift in the average temperature to have an ice age or global warming. A range of 3% to 15% margins (typical of our "cultivation differentials") in a large and otherwise stable field often signals a landslide, a market takeover, or an epidemic, and it certainly tips the scale of any closely balanced choice, vote, or other decision. A slight but pervasive (e.g., generational) shift in the cultivation of common perspectives may alter the cultural climate and upset the balance of social and political decision-making without necessarily changing observable behavior. A single percentage point rating difference in a large market is worth many millions of dollars in advertising revenue—as the networks know only too well.

VARIATIONS IN CULTIVATION

We have noted that cultivation is not a unidirectional flow of influence from television to audience, but part of a continual, dynamic, ongoing process of interaction among messages and contexts. In many cases, those who watch more television (the heavy viewers) are more likely—in all or most subgroups—to give the "television answers." But often the patterns are more complex.

Cultivation is both dependent on and a manifestation of the extent to which television's imagery dominates viewers' sources of information. For example, personal interaction makes a difference. Parental co-viewing patterns and orientations toward television can either increase (Gross & Morgan, 1985) or decrease (Rothschild & Morgan, 1987) cultivation among adolescents. Also, children who are more integrated into cohesive peer or family groups are more resistant to cultivation (Rothschild, 1984).

Direct experience also plays a role. The relationship between amount of viewing and fear of crime is strongest among those who live in high crime urban

---

[3] In all analyses I use a number of demographic variables as controls. These are applied both separately and simultaneously. Included are gender, age, race, education, income, and political self-designation (liberal, moderate, or conservative). Where applicable, other controls, such as urban or rural residence, newspaper reading, and party affiliation are also used.

areas. This is a phenomenon we have called "resonance," in which everyday reality and television provide a "double dose" of messages that "resonate" and amplify cultivation. The relationships between amount of viewing and the tendency to hold exaggerated perceptions of violence are also more pronounced within those real-world demographic subgroups (e.g., minorities) whose fictional counterparts are relatively more frequently victimized on television (Morgan, 1983).

There are many factors and processes that produce systematic and theoretically meaningful variations in cultivation patterns. One process, however, stands out, both as an indicator of differential vulnerability and as a general, consistent pattern representing one of the most profound consequences of living with television. That is the process of mainstreaming.

Mainstreaming

Most cultures consist of many diverse currents. But there is typically a dominant set of attitudes, beliefs, values, and practices. This dominant current is not simply the sum total of all the cross-currents and sub-currents. Rather, it is the most general, functional, and stable mainstream, representing the broadest dimensions of shared meanings and assumptions. It is that which ultimately defines all the other cross-currents and sub-currents, including what Williams (1977) called "residual and emergent strains." Television's central role in our society makes it the primary channel of the mainstream of our culture.

This mainstream can be thought of as a relative commonality of outlooks and values that heavy exposure to the television world tends to cultivate. "Mainstreaming" means that heavy viewing may absorb or override differences in perspectives and behavior which ordinarily stem from other factors and influences. In other words, differences found in the responses of different groups of viewers, differences that usually are associated with the varied cultural, social, and political characteristics of these groups, are diminished in the responses of heavy viewers in these same groups.

As a process, mainstreaming represents the theoretical elaboration and empirical verification of television's cultivation of common perspectives. It represents a relative homogenization, an absorption of divergent views, and an apparent convergence of disparate outlooks on the overarching patterns of the television world.

Figure 1 illustrates some of the different models of the cultivation process that emerge when subgroups are compared. In graph a, the subgroups show different baselines, but the associations are equivalent, and there is no interaction. Graphs b, c, and d show typical instances of mainstreaming, and imply that the light–heavy viewer differences need not point in the same direction or involve all subgroups. The pattern in graph e depicts the kind of interaction we call

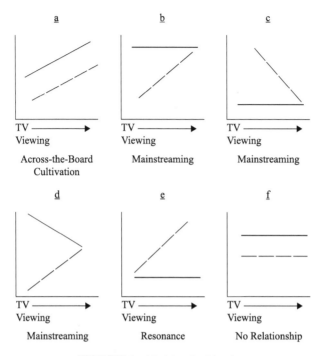

FIGURE 1 Models of cultivation.

resonance, and in graph f there are no relationships within any subgroup. Except for graph f, all these models reflect the cultivation process and relate to its center of gravity, the television mainstream.

The Findings of Cultivation Analysis

Clear-cut divergences between symbolic reality and independently observable ("objective") reality provide convenient tests of the extent to which television's versions of "the facts" are incorporated or absorbed into what heavy viewers take for granted about the world. For example, we found that television drama tends to sharply underrepresent older people. While those over 65 constitute the fastest growing segment of the real-world population in the United States, heavy viewers were more likely to feel that the elderly are a "vanishing breed"—that compared to 20 years ago there are fewer of them, that they are in worse health, and that they do not live as long—all contrary to fact (Gerbner, Gross, Signorielli, & Morgan, 1980).

As another example, consider how likely television characters are to encounter violence compared to the rest of us. Well over half of all major characters on television are involved each week in some kind of violent action. While the FBI statistics have clear limitations, they indicate that in any year less than 1% of people in the United States are victims of criminal violence. We have found considerable support for the proposition that heavy exposure to the world of television cultivates exaggerated perceptions of the number of people involved in violence in any given week (Gerbner, Gross, Morgan, et al., 1980; Gerbner, Gross, Signorielli, Morgan, & Jackson-Beeck, 1979), as well as numerous other inaccurate beliefs about crime and law enforcement.

The "facts" of the television world are evidently learned quite well, whether or not viewers profess a belief in what they see on television or claim to be able to distinguish between factual and fictional presentations. (In fact, most of what we know, or think we know, is a mixture of all the stories we have absorbed. "Factual," which may be highly selective, and "fictional," which may be highly realistic, are more questions of style than function within a total framework of knowledge.) The repetitive "lessons" we learn from television, beginning with infancy, are likely to become the basis for a broader world view, making television a significant source of general values, ideologies, and perspectives as well as specific assumptions, beliefs, and images. Hawkins and Pingree (1982) called this the cultivation of "value systems." (See also Hawkins & Pingree, 1990.)

One example of this is the "mean world syndrome." Our message data say little directly about either the selfishness or altruism of people, and there are certainly no real-world statistics about the extent to which people can be trusted. Yet, I have found that long-term exposure to television, in which frequent violence is virtually inescapable, tends to cultivate the image of a relatively mean and dangerous world. Responses of heavier compared to matching groups of lighter viewers suggest the conception of reality in which greater protection is needed, most people "cannot be trusted," and most people are "just looking out for themselves" (Gerbner, Gross, Morgan, et al., 1980; Signorielli, 1990b).

The Mean World Index, composed of violence-related items, also illustrates the mainstreaming implications of viewing (Signorielli, 1990b). For example, combining data from the 1980, 1983, and 1986 NORC GSSs, heavy and light viewers who have not been to college are equally likely to score high on the Mean World Index: 53% of both the heavy and light viewers agree with two or three of the items. However, among those who have had some college education, television viewing makes a considerable difference: 28% of the light viewers compared to 43% of the heavy viewers in this subgroup have a high score on the Mean World Index. There is thus a 25-percentage point difference between the two subgroups of light viewers but only a 10-point spread between the two subgroups of heavy viewers. The heavy viewers of otherwise different groups are both in the "television mainstream."

Another example of extrapolated assumptions relates to the image of women. The dominant majority status of men on television does not mean that heavy viewers ignore daily experience and underestimate the number of women in society. But underrepresentation in the world of television means a relatively narrow (and thus more stereotyped) range of roles and activities. Most groups of heavy viewers—with other characteristics held constant—score higher on a "sexism scale" using data from the NORC GSSs (Signorielli, 1989).

Several other studies have examined assumptions relating to gender-roles in samples of children and adolescents. Morgan (1982) found that television cultivated such notions as "women are happiest at home raising children" and "men are born with more ambition than women." Rothschild (1984) found that third- and fifth-grade children who watched more television were more likely to stereotype both gender-related activities (e.g., cooking, playing sports) and gender-related qualities (e.g., warmth, independence) along traditional gender role lines. While viewing seems to cultivate adolescents' and children's attitudes about gender-related chores, viewing was not related to actually doing these chores (Morgan, 1987; Signorielli & Lears, 1991).

Other studies have dealt with assumptions about marriage and work. Signorielli (1990a) found that television seems to cultivate rather realistic views about marriage but seemingly contradictory views about work. Heavy viewing adolescents were more likely to want high status jobs that would give them a chance to earn a lot of money but also wanted to have their jobs be relatively easy with long vacations and time to do other things.

Other extrapolations from content patterns involve political views. For example, we have argued that as television seeks large and heterogeneous audiences, its messages are designed to disturb as few as possible. Therefore, they tend to "balance" opposing perspectives, and to steer a "middle course" along the supposedly non-ideological mainstream. We have found that heavy viewers are substantially more likely to label themselves as being "moderate" rather than either "liberal" or "conservative" (see Gerbner, Gross, Morgan, & Signorielli, 1982, 1984).

We have observed this finding in many years of the NORC GSS data. NORC GSS data from 1990 reveal this pattern once again, as shown in Table 1. Heavy viewers in all subgroups tend to see themselves as "moderate" and avoid saying they are either "liberal" or "conservative." Figure 2 shows the patterns for Democrats, Independents, and Republicans. The percentage choosing the "moderate" label is again substantially higher among heavy viewers, regardless of party; and heavy viewing Democrats are less likely to say they are "liberal," while heavy viewing Republicans are less likely to call themselves "conservative." The general pattern shown in these data has appeared every year since 1975.

Yet, looking at the actual positions taken on a number of political issues shows that the mainstream does not mean the "middle of the road." When we analyzed responses to questions in the NORC GSS about attitudes and opinions on such

TABLE 1
Television Viewing and Political Self-Designation in the 1990 General Social Survey

| | | % Who Call Themselves ||||||||||||
| | | Liberal |||| Moderate |||| Conservative ||||
TV Viewing	N	L	M	H	Gamma	L	M	H	Gamma	L	M	H	Gamma
Overall	885	28	29	25	−.04	33	35	45	.17	40	36	30	−.14
Men	394	24	31	23	−.03	32	32	43	.12*	42	37	34	−.09
Women	491	30	27	27	−.05	32	38	47	.20	38	35	27	−.17
Younger	203	38	27	21	−.26	30	38	47	.23	32	35	32	−.00
Middle	515	26	34	28	.05	32	34	42	.11*	42	32	30	−.16
Older	167	18	15	25	.21*	39	33	49	.19*	43	52	26	−.32
Low education	449	19	29	22	−.00	42	39	49	.12*	39	32	29	−.13*
High education	435	33	30	31	−.04	27	31	38	.15	40	39	31	−.11*
Low income	368	27	26	22	−.08	34	35	49	.21	39	39	29	−.16
High income	433	31	31	28	−.04	30	34	40	.13*	39	35	33	−.09
Democrats	320	42	36	33	−.11	33	38	45	.15	25	26	22	−.06
Independents	268	25	31	22	−.04	44	42	58	.18	32	28	20	−.19
Republicans	287	18	20	17	−.00	24	25	32	.13	59	55	51	−.10

Note. L = light viewing (1 hr or less daily); M = medium viewing (2–3 hr daily); H = heavy viewing (4 hr or more daily); younger = 18 to 30 years old; middle = 31 to 64 years old; older = 65 years or older; low education = 12 or fewer years (no college); high education = 13 years or more (at least some college); low income = less than $25,000 yearly; high income = $25,000 or more yearly.

* $p < .10$.

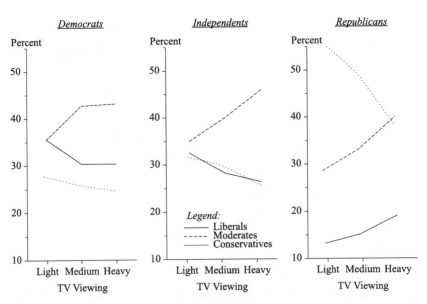

FIGURE 2 Comparisons on political self-designation by amount of television viewing within parties.

topics as racial segregation, homosexuality, abortion, minority rights, and other issues that have traditionally divided liberals and conservatives, we found such division mostly among those who watch little television. Overall, self-styled moderates are much closer to conservatives than they are to liberals. Among heavy viewers, liberals and conservatives are closer to each other than among light viewers. We have also noted (Gerbner et al., 1982, 1984) that while mainstreaming bends toward the right on political issues, it leans toward a populist stance on economic issues (e.g., demanding more social services but lower taxes), reflecting the influence of a marketing orientation and setting up potential conflicts of demands and expectations.

Implications of cultivation for foreign policy were reflected in a study of attitudes toward the war in the Persian Gulf (Lewis, Jhally, & Morgan, 1991). Heavy television viewers were more familiar with the military terminology used and more supportive of the war but less informed about issues and the Middle East in general. Overall amount of viewing was far more important than specific exposure to news.

International Cultivation Analysis

Cultivation analysis is well suited to multinational and cross-cultural comparative study (Gerbner, 1977, 1989; Morgan, 1990). In fact, such study is the best test of systemwide similarities and differences across national boundaries, and of the actual significance of national cultural policies.

Every country's television system reflects the historical, political, social, economic, and cultural contexts within which it has developed (Gerbner, 1958, 1969). Although U.S. films and television are a significant presence on the screens of most countries (Varis, 1984), they combine with local and other productions to compose synthetic "worlds" that are culture-specific. Other media systems and policies may or may not project images and portrayals that are as stable, coherent, and homogeneous as those of U.S. media (for example, as we have found, surprisingly, in the Soviet Union, as we will note below). Therefore, they may or may not lend themselves to the type of cultivation and mainstreaming we find in the United States (see Gerbner, 1990; Morgan, 1990; Tamborini & Choi, 1990).

International work in cultivation analysis attempts to answer the question of whether the medium or the system is the message. It reveals the extent to which, and the ways in which, each message system contributes to conceptions of social reality congruent with its most stable and recurrent messages and images. Of course, given the range of variations in susceptibility to cultivation even within the United States, there is no reason to assume that cultivation patterns will be identical or invariant across cultures.

Pingree and Hawkins (1981) found that exposure to U.S. programs (especially crime and adventure) was significantly related to Australian students' scores on

"Mean World" and "Violence in Society" indexes concerning Australia, but not the United States. Viewing Australian programs was unrelated to these conceptions, but those who watched more U.S. programs were more likely to see Australia as dangerous and mean. Weimann's (1984) study of high school and college students in Israel found that heavy viewers had an idealized, "rosier" image of the standard of living in the United States.

In England, Wober (1978) found little support for cultivation in terms of images of violence. (See also Gunter, 1987; Gunter & Furnham, 1984; Wober, 1984, 1990; Wober & Gunter, 1988). But there was little violence in British programs, and U.S. programs only made up about 15% of British screen time. Piepe, Charlton, and Morey (1990) found evidence of political "homogenization" (mainstreaming) in Britain that was highly congruent with U.S. findings (Gerbner et al., 1982), as did Morgan and Shanahan (1991) in Argentina.

In the Netherlands, Bouwman (1984) found weak associations between amount of viewing and perceptions of violence, victimization, and mistrust. But the findings reveal the importance of cultural context in comparative cultivation research. Content analyses showed a good deal of similarity between U.S. and Dutch television (Bouwman & Signorielli, 1985; Bouwman & Stappers, 1984) and much programming was imported from the United States. Yet, it was found that both light and heavy viewers see about equal amounts of fictional entertainment, but heavy viewers see more "informational" programs, a situation quite different from that in the United States (see also Bouwman, 1982; Stappers, 1984).

Cultivation analyses about conceptions of violence, sex-roles, political orientations, "traditional" values, social stereotypes, and other topics have been conducted in numerous other countries, including Sweden (Hedinsson & Windahl, 1984; Reimer & Rosengren, 1990), Argentina (Morgan & Shanahan, 1991), the Philippines (Tan, Tan, & Tan, 1987), Taiwan and Mexico (Tan, Li, & Simpson, 1986), Japan (Saito, 1991), and Thailand (Tan & Suarchavarat, 1988). These studies show the complex ways in which the viewing of local or imported programming can interact with distinct cultural contexts. For example, in Korea, Kang and Morgan (1988) found that exposure to U.S. television was associated with more "liberal" perspectives about gender-roles and family values among females. At the same time, more viewing of U.S. television among Korean male students correlated with greater hostility toward the United States and protectiveness toward Korean culture, suggesting a "backlash" of nationalism among the more politicized college students.

Most of these studies examined single countries. Comparative cross-cultural research typically requires complex joint development and collaboration. It takes longer, costs more, and is more difficult to fund. Nevertheless, recent research has begun to emphasize the comparative aspects of cultivation analysis. Morgan and Shanahan (1996) analyzed adolescents in Taiwan and Argentina. In Argentina, where television is supported by commercials and features many U.S. programs, heavy viewing cultivates traditional gender roles and authoritarianism. In Taiwan, where media are more state-controlled, with fewer U.S. imports, and where overall viewing is much lighter, cultivation was much less apparent. Also, Morgan (1990) compared the cultivation of sex-role stereotypes in five different countries.

Large-scale comparative cultivation analyses involving many countries were underway or planned in the early 1990s. One of the first to be concluded, a study of U.S. and Soviet television conducted in 1989 and 1990, found that television plays a different role in the two countries. In the United States, but not in the former Soviet Union, television heightens anxieties about neighborhood safety (including comparisons of light and heavy viewers in the same types of neighborhoods), perhaps as a result of the much lower frequency of violence on Soviet television. In both countries, but especially in the former Soviet Union, the more people watch television, the more they are likely to say that housework is primarily the responsibility of the woman. General satisfaction with life is consistently lower among heavy than among light television viewers in the United States but not in the former Soviet Union (where it is relatively low for everyone).

Both U.S. and Soviet television systems reduce social and economic differences in attitudes, but this is especially so in the United States where such differences are greater. Lacking regular prime-time dramatic series and relying more on movies, theater, documentaries, and the classics, Soviet television may, in fact, present more diversified dramatic fare than U.S. television. At any rate, television viewing seems to have greater mainstreaming consequences in the United States than in the former Soviet Union. The availability of different cultural and language programming in the different republics of the former USSR may also contribute to the relative diversity of Soviet television—and to the centrifugal forces tearing the Union apart.

In sum, in countries in which television's portrayals are less repetitive and homogeneous than in the United States, the results of cultivation analysis also tend to be less predictable and consistent. The extent to which cultivation will occur in a given country will also depend on various structural factors, such as the number of channels available, overall amount of broadcasting time, and amount of time audiences spend viewing. However, it will especially depend on the amount of diversity in the available content, which is not necessarily related to the number of channels. A single channel with a diverse and balanced program structure can foster (and, in fact, compel) more diversified viewing, than many channels competing for the same audience, using similar appeals, and lending themselves to viewer selection of the same "preferences" most of the time.

Different media systems differ along all these dimensions, and complex interactions among these elements may account for substantial cross-cultural variations in cultivation. Imported U.S. programs can augment, diminish, or be irrelevant to these dynamics. The key questions are: (a) How important television is in the culture, and (b) How consistent and coherent the total system of its messages? The more important, consistent, and coherent, the more cultivation can be expected.

CONCLUSIONS

Television pervades the symbolic environment. Cultivation analysis focuses on the consequences of exposure to its recurrent patterns of stories, images, and messages. Our theories of the cultivation process attempt to understand and explain the dynamics of television as the distinctive and dominant cultural force of our age.

Our explorations and formulations have been challenged, enriched, confirmed, and extended by studies of numerous independent investigators in the United States and abroad, and are still evolving especially as they are being applied in more and more countries.

Cultivation analysis is not a substitute for but a complement to traditional approaches to media effects. Traditional research is concerned with change rather than stability and with processes more applicable to media that enter a person's life at later stages (with mobility, literacy, etc.) and more selectively.

Neither the "before and after exposure" model, nor the notion of "predispositions" as intervening variables, so important in traditional effects studies, applies in the context of cultivation analysis. Television enters life in infancy; there is no "before exposure" condition. Television plays a role in the formation of those very "predispositions" that later intervene (and often resist) other influences and attempts at persuasion.

Cultivation analysis concentrates on the enduring and common consequences of growing up and living with television. Those are the stable, resistant, and widely shared assumptions, images, and conceptions expressing the institutional characteristics and interests of the medium itself.

Television has become the common symbolic environment that interacts with most of the things we think and do. Exploring its dynamics can help develop an understanding of the forces of social cohesion, cultural dependence, and resistance to change, as well as the requirements of developing alternatives and independence essential for self-direction and self-government in the television age.

REFERENCES

Bouwman, H. (1982). "Cultural Indicators:" Die Gerbnersche Konzeption der "Message System Analysis" und Erste Empirische Befunde aus den Niederlanden [Gerbner's concept of cultivation analysis and its first empirical demonstration in the Netherlands]. *Rundfunk und Fernsehen, 30*, 341–355.

Bouwman, H. (1984). Cultivation analysis: The Dutch case. In G. Melischek, K. E. Rosengren, & J. Stappers (Eds.), *Cultural indicators: An international symposium* (pp. 407–422). Vienna, Austria: Verlag der Osterreichischen Akademie der Wissenschaften.

Bouwman, H., & Signorielli, N. (1985). A comparison of American and Dutch programming. *Gazette, 35*, 93–108.

Bouwman, H., & Stappers, J. (1984). The Dutch violence profile: A replication of Gerbner's message system analysis. In G. Melischek, K. E. Rosengren, & J. Stappers (Eds.), *Cultural indicators: An international symposium* (pp. 113–128). Vienna, Austria: Verlag der Osterreichischen Akademie der Wissenschaften.

Gerbner, G. (1958). On content analysis and critical research in mass communication. *AV Communication Review, 6*, 85–108.

Gerbner, G. (1969). Toward "cultural indicators:" The analysis of mass mediated message systems. *AV Communication Review, 17*, 137–148.

Gerbner, G. (1970). Cultural indicators: The case of violence in television drama. *The Annals of the American Academy of Political and Social Science, 388*, 69–81.

Gerbner, G. (1972a). Communication and social environment. *Scientific American, 227*, 152–160.

Gerbner, G. (1972b). The structure and process of television program content regulation in the U.S. In *Television and social behavior: Vol. 1. Content and control*. Washington, DC: U.S. Government Printing Office.

Gerbner, G. (1973). Cultural indicators: The third voice. In G. Gerbner, L. Gross, & W. H. Melody (Eds.), *Communications technology and social policy* (pp. 555–573). New York: Wiley.

Gerbner, G. (1977). Comparative cultural indicators. In G. Gerbner (Ed.), *Mass media policies in changing cultures* (pp. 199–205). New York: Wiley.

Gerbner, G. (1988). *Violence and terror in the mass media* (Reports and Papers in Mass Communication, No. 102). Paris: Unesco.

Gerbner, G. (1989). Cross-cultural communications research in the age of telecommunications. In Christian Academy (Ed.), *Continuity and change in communications in post-industrial society* (Vol. 2). Seoul, Korea: Wooseok.

Gerbner, G. (1990). Epilogue: Advancing on the path of righteousness (maybe). In N. Signorielli & M. Morgan (Eds.), *Cultivation analysis: New directions in media effects research* (pp. 249–262). Newbury Park, CA: Sage.

Gerbner, G., Gross, L., Morgan, M., & Signorielli, N. (1980). The "mainstreaming" of America: Violence profile no. 11. *Journal of Communication, 30*(3), 10–29.

Gerbner, G., Gross, L., Morgan, M., & Signorielli, N. (1982). Charting the mainstream: Television's contributions to political orientations. *Journal of Communication, 32*(2), 100–127.

Gerbner, G., Gross, L., Morgan, M., & Signorielli, N. (1984). Political correlates of television viewing. *Public Opinion Quarterly, 48*(1), 283–300.

Gerbner, G., Gross, L., Signorielli, N., & Morgan, M. (1980). Aging with television: Images on television drama and conceptions of social reality. *Journal of Communication, 30*(1), 37–47.

Gerbner, G., Gross, L., Signorielli, N., Morgan, M., & Jackson-Beeck, M. (1979). The demonstration of power: Violence profile no. 10. *Journal of Communication, 29*(3), 177–196.

Gross, L., & Morgan, M. (1985). Television and enculturation. In J. R. Dominick & J. E. Fletcher (Eds.), *Broadcasting research methods* (pp. 221–234). Boston: Allyn & Bacon.

Gunter, B. (1987). *Television and the fear of crime*. London: Libbey.

Gunter, B., & Furnham, A. (1984). Perceptions of television violence: Effects of programme genre and type of violence on viewers' judgements of violent portrayals. *British Journal of Social Psychology, 23*(2), 155–164.

Hawkins, R. P., & Pingree, S. (1982). Television's influence on social reality. In D. Pearl, L. Bouthilet, & J. Lazar (Eds.), *Television and behavior: Ten years of scientific progress and implications for the 80's: Vol. 2. Technical reviews* (pp. 224–247). Rockville, MD: National Institute of Mental Health.

Hawkins, R. P., & Pingree, S. (1990). Divergent psychological processes in constructing social reality from mass media content. In N. Signorielli & M. Morgan (Eds.), *Cultivation analysis: New directions in media effects research* (pp. 35–50). Newbury Park, CA: Sage.

Hedinsson, E., & Windahl, S. (1984). Cultivation analysis: A Swedish illustration. In G. Melischek, K. E. Rosengren, & J. Stappers (Eds.), *Cultural indicators: An international symposium* (pp. 389–406). Vienna, Austria: Verlag der Osterreichischen Akademie der Wissenschaften.

Jackson-Beeck, M. (1977). The non-viewers: Who are they? *Journal of Communication, 27*(3), 65–72.

Kang, J. G., & Morgan, M. (1988). Culture clash: US television programs in Korea. *Journalism Quarterly, 65*, 431–438.

Lewis, J., Jhally, S., & Morgan, M. (1991). *The Gulf War: A study of the media, public opinion, and public knowledge.* Unpublished manuscript, University of Massachusetts, Amherst, Center for the Study of Communication, Department of Communication.

Morgan, M. (1982). Television and adolescents' sex-role stereotypes: A longitudinal study. *Journal of Personality and Social Psychology, 43*, 947–955.

Morgan, M. (1983). Symbolic victimization and real-world fear. *Human Communication Research, 9*(2), 146–157.

Morgan, M. (1987). Television, sex-role attitudes, and sex-role behavior. *Journal of Early Adolescence, 7*, 269–282.

Morgan, M. (1990). International cultivation analysis. In N. Signorielli & M. Morgan (Eds.), *Cultivation analysis: New directions in media effects research* (pp. 225–248). Newbury Park, CA: Sage.

Morgan, M., Alexander, A., Shanahan, J., & Harris, C. (1990). Adolescents, VCRs, and the family environment. *Communication Research, 17*(1), 83–106.

Morgan, M., & Shanahan, J. (1991). Television and the cultivation of political attitudes in Argentina. *Journal of Communication, 41*(1), 88–103.

Morgan, M., & Shanahan, J. (1996). Two decades of cultivation analysis: An appraisal and a meta-analysis. In B. Burleson (Ed.), *Communication yearbook 2020* (pp. 1–45). Thousand Oaks, CA: Sage.

Piepe, A., Charlton, P., & Morey, J. (1990). Politics and television viewing in England: Hegemony or pluralism? *Journal of Communication, 40*(1), 24–35.

Pingree, S., & Hawkins, R. P. (1981). U.S. programs on Australian television: The cultivation effect. *Journal of Communication, 31*(1), 97–105.

Reimer, B., & Rosengren, K. E. (1990). Cultivated viewers and readers: A life-style perspective. In N. Signorielli & M. Morgan (Eds.), *Cultivation analysis: New directions in media effects research* (pp. 181–206). Newbury Park, CA: Sage.

Rothschild, N. (1984). Small group affiliation as a mediating factor in the cultivation process. In G. Melischek, K. E. Rosengren, & J. Stappers (Eds.), *Cultural indicators: An international symposium* (pp. 377–387). Vienna, Austria: Verlag der Osterreichischen Akademie der Wissenschaften.

Rothschild, N., & Morgan, M. (1987). Cohesion and control: Relationships with parents as mediators of television. *Journal of Early Adolescence, 7*, 299–314.

Saito, S. (1991). *Does cultivation occur in Japan? Testing the applicability of the cultivation hypothesis on Japanese television viewers.* Unpublished master's thesis, University of Pennsylvania, Philadelphia.

Signorielli, N. (1989). Television and conceptions about sex roles: Maintaining conventionality and the status quo. *Sex Roles, 21*, 337–356.

Signorielli, N. (1990a, November). *Television's contribution to adolescents' perceptions about work.* Paper presented at the annual conference of the Speech Communication Association, Chicago.

Signorielli, N. (1990b). Television's mean and dangerous world: A continuation of the cultural indicators perspective. In N. Signorielli & M. Morgan (Eds.), *Cultivation analysis: New directions in media effects research* (pp. 85–106). Newbury Park, CA: Sage.

Signorielli, N., & Lears, M. (1991). *Children, television and conceptions about chores: Attitudes and behaviors*. Unpublished manuscript, University of Delaware, Dover.

Stappers, J. G. (1984). De eigen aard van televisie; tien stellingen over cultivatie en culturele indicatoren [The debate over cultural indicators]. *Massacommunicatie, 12,* 249–258.

Tamborini, R., & Choi, J. (1990). The role of cultural diversity in cultivation research. In N. Signorielli & M. Morgan (Eds.), *Cultivation analysis: New directions in media effects research* (pp. 157–180). Newbury Park, CA: Sage.

Tan, A. S., Li, S., & Simpson, C. (1986). American television and social stereotypes of Americans in Taiwan and Mexico. *Journalism Quarterly, 63,* 809–814.

Tan, A. S., & Suarchavarat, K. (1988). American TV and social stereotypes of Americans in Thailand. *Journalism Quarterly, 65,* 648–654.

Tan, A. S., Tan, G. K., & Tan, A. S. (1987). American television in the Philippines: A test of cultural impact. *Journalism Quarterly, 64,* 65–72.

Varis, T. (1984). The international flow of television programs. *Journal of Communication, 34*(1), 143–152.

Weimann, G. (1984). Images of life in America: The impact of American TV in Israel. *International Journal of Intercultural Relations, 8*(2), 185–197.

Williams, R. (1977). *Marxism and literature*. Oxford, England: Oxford University Press.

Wober, J. M. (1978). Televised violence and paranoid perception: The view from Great Britain. *Public Opinion Quarterly, 42*(3), 315–321.

Wober, J. M. (1984). Prophecy and prophylaxis: Predicted harms and their absence in a regulated television system. In G. Melischek, K. E. Rosengren, & J. Stappers (Eds.), *Cultural indicators: An international symposium* (pp. 423–440). Vienna, Austria: Verlag der Osterreichischen Akademie der Wissenschaften.

Wober, J. M. (1990). Does television cultivate the British? Late 80s evidence. In N. Signorielli & M. Morgan (Eds.), *Cultivation analysis: New directions in media effects research* (pp. 207–224). Newbury Park, CA: Sage.

Wober, J. M., & Gunter, B. (1988). *Television and social control*. New York: St. Martin's.

Uses and Gratifications Theory in the 21st Century

Thomas E. Ruggiero
Communications Department
University of Texas at El Paso

Some mass communications scholars have contended that uses and gratifications is not a rigorous social science theory. In this article, I argue just the opposite, and any attempt to speculate on the future direction of mass communication theory must seriously include the uses and gratifications approach. In this article, I assert that the emergence of computer-mediated communication has revived the significance of uses and gratifications. In fact, uses and gratifications has always provided a cutting-edge theoretical approach in the initial stages of each new mass communications medium: newspapers, radio and television, and now the Internet. Although scientists are likely to continue using traditional tools and typologies to answer questions about media use, we must also be prepared to expand our current theoretical models of uses and gratifications. Contemporary and future models must include concepts such as interactivity, demassification, hypertextuality, and asynchroneity. Researchers must also be willing to explore interpersonal and qualitative aspects of mediated communication in a more holistic methodology.

What mass communication scholars today refer to as the *uses and gratifications* (U&G) *approach* is generally recognized to be a subtradition of media effects research (McQuail, 1994). Early in the history of communications research, an approach was developed to study the gratifications that attract and hold audiences to the kinds of media and the types of content that satisfy their social and psychological needs (Cantril, 1942). Much early effects research adopted the experimental or quasi-experimental approach, in which communication conditions were manipulated in search of general lessons about how better to communicate, or about the unintended consequences of messages (Klapper, 1960).

Other media effects research sought to discover motives and selection patterns of audiences for the new mass media. Examples include Cantril and Allport (1935) on the radio audience; Waples, Berelson, and Bradshaw (1940) on reading; Herzog (1940, 1944) on quiz programs and the gratifications from radio daytime serials; Suchman (1942) on the motives for listening to serious music; Wolfe and Fiske (1949) on children's interest in comics; Berelson (1949) on the functions of newspaper reading; and Lazarsfeld and Stanton (1942, 1944, 1949) on different media genres. Each of these studies formulated a list of functions served either by some specific content or by the medium itself:

> To match one's wits against others, to get information and advice for daily living, to provide a framework for one's day, to prepare oneself culturally for the demands of upward mobility, or to be reassured about the dignity and usefulness of one's role. (Katz, Blumler, & Gurevitch, 1974, p. 20)

This latter focus of research, conducted in a social-psychological mode, and audience based, crystallized into the U&G approach (McQuail, 1994).

Some mass communication scholars cited "moral panic" and the Payne Fund Studies as the progenitor of U&G theory. Undertaken by the U.S. Motion Picture Research Council, the Payne Fund Studies were carried out in the late 1920s. Leading sociologists and psychologists including Herbert Blumer, Philip Hauser, and L. L. Thurstone sought to understand how movie viewing was affecting the youth of America (Lowery & DeFleur, 1983). Rosengren, Johnsson-Smaragdi, and Sonesson (1994), however, argued that the Payne Fund Studies were primarily effects-oriented propaganda studies, as opposed to the U&G tradition, which focuses on research of individual use of the media. Likewise, Cantril's (1940) study of Orson Welles's "War of the Worlds" radio broadcast was more narrowly interested in sociological and psychological factors associated with panic behavior than in developing a theory about the effects of mass communication (Lowery & DeFleur, 1983).

Wimmer and Dominick (1994) proposed that U&G began in the 1940s when researchers became interested in why audiences engaged in various forms of media behavior, such as listening to the radio or reading the newspaper. Still others credit the U&G perspective with Schramm's (1949) immediate reward and delayed reward model of media gratifications (Dozier & Rice, 1984).

Regardless, early U&G studies were primarily descriptive, seeking to classify the responses of audience members into meaningful categories (Berelson, Lazarsfeld, & McPhee, 1954; Katz & Lazarsfeld, 1955; Lazarsfeld, Berelson, & Gaudet, 1948; Merton, 1949).

Most scholars agree that early research had little theoretical coherence and was primarily behaviorist and individualist in its methodological tendencies (McQuail, 1994). The researchers shared a qualitative approach by attempting to group gratification statements into labeled categories, largely ignoring their frequency distribution in the population. The earliest researchers for the most part did not attempt to explore the links between the gratifications detected and the psychological or sociological origins of the needs satisfied. They often failed to search for the interrelations among the various media functions, either quantitatively or conceptually, in a manner that might have led to the detection of the latent structure of media gratifications.

Criticisms of early U&G research focus on the fact that it (a) relied heavily on self-reports, (b) was unsophisticated about the social origin of the needs that audiences bring to the media, (c) was too uncritical of the possible dysfunction both for self and society of certain kinds of audience satisfaction, and (d) was too captivated by the inventive diversity of audiences used to pay attention to the constraints of the text (Katz, 1987). Despite severe limitations, early researchers, especially those at the Bureau of Applied Social Research of Columbia University, persevered, particularly in examining the effects of the mass media on political behavior. They studied voters in Erie County, Ohio, during the 1940 election between Roosevelt and Wilkie (Lazarsfeld et al., 1948) and voters in Elmira, New York, during the 1948 Truman–Dewey election (Berelson et al., 1954). Both studies suggested that the mass media played a weak role in election decisions compared with personal influence and influence of other people. As a result, Berelson et al. began amplifying the two-step flow theory, moving away from the concept of an "atomized" audience and toward the impact of personal influence (Katz, 1960).

1950S AND 1960S RESEARCH

Despite disagreement by communication scholars as to the precise roots of the approach, in the next phase of U&G research, during the 1950s and 1960s, researchers identified and operationalized many social and psychological variables that were presumed to be the precursors of different patterns of consumption of gratifications (Wimmer & Dominick, 1994). Accordingly, Schramm, Lyle, and Parker (1961) concluded that children's use of television was influenced by individual mental ability and relationships with parents and peers. Katz and Foulkes (1962) conceptualized mass media use as escape. Klapper (1963) stressed the importance of analyzing the consequences of use rather than simply labeling the use as earlier researchers had done. Mendelsohn (1964) identified several generalized functions of radio listening: companionship, bracketing the day, changing mood, counteracting loneliness or boredom, providing useful news and information, allowing vicarious participation in events, and aiding social interaction. Gerson (1966) introduced the variable of race and suggested that race was important in predicting how adolescents used the media. Greenberg and Dominick (1969) concluded that race and social class predicted how teenagers used television as an informal source of learning.

These studies and others conducted during this period reflected a shift from the traditional effects model of mass media research to a more functionalist perspective. Klapper (1963) called for a more functional analysis of U&G studies that would restore the audience member to "his rightful place in the dynamic, rather than leaving him in the passive, almost inert, role to which many older studies relegated him" (p. 527). Markedly, Geiger and Newhagen (1993) credited Klapper with ushering in the "cognitive revolution" in the communication field. From the 1950s forward, cross-disciplinary work between U&G researchers and psychologists has produced abundant research on the ways human beings interact with the media.

1970S RESEARCH

Until the 1970s, U&G research concentrated on gratifications sought, excluding outcomes, or gratifications obtained (Rayburn, 1996). During the 1970s, U&G researchers intently examined audience motivations and developed additional typologies of the uses people made of the media to gratify social and psychological needs. This may partially have been in response to a strong tide of criticism from other mass communication scholars. Critics such as Elliott (1974), Swanson (1977), and Lometti, Reeves, and Bybee (1977) stressed that U&G continued to be challenged by four serious conceptual problems: (a) a vague conceptual framework, (b) a lack of precision in major concepts, (c) a confused explanatory apparatus, and (d) a failure to consider audiences' perceptions of media content.

U&G researchers produced multiple responses. Katz, Gurevitch, and Haas (1973) assembled a comprehensive list of social and psychological needs said to be satisfied by exposure to mass media. Rosengren (1974), attempting to theoretically refine U&G, suggested that certain basic needs interact with personal characteristics and the social environment of the individual to produce perceived problems and perceived solutions. Those problems and solutions constitute different motives for gratification behavior that can come from using the media or other activities. Together media use or other behaviors produce gratification (or nongratification) that has an impact on the individual or society, thereby starting the process anew. Seeking to more closely define the relation between psychological motives and communication gratifications, Palmgreen and Rayburn (1979) studied viewers' exposure to public television and concluded that the U&G approach served well as a complement to other determinant factors such as media availability, work schedules, and social constraints. Palmgreen and Rayburn argued that the primary task facing media researchers was to "integrate the roles played by gratifications and other factors into a general theory of media consumption" (p. 177). Essentially, Palmgreen and Rayburn were responding to earlier researchers' (Greenberg, 1974; Lometti et al., 1977) call to investigate gratification sought and gratifications received. Blumler (1979) identified three primary social origins of media gratifications: normative influences, socially distributed life changes, and the subjective reaction of the individual to the social situation. Also, in response, McLeod, Bybee, and Durall (1982) theoretically clarified audience satisfaction by concluding that gratifications sought and gratifications received were two different conceptual entities that deserved independent treatment in any future U&G research.

Another related theoretical development was the recognition that different cognitive or affective states facilitate the use of media for various reasons, as predicted by the U&G approach. Blumler (1979) proposed that cognitive motivation facilitated information gain and that diversion or escape motivation facilitated audience perceptions of the accuracy of social portrayals in entertainment programming. In related research, McLeod and Becker (1981) found that individuals given advanced notice that they would be tested made greater use of public affairs magazines than did a control group. Bryant and Zillmann (1984) discovered that stressed individuals watched more tranquil programs and bored participants opted for more exciting fare.

1980S AND 1990S RESEARCH

Rubin (1983) noted that gratifications researchers were beginning to generate a valid response to critics. He concluded that his colleagues were making a systematic attempt to (a) conduct modified replications or extensions of studies, (b) refine methodology, (c) comparatively analyze the findings of separate investigations, and (d) treat mass media use as an integrated communication and social phenomenon. Examples include Eastman's (1979) analysis of the multivariate interactions among television viewing functions and lifestyle attributes, Ostman and Jeffers's (1980) examination of the associations among television viewing motivations and potential for lifestyle traits and television attitudes to predict viewing motivations, Bantz's (1982) exploration of the differences between general medium and specific program television viewing motivations and the comparability of research findings, Rubin's (1981) consideration of viewing motivations scale validity and the comparability of research results in U&G research, and Palmgreen and Rayburn's (1985) empirical comparison of alternative gratification models.

Likewise, Windahl (1981) also sought to advance U&G theoretically. In his "Uses and Gratifications at the Crossroads," he argued that the primary difference between the traditional effects approach and the U&G approach is that a media effects researcher usually examines mass communication from the perspective of the communicator, whereas the U&G researcher uses the audience as a point of departure. Believing it was more beneficial to emphasize similarities than differences, Windahl coined the term *conseffects* and argued for a synthesis of the two approaches. Thus, he suggested, observations that are partly results of content use in itself and partly results of content mediated by use would serve as a more useful perspective. Windahl's approach served to link an earlier U&G approach to more recent research.

Aspiring to heighten the theoretical validity of structural determinants, Webster and Wakshlag (1983) integrated the dissimilar perspectives of U&G and "models of choice," attempting to locate the interchange between programming structures, content preferences, and viewing conditions in the program choice process. Likewise, Dobos (1992), using U&G models applied to media satisfaction and choice in organizations, predicted television channel choice and satisfaction within specific communication technologies.

ACTIVE AUDIENCE

Also, in the 1980s, researchers reevaluated the long-held notion of an active audience. During this time, some researchers reiterated that although both uses and effects sought to explain the outcomes or consequences of mass communication, they did so by recognizing the potential for audience initiative and activity (Rubin, 1994b). Levy and Windahl (1984) attempted to articulate a theoretically more complete notion of audience activity and to test a model of audience orientations that linked activity to U&G, and Rubin (1984) suggested that audience activity is not an absolute concept, but a variable one. Notably, Windahl (1981) argued that "the notion of activeness leads a picture of the audience as superrational and very selective, a tendency which invites criticism" (p. 176). Instead, he argued audience activity covers a range of possible orientations to the communication process, a range that "varies across phases of the communication sequence" (Levy & Windahl, 1984, p. 73). More succinctly, different individuals tend to display different types and amounts of activity in different communication settings and at different times in the communication process.

In support of this, theoretical active audience models have increasingly emerged that range from high audience activity to low levels of involvement. For example, both dependency and deprivation theories suggest that some individuals under certain conditions such as confinement to home, low income, and some forms of stress form high levels of attachment to media. These include television (Grant, Guthrie, & Ball-Rokeach, 1991), newspapers (Loges & Ball-Rokeach, 1993), and communication technologies such as remote control devices (Ferguson & Perse, 1994).

DEPENDENCY THEORY

Media dependency theory itself posits that media influence is determined by the interrelations between the media, its audience, and society (DeFleur & Ball-Rokeach, 1982). The individual's desire for information from the media is the primary variable in explaining why media messages have cognitive, affective, or variable effects. Media dependency is high when an individual's goal satisfaction relies on information from the media system (Ball-Rokeach, 1985). Rubin and Windahl (1986) augmented the dependency model to include the gratifications sought by the audience as an interactive component with media dependency. For Rubin and Windahl, the combination of gratifications sought and socially determined dependency produced media effects. They argued that dependency on a medium or a message results when individuals either intentionally seek out information or ritualistically use specific communication media channels or messages. For example, McIlwraith (1998) found that self-labeled "TV addicts" often used television to distract themselves from unpleasant thoughts, to regulate moods, and to fill time. This link between dependency and functional alternatives illustrates how U&G is a theory "capable of interfacing personal and mediated communication" (Rubin, 1994b, p. 428).

DEPRIVATION THEORY

Deprivation theory has an even longer history in U&G research than dependency theory. Berelson (1949) studied the effects of the 1945 strike of eight major New York City daily newspapers on audience behavior. Since that time, additional studies of media strikes have emerged: Kimball (1959) replicated Berelson's study during the 1958 New York City newspaper strike; de Bock (1980) studied the effects of newspaper and television strikes in the Netherlands in 1977; Cohen (1981) examined a general media strike; and Walker (1990) analyzed viewers' reactions to the 1987 National Football League players' strike.

Related, Windahl, Hojerback, and Hedinsson (1986) suggested that the consequences of a media strike for adolescents were connected to the total degree of perceived deprivation of television as well as the specific content such as entertainment, information, and fiction. These deprivations are related both to media variables like exposure, involvement, and motives, and nonmedia variables such as socioconcept orientation and activities with friends and parents. Windahl et al. found that individuals in more socially oriented environments tended to feel more deprived than those in conceptually oriented settings.

THEORIES OF LOW-LEVEL AND VARIABLE AUDIENCE ACTIVITY

Conversely, other factors such as (a) different time relations (advance expectations, activity during the experience, postexposure), (b) variability of involvement (as background noise, companionship), and (c) ritualistic or habitual use (as mild stimulation) suggest a much less active audience than traditionally believed. Specifically, time relations theory argues that individuals are differentially selective and goal directed at different times: before, during, and after exposure to media (Levy & Windahl, 1984). For example, Lemish (1985) discovered that college students arranged their busy schedules to view a specific soap opera, formed program-centered groups, paid attention to the program, and discussed the content with others.

Variability of involvement suggests that the motivation to use any mass medium is also affected by how much an individual relies on it (Galloway & Meek, 1981), and how well it satisfies her or his need (Lichtenstein & Rosenfeld, 1983). Thus, many U&G researchers have included some aspect of expectancy in their models and have turned to established theories of expectancy to explain media consumption (Rayburn, 1996). Rayburn cited Fishbein and Ajzen's (1975) expectancy value theory as illustrative. Fishbein and Ajzen's model poses three beliefs: (a) Descriptive beliefs result from direct observation of an object, (b) informational beliefs are formed by accepting information from an outside source that links certain objects and attributes, and (c) inferential beliefs are about the characteristics of objects not yet directly observed, or that are not directly observable. Palmgreen and Rayburn (1982) developed an expectancy model that successfully predicted gratifications sought from television news. Rayburn and Palmgreen combined U&G with expectancy value theory to generate an expectancy value model of gratifications sought (GS) and gratifications obtained (GO).

For example, a study about talk radio by Armstrong and Rubin (1989) concluded that individuals who called in found face-to-face communication less rewarding, were less mobile, believed talk radio was more important to them, and listened for more hours a day than listeners who did not call in.

In terms of ritualistic and habitual media use, audience activity involves the concept of utility, an individual's reasons and motivations for communicating, but little intentionality or selectivity (Blumler, 1979; Hawkins & Pingree, 1981). Rubin (1984) suggested that ritualized viewing involved more habitual use of television for diversionary reasons and a greater attachment with the medium itself. Instrumental viewing, on the other hand, reflected a more goal-oriented use of television content to gratify information needs or motives. Notably, however, Rubin (1984) cautioned that ritualized and instrumental media use are not neatly dichotomous but are more likely interrelated. Just as audience activity is variable, individuals may use media ritualistically or instrumentally depending on background, time, and situational demands. Thus, Perse and Rubin (1988) suggested a multidimensional view of audience activity, reinforcing an emphasis on media use instead of media exposure. Additionally, Rubin (1994a) argued that U&G research needed to "continue its progression from simple exposure explanations of effects and typologies of media motivation to conceptual models that explain the complexity of the media effects process" (p. 103).

ATTEMPTS TO REFINE U&G

Paradoxically, U&G scholars may have been their own toughest critics. Throughout the decades, U&G researchers challenged their own model and argued for a more comprehensive theoretical grounding (Klapper, 1963; Rubin, 1994a; Schramm et al., 1961). Rubin (1986) called for a clearer picture of the relation between media and personal channels of communication and sources of potential influence. Swanson (1987) urged that research focus on three areas: the role of gratification seeking in exposure to mass media, the relation between gratification and the interpretive frames through which audiences understand media content, and the link between gratifications and media content. Windahl (1981) argued that a synthesis of several viewpoints would be most productive: (a) that media perceptions and expectations guide people's behavior; (b) that besides needs, motivation is derived from interests and externally imposed constraints; (c) that there are functional alternatives to media consumptions; and (d) that media content plays an important role in media effects. Rubin (1994b) agreed that a fruitful direction was a synthesis between U&G and media effects research as proposed by Windahl.

CONTINUED CRITICISMS OF U&G

Thus, during the last several decades, U&G researchers have continued to conceptually refine their perspective. Nevertheless, critics such as Stanford (1983) have assailed perceived deficiencies such as the confusing of operational definitions and the analytical model, a lack of internal consistency, and a lack of theoretical justification for the model offered. Stanford complained, "the discussion ranges far from the results, which do not support their theoretical underpinnings" (p. 247). Likewise, media hegemony advocates have contended that the U&G theory overextends its reach in asserting that people are free to choose the media fare and interpretations they want (White, 1994). J. A. Anderson (1996) conceded that U&G is an "intelligent splice of psychological motivations and sociological functions, [but nonetheless noted that] materialism, reductionism, and determinism, as well as foundational empiricism, are all firmly in place" (p. 212).

Thus, much contemporary criticism of U&G challenges assumptions that include (a) media selection initiated by the individual; (b) expectations for media use that are produced from individual predispositions, social interaction, and environmental factors; and (c) active audiences with goal-directed media behavior (Wimmer & Dominick, 1994).

Outside of the United States, particularly in non-Western countries, even a diffused notion of an active audience has limited acceptability and U&G scholars differ in their methodological approach. For example, Cooper (1997) noted that Japan's communication researchers view media's individual-level impact as a limited effects perspective, in that media serve only to reinforce preexisting attitudes and behaviors.

CONTINUED FLAWS IN U&G THEORY

Thus, despite attempts to produce a more rigorous and comprehensive theory, several flaws continue to plague the perspective, and U&G researchers have acknowledged this. First, by focusing on audience consumption, U&G is often too individualistic (Elliott, 1974). It makes it difficult to explain or predict beyond the people studied or to consider societal implications of media use. Second, some studies are too compartmentalized, producing separate typologies of motives. This hinders conceptual development because separate research findings are not synthesized. Third, there still exists a lack of clarity among central concepts such as social and psychological backgrounds, needs, motives, behavior, and consequences. Fourth, U&G researchers attach different meanings to concepts such as motives, uses, gratifications, and functional alternatives, contributing to fuzzy thinking and inquiry. Fifth, the cornerstones of U&G theory, the notion of an active audience and the validity of self-report data to determine motives, are assumed by researchers, and that assumption may be "a little simplistic or naive" (Severin & Tankard, 1997, p. 335). Thus, some critics continue to argue that traditional U&G methodologies, particularly those dependent on self-reported typologies and relying on interpretation of lifestyle and attitude variables rather than observable audience behavior, are suspect (Rosenstein & Grant, 1997). Self-reports may not be measuring the individual's actual behavior so much as his or her awareness and interpretation of the individual's behavior. This dilemma is further complicated by evidence that suggests that individuals may have little direct introspective access to the higher order cognitive processes that mediate their behavior (Nisbett & Wilson, 1977), and therefore may base their self-reports on "a priori, casual theories influenced by whatever stimuli happen to be salient" (Rosenstein & Grant, 1997, p. 4).

U&G THEORY BUILDING

Despite these perceived theoretical and methodological imperfections, I would argue that reproach of U&G must be tempered with encouragement. A typology of uses, although not providing what some scholars would consider a refined theoretical perspective, furnishes a benchmark base of data for other studies to further examine media use. Furthermore, Finn (1997) suggested that due to a contemporary preference for more parsimonious models of human personality, the design of U&G studies committed to a "broad range of personality traits has become a more tractable endeavor" (p. 1). For example, current scholars favor a typology of five (K. J. Anderson & Revelle, 1995; Costa & McCrae, 1988), and in some cases as few as three fundamental personality traits (Eysenck, 1991). Contrast this to the earlier system of 16 primary personality factors as advanced by Cattell, Edger, and Tatsuoka (1970) and McGuire (1974).

Second, there has been a trend toward enlarging and refining theories concerning affective motivations toward media use (Finn, 1997). For instance, Finn noted that the rigid dichotomy between instrumental and ritualistic behaviors that formerly esteemed information-seeking over entertainment-seeking behaviors has been infused with new motivational theories. These take into consideration the individuals' need to manage affective states (D. R. Anderson, Collins, Schmitt, & Jacobvitz, 1996; Kubey & Csikszentmihalyi, 1990) or achieve optimum levels of arousal (Donohew, Finn, & Christ, 1988; Zillmann & Bryant, 1994).

Third, fully focusing on the social and cultural impacts of new communication technologies may be premature until we grasp more fully how and why people are making use of these media channels (Perse & Dunn, 1998). It stands to reason that in the information age, media users will seek information. Equally reasonably, World Wide Web (Web) survey respondents are most attracted to information formats that speak to them in a more personalized voice and in a broader entertaining context (Eighmey & McCord, 1995).

Thus, the media uses and effects process is an increasingly complex one that requires careful attention to antecedent, mediating, and consequent conditions (Rubin, 1994b). A continued emphasis on theory building must proceed, particularly by scholars who will attempt to develop theories that explain and predict media consumption of the public based on sociological, psychological, and structural variables. Some current research illustrates the plausibility of changing the scope of U&G research from an "exaggerated emphasis on using mass media to meet social deficits, to the function it fulfills," as Blumler (1985, p. 41) previously suggested to aiding people in promoting social identities (Finn, 1997). A serious potential problem facing U&G researchers, however, may be the practical impossibility of probability sampling on the Internet. At this point, studies may only be able to tentatively generalize to a very specific population. Also, Web-administered surveys may pose problems with tracking precise and reliable response rates. Additionally, a current lack of standardization among browsers, servers, and operating systems may create a serious challenge to methodically sound quantitative research. However, as we invent more sophisticated methods of tracking users and become more familiar with their demographics, generalizability to well-studied segments of the overall population should become less problematic (Smith, 1997).

TELECOMMUNICATIONS TECHNOLOGY AND THE REVIVAL OF U&G

U&G fell out of favor with some mass communication scholars for several decades, but the advent of telecommunications technology may well have revived it from dormancy. The deregulation of the communications industry and the convergence of mass media and digital technology have altered the exposure patterns of many media consumers (Finn, 1997). Improved compression algorithms now allow for the compression of video data for online transmission down telephone copper wire, coaxial, fiber optic cable, and by broadcast satellite, cellular, and wireless technologies (Chamberlain, 1994, p. 279). As new technologies present people with more and more media choices, motivation and satisfaction become even more crucial components of audience analysis. Not surprisingly, researchers have been busy applying U&G theory to a wide range of newly popularized video media technologies. For example, Donohew, Palmgreen, and Rayburn (1987) explored how the need for activation interacts with social and psychological factors to affect media U&G sought by cable television audiences. They identified four lifestyle types whose members differed significantly on a wide range of variables, including newspaper and newsmagazine readership and gratifications sought from cable television. They found that individuals with a high need for activation had lifestyles involving greater exposure to media sources of public affairs information than individuals with a lower need for activation and less cosmopolitan lifestyles. LaRose and Atkin (1991) also examined cable subscribership in U.S. households, including the factors that lead to initial subscription and to subscription retention. Walker and Bellamy (1991) related television remote control devices to audience member interest in types of program content. Lin (1993) conducted a study to determine if VCR satisfaction, VCR use, and interpersonal communication about VCRs were related to three functions: home entertainment, displacement, and social utility. James, Wotring, and Forrest (1995) investigated adoption and social impact issues possessed by the characteristic bulletin board user and how board use affected other communication media. Jacobs (1995) examined the relation between sociodemographics and satisfaction by studying the determinants of cable television viewing satisfaction. Jacobs identified antecedents in the study that included performance attributes, complaint call frequencies, and cable system characteristics. Funk and Buchman (1996) explored the effects of computer and video games on adolescents' self-perceptions. Perse and Dunn (1998) examined home computer use, and how CD–ROM ownership and Internet capability were linked to computer utility. Each of these scholars questioned whether new telecommunications media are used to satisfy the same needs they had been theorized to satisfy with traditional communication media (Williams, Phillips, & Lum, 1985). For example, the parasocial aspects of television soap opera viewing may soon pale in comparison to the interactive relation possibilities offered by electronic chat rooms and multiuser domains. Researchers are now being challenged to "decode the uses and gratifications of such communication experiences" (Lin, 1996, p. 578).

This increasing interest by communication scholars in online audiences may be particularly intense because of the makeup of these newer media forms: interactive media obscure the line between the sender and receiver of mediated messages (Singer, 1998). Furthermore, new media like the Internet possess at least three attributes of data not commonly associated with traditional media: interactivity, demassification, and asynchroneity.

INTERACTIVITY

Interactivity significantly strengthens the core U&G notion of active user because it has been defined as "the degree to which participants in the communication process have control over, and can exchange roles in their mutual discourse" (Williams, Rice, & Rogers, 1988, p. 10). Communication literature reflects six user-oriented dimensions of interactivity that should be useful for the U&G approach: threats (Markus, 1994), benefits (S. Ang & Cummings, 1994), sociability (Fulk, Flanagin, Kalman, Monge, & Ryan, 1996), isolation (Dorsher, 1996), involvement (Trevino & Webster, 1992), and inconvenience (Stolz, 1995; Thomas, 1995). Additionally, Ha and James (1998) cited five dimensions of interactivity: playfulness, choice, connectedness, information collection, and reciprocal communication. Ha and James suggested that for "self-indulgers" and "Web surfers," the playfulness and choice dimensions of interactivity fulfill self-communication and entertainment needs. For task-oriented users, the connectedness dimension fulfills information needs. For expressive users, the information collection and reciprocal communication dimensions allow them to initiate communication with others of common online interests. Ha and James assessed dimensions such as information collection and reciprocal communication as higher levels of interactivity. Playfulness, choice, and connectedness were viewed as lower levels of interactivity.

Heeter (1989) also defined interactivity as a multidimensional concept: amount of choice provided to users, amount of effort a user must exert to access information, how actively responsive a medium is to users, potential to monitor system use, degree to which users can add information to the system that a mass undifferentiated audience can access, and degree to which a media system facilitates interpersonal communication between specific users.

Thus, the real advantage to interactivity for individual users is not simply multimedia videos, online shopping, or obtaining information on demand. Just as the Lotus 1-2-3 spreadsheet allowed users to create their own business plans and models, interactivity may offer users the means to develop new means of communication (Dyson, 1993) and greatly increase user activity. After all, interactivity is not only the ability to select from a wide array of Internet merchandise or "surf" 500 or more television channels. Technologists such as Nelson (1990) argued that human–computer activities represent the human impulse to create interactive representation. Dutton, Rogers, and Jun (1987) suggested that interactivity displays "the degree to which the new communication systems are capable of responding to user commands" (p. 234). However, interactivity, at least on the Internet with current technology, does pose some serious practical limitations for users. The ability to access information is limited to three means: entering the address of a location the user already knows, scrolling through a single document, and following a hypertext link (Jackson, 1997). A further serious downside to interactivity continues to exist. More and more often, a Web search using a keyword or a hypertext link results in an extensive list and the user must choose from hundreds or even thousands of destinations, often with few or no contextual clues (Bergeron & Bailin, 1997).

DEMASSIFICATION

Williams et al. (1988) defined *demassification* as the control of the individual over the medium, "which likens the new media to face-to-face interpersonal communication" (p. 12). Demassification is the ability of the media user to select from a wide menu. Chamberlain (1994) argued that we have entered an era of demassification in which the individual media user is able, through newer technologies, to pick from a large selection of media, previously shared only with other individuals as mass media. Unlike traditional mass media, new media like the Internet provide selectivity characteristics that allow individuals to tailor messages to their needs. Kuehn (1994) cited *The New York Times* as an example. Those who wish to receive the paper version of *The New York Times* must pay for the whole paper, whereas those receiving the electronic version may select only those articles of interest to them. Mass messages will be able to be viewed as second-class by recipients and "individual, one-on-one dialogue will be the preferred mode of communication" (Chamberlain, 1994, p. 274).

ASYNCHRONEITY

Asynchroneity refers to the concept that messages may be staggered in time. Senders and receivers of electronic messages can read mail at different times and still interact at their convenience (Williams et al., 1988). It also means the ability of an individual to send, receive, save, or retrieve messages at her or his convenience (Chamberlain, 1994). In the case of television, asynchroneity meant the ability of VCR users to record a program for later viewing. With electronic mail (e-mail) and the Internet, an individual has the potential to store, duplicate, or print graphics and text, or transfer them to an online Web page or the e-mail of another individual. Once messages are digitized, manipulation of media becomes infinite, allowing the individual much more control than traditional means.

For U&G researchers, each of these accelerated media aspects—interactivity, demassification, and asynchroneity—offer a vast continuum of communication behaviors to examine.

TRADITIONAL MODELS OF U&G

Rogers (1986) concluded that these novel attributes make it nearly impossible to investigate the effects of a new communication system using earlier research. Rogers argued that "conventional research methodologies and the traditional models of human communication are inadequate. That's why the new communication technologies represent a new ball game for communication research" (p. 7).

Other mass media scholars, however, suggested that traditional models of U&G may still provide a useful framework from which to begin to study Internet and new media communication (December, 1996; Kuehn, 1994; Morris & Ogan, 1996). All four of these scholars contend that a U&G model provides a productive method of examining Internet use at this time. Much of the current activity on the Web involves exploratory behavior, offering an environment in which users can contact thousands of sources, find information presented in a wide range of formats, and interact with many of the sources they contact (Eighmey, 1997). Kuehn (1994) emphasized this interactive capacity of computer-mediated communication and suggested a group of U&G statements be used as rating scales to evaluate computer-aided instructional programs. His typology included convenience, diversion, relationship development, and intellectual appeal.

For December (1996), more traditional typologies of mass media consumption translate appropriately to the Internet. U&G researchers can continue to use categories such as surveillance, entertainment and diversion, interpersonal utility, and parasocial interaction to test people's attitudes toward media consumption through such variables as GO and GS. Also in line with previous U&G scholars, Morris and Ogan (1996) argued that the concept of active audience, whether instrumental or ritualized, should continue to be included in current and future Internet research.

Perse and Dunn (1998) also suggested that U&G offers a convincing theoretical explanation for changes in media use patterns following the adoption of new communication technologies such as personal computers. Because they are increasingly filling similar needs, personal computers may be displacing the use of traditional media like newspapers and television. When television was adopted, for instance, it tended to replace other entertainment activities such as radio, movies, and comics. A more recent study concluded that displacement of other media and forms of television occurred with an individual's acquisition of a VCR (Anonymous, 1989). Significantly, some predict that television, the Internet, and the telephone may soon merge into one instrument, displacing other media choices.

TWO THEORETICAL DICHOTOMIES

In general, although the media industry is based on the strategy that audiences are at least somewhat active, two dichotomies concerning media and U&G research have long prevailed (Zillman & Bryant, 1985). In the first group are those scholars who view the mass audience as predominantly passive and those who hold that audience members are active and discriminating. In the second group are those studies that underscore the explanatory power of individual characteristics and those that attribute power to structural factors (Cooper, 1996).

Those scholars that supported a passive audience conception often cite the escapist model of media use, particularly in television viewing (Stone & Stone, 1990). The escapist model presumes that television viewing consists largely of a leisurely way to pass the time (Barwise, Ehrenberg, & Goodhardt, 1982; Kubey, 1986) and that television programming is primarily homogeneous in gratifying a time-filling behavior (McQuail, Blumler, & Brown, 1972). Goodhardt, Ehrenberg, and Collins's (1987) study of British television audience behavior is frequently cited as corroboration that audience availability, not selectivity, is paramount in shaping patterns of viewing. In their study, the researchers examined three variables: repeat viewing, audience duplication, and audience appreciation. They discovered that (a) 55% of the viewers of one episode of a television program also watched the following episode; (b) for any two programs, the level of audience viewing duplication depends on the programs' ratings and not their content; and (c) a viewer's average appreciation score does not depend on the program's rating or its incidence of repeat viewing. Goodhardt et al. concluded that television viewing behavior and audience appreciation appeared to follow "a few very general and simple patterns" (p. 116) rather than involving great differentiation between distinct groups of viewers and between the audiences of different programs. Horna (1988) found specific relations between leisure and an individual's U&G of mass media. Specifically, the majority of media audiences are seeking entertainment, relaxation, or escape, and for most people, leisure and mass media are nearly synonymous.

Conversely, a chief tenet of U&G theory of audience behavior is that media use is selective and motivated by rational self-awareness of the individual's own needs and an expectation that those needs will be satisfied by particular types of media and content (Katz et al., 1974). Rubin (1983) argued that "viewing motivations are not isolated static traits, but rather, comprise a set of interactive needs and expectations" (p. 39). Studies by scholars such as Garramone (1984, 1985) suggested that motivation leads to higher knowledge regardless of attention to a specific medium. Other studies that support the active audience assumption include work by Fry and McCain (1983), who found that a person's expectations, evaluations, and motivations determined the usefulness of a medium; and work by Gandy, Matabane, and Omachonu (1987), who discovered that the strongest factors predicting knowledge from a medium were an individual's gender and personal interest in the issues. Furthermore, Grunig (1979) suggested that people sometimes seek media content that has a functional relation to situations in which they are involved. Perse and Courtright (1993) concluded that individuals are aware of communication alternatives and select channels based on the normative images those channels are perceived to have.

STRUCTURAL MODELS OF U&G

On the other hand, those scholars who attribute media use behavior to structural factors, particularly in television viewing, have used complex statistical procedures to show that channel loyalty, inheritance effects, repeat viewing, and availability are stronger predictors of program choice than any measure of program typology (Goodhardt et al., 1987; Webster & Wakshlag, 1983). Supporting this perspective, in Heeter's (1989) study of program choice and channel selection, 23% of all respondents were unable to identify what channels they commonly viewed. Structural scholars interpret this to mean that most audience members pay little attention to content or channel but use television in a relatively undiscriminating fashion. A viewer's primary relation may be with the medium itself rather than with any specific channel or program (Rosenstein & Grant, 1997). This has serious ramifications, particularly for critical scholars, who argue that "new media technologies will be funded almost exclusively by private enterprise" (Chamberlain, 1994, p. 280). This will restrict the use of the latest technology to those who can afford it, widening the gap between the haves and have nots, perpetuating information-rich and information-poor individuals, groups, and societies.

Despite their usefulness, however, most structural models should be viewed as "a set of complex, surrogate variables that can have great predictive power" (Cooper, 1996, p. 10) but lack ability to explain the underlying processes. Research has yet to fully explicate how the structure of television program offerings, for example, influence the actual choices made by individual viewers. Thus, U&G continues to be exceedingly useful in explaining audience activity when individuals are most active in consciously making use of media for intended purposes. For example, Lind's (1995) study concluded that television viewers did not want their news fare limited by the government, the industry, or even concerned viewers.

NEWER COMMUNICATION MEDIA

Additionally, the active audience concept is gaining credibility with newer media researchers. As emerging technologies provide users with a wider range of source selection and channels of information, individuals are selecting a media repertoire in those areas of most interest. Heeter and Greenburg (1985) suggested that given the many entertainment options on cable television, most viewers choose a subset of channels, or a repertoire, that they prefer. Ferguson (1992) discovered that the main component of television channel repertoire was whether the viewer subscribed to cable television. Atkin (1993) identified the phenomenon of repertoire when studying the interrelations between cable and noncable television, and subscriptions to them by owners of VCRs, camcorders, personal computers, walkman radios, and cellular telephones. Reagan (1996) argued that each individual is now able to rely on easy-to-use media for low-interest topics and more complex repertoires for higher interest topics. He suggested that researchers should move away from labeling media users as television oriented or newspaper oriented, and consider them more as users of "cross-channel clusters of information sources" (p. 5).

Similarly, some communications scholars are viewing the Internet as the ultimate in individualism, "a medium with the capability to empower the individual in terms of both the information he or she seeks and the information he or she creates" (Singer, 1998, p. 10). Inversely, others see the Web as the ultimate in community building and enrichment, through which users can create relationships online in ways that have never been possible through traditional media. Despite this optimistic portrait, Rafaeli (1986) speculated that computer-mediated communication by individuals may lead to loneliness and isolation. Moreover, Young (1996) raised concern that excessive use of new media such as the personal computer may leave users vulnerable to technological dependencies like "Internet addiction."

Whatever the approach, most U&G scholars agree that concepts such as *active* and *audience* will have to be revised when applied to Internet communication. Reasons for using the Internet differ from person to person. Some individuals are goal directed and may want to complete a task through visiting specific Web sites. Others may only be curious and surf the Web for fun. Additionally, in electronic discussion groups, for example, some users are quiet observers and "lurkers" who never participate, whereas others frequently participate in the discussion (Ha, 1995). Fredin and David (1998) argued that audience activity, as it applies to hypermedia use, has three interrelated components that place elevated demands on individual user interaction. First, hypermedia obligate frequent audience responses because, unlike radio or television, hypermedia freeze or halt if responses are not made. Second, the audience is presented with a seemingly unending variety of options from which they must choose. Third, an individual's choices are often highly contingent on a series of earlier responses. Moreover, differences in quality and quantity of activity exist among individual online users. Sundar (1998) contended that experienced Internet users make different choices than do novices, particularly in matters such as attentiveness to sources in electronic news stories.

THE INTERNET AND U&G

Additionally, some media scholars argued that even the traditional audience concept must be radically amended because of novel informational characteristics of the Internet. Abrahamson (1998) envisioned the Internet moving from a mass-market medium to a "vehicle for the provision of very specific high-value information to very specific high-consumption audiences" (p. 15). Specifically, he theorized a mass Internet audience "fractionated" into smaller, more elite audiences, such as occurred with consumer magazines in the 1960s. Ha and James (1998) believed the medium will evolve from a mass-produced and mass-consumed commodity to an "endless feast of niches and specialties" (p. 2). Weaver (1993) forecasted a tiered communication system emerging, with some messages reaching the masses (presidential speeches, war coverage), others reaching a significant segment of society (business news, some sporting events), and others reaching relatively small, special-interest groups (music, art, and hobbies). Dicken-Garcia (1998) envisioned common interests rather than geographic space defining much of the Internet audience. Yet, she asserted, the Internet, unlike other media, has no targeted community as a primary audience or as a result of its function.

Other scholars have insisted that the traditional audience concept must be modified because of the interpersonal potential of the Internet. Ironically, interpersonal relationships, one of the two mediating variables of the early persuasion model (selectivity being the other), and the forerunner of diffusion of innovations, is reemerging as a serviceable U&G variable. This concept of "personalness," social presence, or the degree of salience in interpersonal relationships is being explored increasingly by U&G researchers, particularly in relation to interactivity. Cowles (1989) found that interactive media (teletext and videotext) possessed more personal characteristics than noninteractive electronic media. She predicted media gratifications theory is ripe for future research involving new media and that such research "might best occur within the context of an individual's total media environment" (p. 83). Dicken-Garcia (1998) contended that the Internet places stronger emphasis on informal, interpersonal conversation than has been true of earlier media. A notable and novel characteristic of Internet audience behavior according to Dicken-Garcia lies in the phenomenon that users communicate electronically what they might never say in person or on the phone. Internet users sometimes take on new personalities, ages, and genders, all of these exemplified by less inhibited behavior. She also noted that Internet talk more resembles word of mouth than newspapers and television, and that, often, "users unquestionably accept information via the Internet that they would not accept so readily from another medium" (p. 22).

The Internet may also have important ramifications for the communication gratifications traditionally sought by consumers of news information. The news, particularly as provided by traditional media institutions, has been linked with the creation of an informed electorate in areas including politics and international events, and to the perpetuation of a democratic society (Wenner, 1985).

What Dunleavy and Weir (1998) called *open-book government* could also form a significant part of a new era of electronic democracy. Not only does the Internet have the potential to improve access to the government, it could also invigorate representative democracy:

> Electronic advances could make public consultation and participation wider, easier and more diverse; and provide new media opportunities which could both focus and diversify the information people receive and obtain for themselves, as the old media

fragment into more and more apolitical and specialised forms—sports channels, gardening channels, fashion channels, golf channels and so on. (p. 72)

As an example, Dunleavy and Weir (1998) cited the British Broadcasting Company's Election 97 Web site, which on election night recorded more than 1.5 million hits. During the election, the Web site not only provided far more reliable basic information than any conventional mass media source, it also allowed individuals to e-mail queries and get answers. Political experts were shocked by the quality of the questions submitted, the insights they contained, and the appetite for information. Party policies, opinion polls, electoral trajectories, and key issues were clarified and debated in depth.

The Internet may also greatly benefit in the creation of a vibrant "discursive democracy" (Dunleavy & Weir, 1998). Government departments, local councils, and other public bodies can clarify how they sculpt their policies and request interested citizens and specialists to participate directly in determining them.

> Interactive question-and-answer sessions, policy forums, panels and discussion groups, planning consultations, chat-lines, even tabloid-style votes can all generate a great deal more information that policymakers should consider. They could also give far more in-depth information more cheaply and conveniently, respond to people's questions and ideas and encourage the public to submit proposals for action. (p. 2)

Newhagen and Rafaeli (1996) also attempted to theoretically position the Internet as a legitimate subject of mass communication and social science research and they called for a U&G approach to investigate the medium. They suggested that because a tradition in mass communication research of studying U&G already exists, that approach may be useful in laying out a taxonomy of cyberspace. Newhagen and Rafaeli focused on five defining characteristics of communication on the Internet: multimedia, packet switching, hypertextuality, synchroneity, and interactivity.

Besides synchroneity and interactivity, which have already been discussed, the other three properties deserve closer explanation. *Multimedia* is the use of computers to present text, graphics, video, animation, and sound in an integrated way. Long extolled as the future revolution in computing, multimedia applications were, until the mid-1990s, scarce due to the costly hardware required. With increases in performance and decreases in price, multimedia is now ubiquitous. Nearly all current personal computers are capable of displaying video, although the resolution available depends on the power of the computer's video adapter and central processing unit. Because of the storage demands of multimedia applications, the most effective media are CD–ROMs, and now Zip™ disks, which both contain far greater memory capacity than traditional floppy disks.

Packet switching refers to protocols in which messages are divided into packets before they are sent. Each packet is then transmitted individually and can even follow different routes to its destination. Once all the packets forming a message arrive at the destination, they are recompiled into the original message. In contrast, normal telephone service is based on a circuit-switching technology, in which a dedicated line is allocated for transmission between two parties. Circuit switching is ideal when data must be transmitted quickly and must arrive in the same order in which it is sent. This is the case with most real-time data, such as live audio and video. Packet switching is more efficient and robust for data that can withstand some delays in transmission, such as e-mail messages and Web pages (Newhagen & Rafaeli, 1996).

Hypertextuality, which constitutes the core of Internet documents, is created by the simple hypertext markup language (HTML), so that the text represents not a fixed linear sequence, but performs as a network to be actively composed (Sandbothe, 1996). Every building block of text (node) contains an abundance of keywords, pictograms, and pictures, which can be clicked on with a mouse; these are the links. Sandbothe (1996) predicted that hypertext technology already is having profound effects on the use of electronic texts:

> Every reader lays his own trail in the text whilst reading. Or rather, every reader composes the object he reads through the active selection of the links provided. The individual reception perspective determines the succession of text building blocks. Reading is no longer a passive process of reception, but rather becomes a process of creative interaction between reader, author, and text. (p. 2)

Additionally, many contemporary communication researchers seek to legitimize the Internet as a subject of research by framing a theoretical construct of the Internet as a continuum between mass and interpersonal communication. Similar questions appear to exist in the literature for both U&G and interpersonal communication. In both cases, the focus is on the biological, psychological, and sociological motivations behind people taking part in receiving or exchanging messages (Newhagen & Rafaeli, 1996). For example, Rice and Williams (1984) argued that interactive new media have the ability to "co-locate with the interpersonal sources on one or both of the personal dimensions" (p. 65). Garramone, Harris, and Anderson (1986) suggested that social presence mediates the relation between the interactive use and noninteractive use of political computer bulletin boards. Garrison (1995) adopted U&G to quantify a number of important questions about how and why journalists do computer-assisted reporting. Eighmey and McCord (1995) drew on the U&G perspective to examine the audience experience associated with Web sites. Thus, U&G research may well play a major role in answering initial Web-use questions of prurience, curiosity, profit seeking, and sociability. U&G also holds the prospect for understanding the Internet's mutability, or its broad range of communication opportunities, by "laying out a taxonomy of just what goes on in cyberspace" (Newhagen & Rafaeli, 1996, p. 11).

U&G AND QUALITATIVE METHODOLOGIES

Leeds-Hurwitz (1992) suggested that a revolution was occurring in all the fields that study human behavior, including communication. She cited specifically "cultural studies, critical theory, postmodernism, semiotics, phenomenology, structuralism, hermeneutics, naturalistic inquiry, ethnography and social communication" (p. 131). This led Weaver (1993) to sound a note of caution about dismissing quantitative methods. Weaver argued that many communication researchers have spent decades applying quantitative methods and statistical analysis. These methods have told us much about general patterns, trends, and relationships, and "can enable us to generalize with far more accuracy than can our own personal experiences and impressions" (p. 213). Additionally, Dobos (1992) concluded that the U&G approach should prove effective in ascertaining the importance of social context as a factor in the communication experience. Significantly, the way that individuals choose to use media differs accordingly with their position in the social structure (Roe, 1983; Rosengren & Windahl, 1989).

Thus, it is important to remember that U&G theory continues to offer more than a methodological perspective. Dervin (1980) advocated that media planners and those conducting information campaigns should begin with the study of the potential information user and the questions that person is attempting to answer to make sense of the world. After all, Pool (1983) noted that when a medium is in the early stages of development, predictions are often inaccurate. Thus, the U&G approach may serve as the vanguard of an eventual thorough quantitative and qualitative analysis of new media technologies.

This is not to relegate qualitative or interpretive methodologies to a subordinate role. On the contrary, Jensen and Jankowski (1991) suggested that quantitative methodologies could be used quite effectively to inform the more commonly used qualitative audience methodologies of interpretive media research. Different levels of analysis, including individual, small group, organizational, societal, and cultural, may require the use of multiple methods in single studies. Thus, communication researchers should be encouraged to employ U&G more frequently in conjunction with qualitative methodologies in a holistic approach. One case of this is Schaefer and Avery's (1993) study of audience conceptualizations of the *Late Night With David Letterman* television show. The study used both questionnaires and interviews to "combine the strengths of survey data with the richness of depth interviews" (p. 271). Additionally, Massey (1995) used a ninefold U&G typology to operationalize her qualitative study of audience media use during the 1989 Loma Prieta earthquake disaster.

Newhagen and Rafaeli (1996) suggested that in time, questions at cultural and societal levels may offer the greatest contribution to communications research. For example, Morley's (1980, 1986, 1992) studies of family TV viewing and domestic power in the working class, Radway's (1984) account of female empowerment linked to reading romance novels, I. Ang's (1985) analysis of Dutch women's interpretations and use of the international television series *Dallas,* Liebes and Katz's (1990) analysis of ethnic and cultural variation in *Dallas* audiences, and Lull's (1991) study of Chinese viewers' resistive engagements with television all document culturally and historically specific ways in which audiences actively interpret and use mass media (Lull, 1995). However, to truly understand new media technologies, critical scholars should learn to embrace multiple levels of analysis. Empiricists, on the other hand, Newhagen and Rafaeli argued, "will have to show a greater, more eclectic tolerance for experimental science" (p. 9).

THEORETICAL SYNOPSIS OF U&G

More than a decade ago, after reviewing the results of approximately 100 U&G studies, Palmgreen (1984) proclaimed that a complex theoretical structure was emerging. Palmgreen's statement has significance for contemporary and future mass communication researchers in at least two ways. First, he was proposing an integrative gratifications model that suggested a multivariate approach (Wimmer & Dominick, 1994); that is, a commitment for researchers to investigate the relation between one or more independent variables and more than one dependent variable. He noted emergent research techniques such as hierarchical regression, canonical correlation, multiple classification analysis, and structural equation modeling to control for media exposure and other intervening variables (Rayburn, 1996). Second, Palmgreen was answering critics who had long argued that the U&G perspective was more a research strategy or heuristic orientation than a theory (Elliott, 1974; Swanson, 1977; Weiss, 1976). He suggested that audience GS and GO were associated with a broad variance of media effects including knowledge, dependency, attitudes, perceptions of social reality, agenda setting, discussion, and politics (Rayburn, 1996).

Thus, if anything, one of the major strengths of the U&G perspective has been its capacity to develop over time into a more sophisticated theoretical model. Historically, the focus of inquiry has shifted from a mechanistic perspective's interest in direct effects of media on receivers to a psychological perspective that stresses individual use and choice (Rubin, 1994b). U&G researchers have also moved from a microperspective toward a macroanalysis. Thus, although the microunit of data collection has primarily remained the individual, the focus of inquiry has been transformed over time. Interpretation of the individual's response by researchers has shifted from the sender to the receiver, from the media to the audience. The primary unit of data collection of U&G continues be the individual, but that individual's activity is now analyzed in a plethora of psychological and social contexts including media dependency, ritualization, instrumental, communication facilitation, affiliation or avoidance, social learning, and role reinforcement. U&G research continues to typologize motivations for media use in terms of diversion (i.e., as an escape from routines or for emotional release), social utility (i.e., to acquire information for conversations), personal identity (i.e., to reinforce attitudes, beliefs, and values), and surveillance (i.e., to learn about one's community, events, and political affairs).

Furthermore, previous U&G researchers have primarily concentrated on choice, reception, and manner of response of the media audience. A key assumption has been that the audience member makes a conscious and motivated choice among media channel and content (McQuail, 1994). Yet, recent U&G researchers have even begun to question stock assumptions about the active audience concept. Although researchers continue to regard audience members as universally active, some now suggest that all audience members are not equally active at all times (Rubin, 1994b). This assertiveness of U&G researchers to continuously critique basic assumptions suggests a dynamic and evolving theoretical atmosphere, especially as we depart the industrial era for the postindustrial age.

U&G AS LEGITIMATE THEORY

Perhaps endlessly, scholars will continue to debate which prevailing theories should be acknowledged as "legitimate" communication theories. U&G detractors may well continue to label it as an approach rather than an authentic theory. Skeptics may question the theory for a lack of empirical distinction between needs and motivations and the obstacles of measuring the gratification of needs. They may argue that the theory posits a rigid teleology within a functionalist approach (Cazeneuve, 1974). Or, as Carey and Kreiling (1974) argued, the utilitarianistic audience-centered interpretations will not suffice to decode popular culture consumption because "an effective theory of popular culture will require a conception of man, not as psychological or sociological man, but as cultural man" (p. 242). Finally, Finn (1997) questioned the ability of U&G researchers to solve the enigma of "linking personality traits to patterns of mass media use without accounting for alternative sources of gratification in the interpersonal domain" (p. 11). Yet, even critical scholars recognize that U&G research, chiefly pioneered by postwar social psychologists, has brought to the forefront the concept that the audience's perceptions of media messages may be altogether different from the meanings intended by their producers (Stevenson, 1997).

For its advocates, however, U&G is still touted as one of the most influential theories in the field of communication research (Lin, 1998). Furthermore, the concept of *needs,* which most U&G theorists embrace as a central psychological concept, is nearly irreproachable in more established disciplines. Within psychology, need is the bedrock of some of the discipline's most important theoretical work, including cognitive dissonance theory, social exchange theory, attribution theory, and some types of psychoanalytic theory (Lull, 1995). Samuels (1984) suggested physiological and psychological needs such as self-actualization, cognitive needs (such as curiosity), aesthetic needs, and expressive needs are inherent in every individual and central to human experience. Additionally, human needs are influenced by culture, not only in their formation but in how they are gratified. "Thus, culturally situated social experience reinforces basic biological and psychological needs while simultaneously giving direction to their sources of gratification" (Lull, 1995, p. 99). Lull further suggested that the study of how and why individuals use media, through U&G research, may offer clues to our understanding about exactly what needs are, where they originate, and how they are gratified.

Unfortunately, the polemic over whether U&G satisfies the standard of a full-fledged theory continues. In part it may be due to the antiquated perception that any communication theory is inherently deficient to the traditional disciplines of sociology and psychology. Even more acrimonious is continued criticism by critical and cultural scholars that the perspective embodies a functionalist approach. Certainly, early U&G emanated from a functionalist theoretical framework; a sociological theory that theorized patterned social phenomena leading to specific social consequences. However, Lin (1996) argued that this functionalist approach provides the "means–ends orientation [for the perspective and] opens up a world of opportunities for studying mediated communication as a functional process that is purposive and leads to specific psychological or social consequences" (p. 2). Additionally, Massey (1995) contended that qualitative communication scholars may find it difficult to advance the "illumination of audience interaction with the media" (p. 17) if they reject the questions, methods, and determinist results of U&G research. Newhagen and Rafaeli (1996) suggested that mass media scholars will eventually have to address profound societal ramifications of new media. However, U&G theory offers researchers the ability to examine challenges and barriers to access that individual users are currently experiencing.

U&G: A CUTTING-EDGE THEORY

By and large, U&G has always provided a cutting-edge theoretical approach in the initial stages of each new mass communications medium: newspapers, radio, television, and now the Internet. It may be argued that the timely emergence of computer-mediated communication has only bolstered the theoretical potency of U&G by allowing it to stimulate productive research into a proliferating telecommunications medium. Lin (1996) argued that the primary strength of U&G theory is its ability to permit researchers to investigate "mediated communication situations via a single or multiple sets of psychological needs, psychological motives, communication channels, communication content, and psychological gratifications within a particular or cross-cultural context" (p. 574). For example, the use of personal computers has been linked to individuals' motivations to use the Internet for communication purposes linked to the fulfillment of gratifications such as social identity, interpersonal communication, parasocial interaction, companionship, escape, entertainment, and surveillance. As new communication technologies rapidly materialize, the range of possible topics for U&G research also multiplies. This flexibility is particularly important as we enter an information age in which computer-mediated communication permeates every aspect of our individual and social lives.

U&G AND ITS ROLE IN THE 21ST CENTURY

The Internet lies at the locus of a new media ecology that has "altered the structural relations among traditional media such as print and broadcast and unites them around the defining technologies of computer and satellite" (Carey, 1998, p. 34). This convergence makes the old print–electronic and verbal–nonverbal distinctions, so long the focus of communication researchers, less relevant in light of messages that combine writing, still and animated images, and voices and other sounds (Weaver, 1993). For users, text, voice, pictures, animation, video, virtual reality motion codes, and even smell have already become part of the Internet experience (Newhagen & Rafaeli, 1996). Communication on the Internet travels at unparalleled velocity. The Internet offers its audience an immense range of communication opportunities. Networks are always "up," allowing 24-hour asynchronous or synchronous interactions and information retrieval and exchange among individuals and groups (Kiesler, 1997). Fortuitous for U&G researchers, communication on the Internet also leaves a trail that is easily traceable. Messages have time stamps, accurate to one hundredth of a second. Content is readily observable, recorded, and copied. Participant demography and behaviors of consumption, choice, attention, reaction, and learning afford extraordinary research opportunities (Newhagen & Rafaeli, 1996). James et al. (1995) suggested Internet forums such as electronic bulletin boards fulfill many expectations of both mass and interpersonal communication. Hence, if the Internet is a new dominion of human activity, it is also a new dominion for U&G researchers.

If the Internet is a technology that many predict will be genuinely transformative, it will lead to profound changes in media users' personal and social habits and roles. The Internet's growth rates are exponential. The number of users has doubled in each of the last 6 years. If this development continues at the same rate, the Internet will soon be as widely disseminated a medium in daily usage as television or the telephone (Quarterman & Carl-Mitchell, 1993). Thus, electronic communication technology may sufficiently alter the context of media use that current mass communication theories do not yet address. Some foresee, for example, that soon the novelty of combining music, video, graphics, and text will wane, and more natural methods will be created for Web users to interact in, such as data "landscapes" (Aldersey-Williams, 1996). Others predict a move beyond studying single users, two-person ties, and small groups, to analyzing the computer-supported social networks that flourish in areas as diverse as the workplace and in virtual communities (Garton, Haythornthwaite, & Wellman, 1997). Gilder (1990) argued that the new media technologies like the Internet will empower individuals by "blowing apart all monopolies, hierarchies, pyramids, and power grids of established society" (p. 32). Others caution that the Internet is becoming more institutionally and commercially driven and is beginning to be "less the egalitarian cyberspace of recent memory than it does a tacky, crowded-with-billboards freeway exit just before any major tourist destination in the U.S." (Riley, Keough, Christiansen, Meilich, & Pierson, 1998, p. 3).

Theoretically and practically, for U&G scholars, however, the basic questions remain the same. Why do people become involved in one particular type of mediated communication or another, and what gratifications do they receive from it? Although we are likely to continue using traditional tools and typologies to answer these questions, we must also be prepared to expand our current theoretical models of U&G to include concepts such as interactivity, demassification, hypertextuality, asynchroneity, and interpersonal aspects of mediated communication. Then, if we are able to situate a "modernized" U&G theory within this new media ecology, in an evolving psychological, sociological, and cultural context, we should be able to anticipate a highly serviceable theory for the 21st century.

REFERENCES

Abrahamson, D. (1998). The visible hand: Money, markets, and media evolution. *Journalism and Mass Communication Quarterly, 75,* 14–18.
Aldersey-Williams, H. (1996). Interactivity with a human face. *Technology Review, 99,* 34–40.
Anderson, D. R., Collins, P. A., Schmitt, K. L., & Jacobvitz, R. S. (1996). Stressful life events and television viewing. *Communication Research, 23,* 243–260.
Anderson, J. A. (1996). *Communication theory: Epistemological foundations.* New York: Guilford.
Anderson, K. J., & Revelle, W. (1995). Personality processes. *Annual Review of Psychology, 46,* 295–328.
Ang, I. (1985). *Watching Dallas: Soap opera and the melodramatic imagination.* London: Routledge.
Ang, S., & Cummings, L. L. (1994). Panel analysis of feedback-seeking patterns in face-to-face, computer-mediated, and computer-generated communication environments. *Perceptual and Motor Skills, 79,* 67–73.
Anonymous. (1989). Functional displacement of traditional TV viewing by VCR owners. *Journal of Advertising Research, 29*(2), 18–23.
Armstrong, C. B., & Rubin, A. M. (1989). Talk radio as interpersonal communication. *Journal of Communication, 39*(2), 84–94.
Atkin, D. (1993). Adoption of cable amidst a multimedia environment. *Telematics & Informatics, 10,* 51–58.

MILESTONE MASS COMMUNICATIONS THEORIES

Ball-Rokeach, S. (1985). The origins of individual media-system dependency: A sociological framework. *Communication Research, 12,* 485–510.

Bantz, C. R. (1982). Exploring uses and gratifications: A comparison of reported uses of television and reported uses of favorite program type. *Communication Research, 9,* 352–379.

Barwise, T. P., Ehrenberg, A. S. C., & Goodhardt, G. J. (1982). Glued to the box. *Journal of Communication, 32*(4), 22–29.

Berelson, B. (1949). What "missing the newspaper" means. In P. F. Lazarsfeld & F. N. Stanton (Eds.), *Communication research 1948–1949* (pp. 111–129). New York: Harper.

Berelson, B., Lazarsfeld, P. F., & McPhee, W. N. (1954). *Voting: A study of opinion formation in a presidential campaign.* Chicago: University of Chicago Press.

Bergeron, B. P., & Bailin, M. T. (1997). The contribution of hypermedia link authoring. *Technical Communication, 44,* 121–128.

Blumler, J. G. (1979). The role of theory in uses and gratifications studies. *Communication Research, 6,* 9–36.

Blumler, J. G. (1985). The social character of media gratifications. In K. E. Rosengren, L. A. Wenner, & P. Palmgreen (Eds.), *Media gratifications research: Current perspectives* (pp. 41–59). Beverly Hills, CA: Sage.

Bryant, J., & Zillman, D. (1984). Using television to alleviate boredom and stress. *Journal of Broadcasting, 28,* 1–20.

Cantril, H. (1940). *The invasion from Mars: A study in the psychology of panic.* Princeton, NJ: Princeton University Press.

Cantril, H. (1942). Professor quiz: A gratifications study. In P. F. Lazarsfeld & F. Stanton (Eds.), *Radio research 1941* (pp. 34–45). New York: Duell, Sloan & Pearce.

Cantril, H., & Allport, G. (1935). *The psychology of radio.* New York: Harper.

Carey, J. W. (1998). The Internet and the end of the National Communication System: Uncertain predictions of an uncertain future. *Journalism and Mass Communication Quarterly, 75*(1), 28–34.

Carey, J. W., & Kreiling, A. L. (1974). Popular culture and uses and gratifications: Notes toward an accommodation. In J. G. Blumler & E. Katz (Eds.), *The uses of mass communications: Current perspectives on gratifications research* (pp. 225–248). Beverly Hills, CA: Sage.

Cattell, R. B., Edger, H. W., & Tatsuoka, M. M. (1970). *Handbook for the Sixteen Personality Factor Questionnaire.* Champaign, IL: Institute of Personality and Ability Testing.

Cazeneuve, E. (1974). Television as a functional alternative to traditional sources of need satisfaction. In J. G. Blumler & E. Katz (Eds.), *The uses of mass communications: Current perspectives on gratifications research* (pp. 213–224). Beverly Hills, CA: Sage.

Chamberlain, M. A. (1994). New technologies in health communication. *American Behavioral Scientist, 38,* 271–284.

Cohen, A. A. (1981). People without media: Attitudes and behavior during a general media strike. *Journal of Broadcasting, 25,* 171–180.

Cooper, R. (1996). The status and future of audience duplication research: An assessment of ratings-based theories of audience behavior. *Journal of Broadcasting & Electronic Media, 40,* 96–116.

Cooper, R. (1997). Japanese communication research: The emphasis on macro theories of media in an information based environment. *Journal of Broadcasting & Electronic Media, 41,* 284–288.

Cowles, D. (1989). Consumer perceptions of interactive media. *Journal of Broadcasting & Electronic Media, 33,* 83–89.

de Bock, H. (1980). Gratification frustration during a newspaper strike and a TV blackout. *Journalism Quarterly, 57,* 61–66, 78.

December, J. (1996). Units of analysis for Internet communication. *Journal of Communication, 46*(1), 14–37.

DeFleur, M. L., & Ball-Rokeach, S. (1982). *Theories of mass communication* (4th ed.). New York: Longman.

Dervin, B. (1980). Communication gaps and inequities: Moving toward a reconceptualization. In B. Dervin & M. J. Voight (Eds.), *Progress in communication sciences* (Vol. 2, pp. 73–112). Norwood, NJ: Ablex.

Dicken-Garcia, H. (1998). The Internet and continuing historical discourse. *Journalism and Mass Communication Quarterly, 75,* 19–27.

Dobos, J. (1992). Gratification models of satisfaction and choice of communication channels in organizations. *Communication Research, 19,* 29–51.

Donohew, L., Finn, S., & Christ, W. G. (1988). The nature of news revisited: The roles of affect, schemas, and cognition. In L. Donohew, H. E. Sypher, & E. T. Higgins (Eds.), *Communication, social cognition and affect* (pp. 195–218). Hillsdale, NJ: Lawrence Erlbaum Associates, Inc.

Donohew, L., Palmgreen P., & Rayburn, J. D., II. (1987). Social and psychological origins of media use: A lifestyle analysis. *Journal of Broadcasting & Electronic Media, 31,* 255–278.

Dorsher, M. (1996, August). *Whither the public sphere: Prospects for cybersphere.* Paper presented at the Media, Technology, and Community Conference, Grand Forks, ND.

Dozier, D. M., & Rice, R. E. (1984). Rival theories of electronic newsgathering. In R. E. Rice (Ed.), *The new media: Communication, research, and technology* (pp. 103–128). Beverly Hills, CA: Sage.

Dunleavy, P., & Weir, S. (1998). How to freshen up democracy. *New Statesman, 11,* 535, 571–572.

Dutton, W. H., Rogers, E. M., & Jun, S. (1987). Diffusion and social impact of personal computers. *Communication Research, 14,* 219–249.

Dyson, E. (1993). Interactivity means "active" participation. *Computerworld, 27*(50), 33–34.

Eastman, S. T. (1979). Uses of television viewing and consumer life styles: A multivariate analysis. *Journal of Broadcasting, 23,* 491–500.

Eighmey, J. (1997). Profiling user responses to commercial Web sites. *Journal of Advertising Research, 37*(3), 59–66.

Eighmey, J., & McCord, L. (1995, November). *Adding value in the information age: Uses and gratifications of the World-Wide Web.* Paper presented at the Conference on Telecommunications and Information Markets. Newport, RI.

Elliott, P. (1974). Uses and gratifications research: A critique and a sociological alternative. In J. G. Blumler & E. Katz (Eds.), *The uses of mass communications: Current perspectives on gratifications research* (pp. 249–268). Beverly Hills, CA: Sage.

Eysenck, H. J. (1991). Dimensions of personality: 16, 5, or 3?—Criteria for a taxonomic paradigm. *Personality and Individual Differences, 12,* 773–790.

Ferguson, D. A. (1992). Channel repertoire in the presence of remote control devices, VCRs and cable television. *Journal of Broadcasting & Electronic Media, 36,* 83–91.

Ferguson, D. A., & Perse, E. M. (1994, March). *Viewing television without a remote: A deprivation study.* Paper presented at the annual meeting of the Research Division, Broadcast Education Association, Las Vegas, NV.

Finn, S. (1997). Origins of media exposure: Linking personality traits to TV, radio, print, and film use. *Communication Research, 24,* 507–529.

Fishbein, M., & Ajzen, I. (1975). *Belief, attitude, and behavior.* Reading, MA: Addison-Wesley.

Fredin, E. S., & David, P. (1998). Browsing and the hypermedia interaction cycle: A model of self-efficacy and goal dynamics. *Journalism and Mass Communication Quarterly, 75,* 35–54.

Fry, D. L., & McCain, T. A. (1983). Community influentials' media dependency in dealing with a controversial local issue. *Journalism Quarterly, 60,* 458–463.

Fulk, J., Flanagin, A. J., Kalman, A. E., Monge, P. R., & Ryan, T. (1996). Connective and communal public goods in interactive communication systems. *Communication Theory, 6,* 60–87.

Funk, J. B., & Buchman, D. D. (1996). Playing violent video and computer games and adolescent self-concept. *Journal of Communication, 46*(2), 19–32.

Galloway, J. J., & Meek, F. L. (1981). Audience uses and gratifications: An expectancy model. *Communication Research, 8,* 435–449.

Gandy, O. H., Jr., Matabane, P. W., & Omachonu, J. O. (1987). Media use, reliance, and active participation. *Communication Research, 14,* 644–663.

Garramone, G. (1984). Audience motivation effects: More evidence. *Communication Research, 11,* 79–96.

Garramone, G. (1985). Motivation and selective attention to political information formats. *Journalism Quarterly, 62,* 37–44.

Garramone, G. M., Harris, A. C., & Anderson, R. (1986). Uses of political computer bulletin boards. *Journal of Broadcasting & Electronic Media, 30,* 325–339.

Garrison, B. (1995). Online services as reporting tools: Daily newspaper use of commercial databases in 1994. *Newspaper Research Journal, 16*(4), 74–86.

Garton, L., Haythornthwaite, C., & Wellman, B. (1997). Studying online social networks. *Journal of Computer-Mediated Communication, 3*(1). Retrieved May 1999 from the World Wide Web: http://jcmc.huji/ vol3/issue1/garton.html#ABSTRACT

Geiger, S., & Newhagen, J. (1993). Revealing the black box: Information processing and media effects. *Journal of Communication, 43*(3), 42–50.

Gerson, W. (1966). Mass media socialization behavior: Negro–Whites differences. *Social Forces, 45,* 40–50.

Gilder, G. (1990). *Life after television.* Knoxville, TN: Whittle Direct.

Goodhardt, G. J., Ehrenberg, A. S. C., & Collins, M. A. (1987). *The television audience: Patterns of viewing* (2nd ed.). Aldershot, England: Gower.

Grant, A. E., Guthrie, K. K., & Ball-Rokeach, S. (1991). Television shopping: A media dependency perspective. *Communication Research, 18,* 773–798.

Greenberg, B. S. (1974). Gratifications of television viewing and their correlates for British children. In J. G. Blumler & E. Katz (Eds.), *The uses of mass communications: Current perspectives on gratifications research* (pp. 71–92). Beverly Hills, CA: Sage.

Greenberg, B. S., & Dominick, J. (1969). Race and social class differences in teenager's use of television. *Journal of Broadcasting, 13*(4), 331–344.

Grunig, J. E. (1979). Time budgets, level of involvement and use of the mass media. *Journalism Quarterly, 56,* 248–261.

Ha, L. (1995). Subscriber's behavior in electronic discussion groups: A comparison between academics and practitioners. In *Proceedings of the first annual conference on telecommunications and information markets* (pp. 27–36).

Ha, L., & James, E. L. (1998). Interactivity reexamined: A baseline analysis of early business Web sites. *Journal of Broadcasting & Electronic Media, 42,* 457–474.

Hawkins, R. P., & Pingree, S. (1981). Uniform messages and habitual viewing: Unnecessary assumptions in social reality effects. *Human Communication Research, 7,* 291–301.

Heeter, C. (1989). Implications of new interactive technologies for conceptualizing communication. In J. L. Salvaggio & J. Bryant (Eds.), *Media use in the information age: Emerging patterns of adoption and consumer use* (pp. 217–235). Hillsdale, NJ: Lawrence Erlbaum Associates, Inc.

Heeter, C., & Greenberg, B. (1985). Cable and program choice. In D. Zillman & J. Bryant (Eds.), *Selective exposure to communication* (pp. 203–224). Hillsdale, NJ: Lawrence Erlbaum Associates, Inc.

Herzog, H. (1940). Professor quiz: A gratification study. In P. F. Lazarsfeld & F. N. Stanton (Eds.), *Radio and the printed page* (pp. 64–93). New York: Duell, Sloan & Pearce.

Herzog, H. (1944). What do we really know about daytime serial listeners? In P. F. Lazarsfeld & F. N. Stanton (Eds.), *Radio research 1942–1943* (pp. 3–33). New York: Duell, Sloan & Pearce.

Horna, J. (1988). The mass media as leisure: A western-Canadian case. *Society and Leisure, 11,* 283–301.

Jackson, M. H. (1997). Assessing the structure of communication on the World Wide Web. *Journal of Computer-Mediated Communication, 3.* Retrieved May 1999 from the World Wide Web: http://jcmc.huji.ac. il/vol3/issue1/jackson.html#ABSTRACT

Jacobs, R. (1995). Exploring the determinants of cable television subscriber satisfaction. *Journal of Broadcasting & Electronic Media, 39,* 262–274.

James, M. L., Wotring, C. E., & Forrest, E. J. (1995). An exploratory study of the perceived benefits of electronic bulletin board use and their impact on other communication activities. *Journal of Broadcasting & Electronic Media, 39,* 30–50.

Jensen, K. B., & Jankowski, N. W. (1991). *A handbook of qualitative methodologies for mass communication research.* New York: Routledge.

Katz, E. (1960). The two-step flow of communication. In W. Schramm (Ed.), *Mass communications* (pp. 346–365). Urbana: University of Illinois Press.

Katz, E. (1987). Communication research since Lazarsfeld. *Public Opinion Quarterly, 51,* 525–545.

Katz, E., Blumler, J., & Gurevitch, M. (1974). Utilization of mass communication by the individual. In J. Blumler & E. Katz (Eds.), *The uses of mass communication: Current perspectives on gratifications research* (pp. 19–34). Beverly Hills, CA: Sage.

Katz, E., & Foulkes, D. (1962). On the use of mass media as escape: Clarification of a concept. *Public Opinion Quarterly, 26,* 377–388.

Katz, E., Gurevitch, M., & Haas, H. (1973). On the use of the mass media for important things. *American Sociological Review, 38,* 164–181.

Katz, E., & Lazarsfeld, P. F. (1955). *Personal influence: The part played by people in the flow of mass communications.* Glencoe, IL: Free Press.

Kiesler, S. (Ed.). (1997). *Culture of the Internet.* Mahwah, NJ: Lawrence Erlbaum Associates, Inc.

Kimball, P. (1959). People without papers. *Public Opinion Quarterly, 23,* 389–398.

Klapper, J. T. (1960). *The effects of mass communication.* New York: Free Press.

Klapper, J. T. (1963). Mass communication research: An old road resurveyed. *Public Opinion Quarterly, 27,* 515–527.

Kubey, R. (1986). Television use in everyday life: Coping with unstructured time. *Journal of Communication, 36*(3), 108–123.

Kubey, R., & Csikszentmihalyi, M. (1990). *Television and the quality of life.* Hillsdale, NJ: Lawrence Erlbaum Associates, Inc.

Kuehn, S. A. (1994). Computer-mediated communication in instructional settings: A research agenda. *Communication Education, 43,* 171–182.

LaRose, R., & Atkin, D. (1991). An analysis of pay-per-view versus other movie delivery modalities. *Journal of Media Economics, 4,* 3–17.

Lazarsfeld, P. F., Berelson, B., & Gaudet, H. (1948). *The people's choice* (2nd ed.). New York: Columbia University Press.

Lazarsfeld, P. F., & Stanton, F. (1942). *Radio research, 1942–1943.* New York: Duell, Sloan & Pearce.

Lazarsfeld, P. F., & Stanton, F. (1944). *Radio research, 1941.* New York: Duell, Sloan & Pearce.

Lazarsfeld, P. F., & Stanton, F. (1949). *Communication research 1948–1949.* New York: Harper & Row.

Leeds-Hurwitz, W. (1992). Social approaches to interpersonal communication. *Communication Theory, 2,* 131–139.

Lemish, D. (1985). Soap opera viewing in college: A naturalistic inquiry. *Journal of Broadcasting & Electronic Media, 29,* 275–293.

Levy, M. R., & Windahl, S. (1984). Audience activity and gratifications: A conceptual clarification and exploration. *Communication Research, 11,* 51–78.

Lichtenstein, A., & Rosenfeld, L. B. (1983). Uses and misuses of gratifications research: An explication of media functions. *Communication Research, 10,* 97–109.

Liebes, T., & Katz, E. (1990). *The export of meaning.* New York: Oxford University Press.

Lin, C. A. (1993). Exploring the role of the VCR use in the emerging home entertainment culture. *Journalism Quarterly, 70,* 833–842.

Lin, C. A. (1996). Looking back: The contribution of Blumler and Katz's uses and mass communication to communication research. *Journal of Broadcasting & Electronic Media, 40,* 574–581.

Lin, C. A. (1998). Exploring personal computer adoption dynamics. *Journal of Broadcasting & Electronic Media, 42*, 95–112.

Lind, R. A. (1995). How can TV news be improved?: Viewer perceptions of quality and responsibility. *Journal of Broadcasting & Electronic Media, 39*, 360–375.

Loges, W. E., & Ball-Rokeach, S. (1993). Dependency relations and newspaper readership. *Journalism Quarterly, 70*, 601–614.

Lometti, G. E., Reeves, B., & Bybee, C. R. (1977). Investigating the assumptions of uses and gratifications research. *Communication Research, 4*, 321–328.

Lowery, S., & DeFleur, M. L. (1983). *Milestones in mass communication research.* New York: Longman.

Lull, J. (1991). *China turned on: Television, reform and resistance.* London: Routledge.

Lull, J. (1995). *Media, communication, culture: A global approach.* New York: Columbia University Press.

Markus, M. L. (1994). Finding a happy medium: Explaining the negative effects of electronic communication on social life at work. *ACM Transactions on Information Systems, 14*, 119–149.

Massey, K. B. (1995). Analyzing the uses and gratifications concept of audience activity with a qualitative approach: Media encounters during the 1989 Loma Prieta earthquake disaster. *Journal of Broadcasting & Electronic Media, 39*, 328–342.

McGuire, W. J. (1974). Psychological motives and communication gratifications. In J. G. Blumler & E. Katz (Eds.), *The uses of mass communications: Current perspectives on gratifications research* (pp. 167–196). Beverly Hills, CA: Sage.

McIlwraith, R. D. (1998). "I'm addicted to television": The personality, imagination, and TV watching patterns of self-identified TV addicts. *Journal of Broadcasting & Electronic Media, 42*, 371–386.

McLeod, J. M., & Becker, L. (1981). The uses and gratifications approach. In D. Nimmo & K. Sanders (Eds.), *Handbook of political communication* (pp. 67–100). Beverly Hills, CA: Sage.

McLeod, J. M., Bybee, C. R., & Durall, J. A. (1982). On evaluating news media performance. *Political Communication, 10*, 16–22.

McQuail, D. (1994). The rise of media of mass communication. In D. McQuail (Ed.), *Mass communication theory: An introduction* (pp. 1–29). London: Sage.

McQuail, D., Blumler, J., & Brown, J. (1972). The television audience: A revised perspective. In D. McQuail (Ed.), *Sociology of mass communications* (pp. 135–165). Middlesex, England: Penguin.

Mendelsohn, H. (1964). Listening to the radio. In L. A. Dexter & D. M. White (Eds.), *People, society and mass communication* (pp. 239–248). New York: Free Press.

Merton, R. K. (1949). Patterns of influence: A study of interpersonal influence and communications behavior in a local community. In P. F. Lazarsfeld & F. N. Stanton (Eds.), *Communication research, 1948–1949* (pp. 180–219). New York: Harper.

Morley, D. (1980). *The nationwide audience.* London: Film Institute.

Morley, D. (1986). *Family television: Cultural power and domestic leisure.* London: Routledge.

Morley, D. (1992). *Television, audiences, and cultural studies.* London: Routledge.

Morris, M., & Ogan, C. (1996). The Internet as mass medium. *Journal of Communications, 46*(1), 39–50.

Nelson, T. H. (1990). The right way to think about software design. In B. Laurel (Ed.), *The art of human–computer interface design.* Reading, MA: Addison-Wesley.

Newhagen, J., & Rafaeli, S. (1996). Why communication researchers should study the Internet: A dialogue. *Journal of Communications, 46*(1), 4–13.

Nisbett, R., & Wilson, T. (1977). Telling more than we can know: Verbal reports on mental processes. *Psychological Review, 84*, 231–259.

Ostman, R. E., & Jeffers, D. W. (1980, June). *The relationship of life-stage to motives for using television and the perceived reality of TV.* Paper presented at the International Communication Association convention, Acapulco, Mexico.

Palmgreen, P. (1984). Uses and gratifications: A theoretical perspective. In R. Bostrom (Ed.), *Communication Yearbook 8* (pp. 20–55). Beverly Hills, CA: Sage.

Palmgreen, P., & Rayburn, J. D., II. (1979). Uses and gratifications and exposure to public television. *Communication Research, 6*, 155–180.

Palmgreen, P., & Rayburn, J. D., II. (1982). Gratifications sought and media exposure: An expectancy value model. *Communication Research, 9*, 561–580.

Palmgreen, P., & Rayburn, J. D., II. (1985). A comparison of gratification models of media satisfaction. *Communication Monographs, 52*, 334–346.

Perse, E. M., & Courtright, J. A. (1993). Normative images of communication research. *Human Communication, 19*, 485–503.

Perse, E. M., & Dunn, D. G. (1998). The utility of home computers and media use: Implications of multimedia and connectivity. *Journal of Broadcasting & Electronic Media, 42*, 435–456.

Perse, E. M., & Rubin, A. M. (1988). Audience activity and satisfaction with favorite television soap opera. *Journalism Quarterly, 65*, 368–375.

Pool, I. D. (1983). *Technologies of freedom.* Cambridge, MA: Harvard University Press.

Quarterman, J. S., & Carl-Mitchell, S. (1993). The computing paradigm shift. *Journal of Organizational Computing, 3*, 31–50.

Radway, J. (1984). *Reading the romance: Feminism, and the representation of women in popular culture.* Chapel Hill: University of North Carolina Press.

Rafaeli, S. (1986). The electronic bulletin board: A computer-driven mass medium. *Computers and the Social Sciences, 2*, 123–136.

Rayburn, J. D. (1996). Uses and gratifications. In M. B. Salwen & D. W. Stacks (Eds.), *An integrated approach to communication theory and research* (pp. 97–119). Mahwah, NJ: Lawrence Erlbaum Associates, Inc.

Rayburn, J. D., & Palmgreen, P. (1984). Merging uses and gratifications and expectancy-value theory. *Communication Research, 11*, 537–562.

Reagan, J. (1996). The "repertoire" of information sources. *Journal of Broadcasting & Electronic Media, 40*, 112–119.

Rice, R. E., & Williams, F. (1984). Theories old and new: The study of the new media. In R. E. Rice (Ed.), *The new media: Communication, research, and technology* (pp. 55–80). Beverly Hills, CA: Sage.

Riley, P., Keough, C. M., Christiansen, T., Meilich, O., & Pierson, J. (1998). Community or colony: The case of online newspapers and the Web. *Journal of Computer-Mediated Communication, 4.* Retrieved May 1999 from the World Wide Web: http://jcmc.huji.ac.il/vol4/ issue1/keough.html#ABSTRACT

Roe, K. (1983). *Mass media and adolescent schooling: Conflict or co-existence?* Stockholm, Sweden: Almqvist & Wiksell.

Rogers, E. (1986). *Communication technology: The new media.* New York: Free Press.

Rosengren, K. E. (1974). Uses and gratifications: A paradigm outlined. In J. G. Blumler & E. Katz (Eds.), *The uses of mass communications: Current perspectives on gratifications research* (pp. 269–286). Beverly Hills, CA: Sage.

Rosengren, K. E., Johnsson-Smaragdi, U., & Sonesson, I. (1994). For better and for worse: effects studies and beyond. In K. E. Rosengren (Ed.), *Media effects and beyond: Culture, socialization and lifestyles* (pp. 302–315). New York: Routledge.

Rosengren, K. E., & Windahl, S. (1989). *Media matter: TV use in childhood and adolescence.* Norwood: NJ: Ablex.

Rosenstein, A. W., & Grant, A. E. (1997). Reconceptualizing the role of habit: A new model of television audience. *Journal of Broadcasting & Electronic Media, 41*, 324–344.

Rubin, A. M. (1981). An examination of television viewing motivations. *Communication Research, 8*, 141–165.

Rubin, A. M. (1983). Television uses and gratifications: The interactions of viewing patterns and motivations. *Journal of Broadcasting, 27,* 37–51.

Rubin, A. M. (1984). Ritualized and instrumental television viewing. *Journal of Communication, 34*(3), 67–77.

Rubin, A. M. (1986). Uses, gratifications, and media effects research. In J. Bryant & D. Zillmann (Eds.), *Perspectives on media effects* (pp. 281–301). Hillsdale, NJ: Lawrence Erlbaum Associates, Inc.

Rubin, A. M. (1994a). Audience activity and media use. *Communication Monographs, 60,* 98–105.

Rubin, A. M. (1994b). Media uses and effects: A uses and gratifications perspective. In J. Bryant & D. Zillmann (Eds.), *Media effects: Advances in theory and research* (pp. 417–436). Hillsdale, NJ: Lawrence Erlbaum Associates, Inc.

Rubin, A. M., & Windahl, S. (1986). The uses and dependency model of mass communication. *Critical Studies in Mass Communication, 3,* 184–199.

Samuels, F. (1984). *Human needs and behavior.* Cambridge, MA: Schnenkman.

Sandbothe, M. (1996). *Interactivity—hypertexuality—transversality: A media-philosophical analysis of the Internet.* Retrieved May 1999 from the World Wide Web: http://www.uni-jena.de/ms/tele/part2.html

Schaefer, R. J., & Avery, R. K. (1993). Audience conceptualizations of "Late night with David Letterman." *Journal of Broadcasting & Electronic Media, 37,* 253–273.

Schramm, W. (1949). The nature of news. *Journalism Quarterly, 26,* 259–269.

Schramm, W., Lyle, J., & Parker, E. (1961). *Television in the lives of our children.* Stanford, CA: Stanford University Press.

Severin, W. J., & Tankard, J. W. (1997). *Communication theories: Origins, methods, and uses in the mass media* (4th ed.). New York: Longman.

Singer, J. B. (1998). Online journalists: Foundations for research into their changing roles. *Journal of Computer-Mediated Communication, 4.* Retrieved May 1999 from the World Wide Web: http://jcmc.huji.ac.il/vol4/issue1/smith.html#ABSTRACT

Smith, C. B. (1997). Casting the net: Surveying an Internet population. *Journal of Computer-Mediated Communication, 3.* Retrieved May 1999 from the World Wide Web: http://jcmc.huji.ac.il/vol3/issue1/singer.html#ABSTRACT

Stanford, S. W. (1983). Comments on Palmgreen and Rayburn: Gratifications sought and media exposure. *Communication Research, 10,* 247–258.

Stevenson, N. (1997). Critical perspectives within audience research. In T. O'Sullivan & Y. Jewkes (Eds.), *The media studies reader.* New York: St. Martin's.

Stolz, C. (1995). *Silicon snake oil: Second thoughts on the information highway.* New York: Doubleday.

Stone, G., & Stone, D. (1990). Lurking in the literature: Another look at media use habits. *Mass Communications Review, 17,* 25–33.

Sundar, S. S. (1998). Effect of source attribution on perception of online news stories. *Journalism and Mass Communication Quarterly, 75,* 55–68.

Swanson, D. L. (1977). The uses and misuses of uses and gratifications. *Human Communication Research, 3,* 214–221.

Swanson, D. L. (1987). Gratification seeking, media exposure, and audience interpretations. *Journal of Broadcasting & Electronic Media, 31,* 237–254.

Trevino, L. K., & Webster, J. (1992). Flow in computer-mediated communication: Electronic mail and voice mail evaluation and impacts. *Communication Research, 19,* 539–573.

Thomas, P. J. (1995). Introduction: The social and interactional dimensions of human–computer interfaces. In P. J. Thomas (Ed.), *The social and interactional dimensions of human–computer interfaces* (pp. 1–10). Cambridge, England: Cambridge University Press.

Walker, J. R. (1990). Time out: Viewing gratifications and reactions to the 1987 NFL players' strike. *Journal of Broadcasting & Electronic Media, 34,* 335–350.

Walker, J. R., & Bellamy, R. V. (1991). Gratifications of grazing: An exploratory study of remote control use. *Journalism Quarterly, 68,* 422–431.

Waples, D., Berelson, B., & Bradshaw, F. R. (1940). *What reading does to people.* Chicago: University of Chicago Press.

Weaver, D. H. (1993). Communication research in the 1990s. In P. Gaunt (Ed.), *Beyond agendas: New directions in communication research* (pp. 199–220). Westport, CT: Greenwood.

Webster, J., & Wakshlag, J. (1983). A theory of television program choice. *Communication Research, 10,* 430–446.

Weiss, W. (1976). Review of the uses of mass communications. *Public Opinion Quarterly, 40,* 132–133.

Wenner, L. A. (1985). The nature of news gratification. In K. E. Rosengren, L. A. Wenner, & P. Palmgreen (Eds.), *Media gratifications research: Current perspectives* (pp. 171–194). Beverly Hills, CA: Sage.

White, R. A. (1994). Audience interpretation of media: Emerging perspectives. *Communication Research Trends, 14*(3), 3–36.

Williams, F., Phillips, A. F., & Lum, P. (1985). Gratifications associated with new communication technologies. In K. E. Rosengren, L. A. Wenner, & P. Palmgreen (Eds.), *Media gratification research: Current perspectives* (pp. 241–252). Beverly Hills, CA: Sage.

Williams, F., Rice, R. E., & Rogers, E. M. (1988). *Research methods and the new media.* New York: Free Press.

Wimmer, R. D., & Dominick, J. R. (1994). *Mass media research: An introduction.* Belmont, CA: Wadsworth.

Windahl, S. (1981). Uses and gratifications at the crossroads. *Mass Communication Review Yearbook, 2,* 174–185.

Windahl, S., Hojerback, I., & Hedinsson, E. (1986). Adolescents without television: A study in media deprivation. *Journal of Broadcasting & Electronic Media, 30,* 47–63.

Young, K. (1996, August). *Internet addiction: The emergence of a new addictive disorder.* Poster presented at the annual meeting of the American Psychological Association, Toronto, Canada.

Zillman, D., & Bryant, J. (1985). *Selective exposure to communication.* Hillsdale, NJ: Lawrence Erlbaum Associates, Inc.

Zillman, D., & Bryant, J. (1994). Entertainment as media effect. In J. Bryant & D. Zillman (Eds.), *Media effects: Advances in theory and research* (pp. 437–461). Hillsdale, NJ: Lawrence Erlbaum Associates, Inc.

Agenda-Setting, Priming, and Framing Revisited: Another Look at Cognitive Effects of Political Communication

Dietram A. Scheufele
Department of Communication
Cornell University

Agenda-setting, priming, and framing research generally has been examined under the broad category of cognitive media effects. As a result, studies often either examine all 3 approaches in a single study or employ very similar research designs, paying little attention to conceptual differences or differences in the levels of analysis under which each approach is operating. In this article, I revisit agenda-setting, priming, and framing as distinctively different approaches to effects of political communication. Specifically, I argue against more recent attempts to subsume all 3 approaches under the broad concept of agenda-setting and for a more careful explication of the concepts and of their theoretical premises and roots in social psychology and political psychology. Consequently, it calls for a reformulation of relevant research questions and a systematic categorization of research on agenda-setting, priming, and framing. An analytic model is developed that should serve as a guideline for future research in these areas.

The original formulation of the agenda-setting hypothesis (Cohen, 1963; McCombs & Shaw, 1972) phrased it more like a speculative idea or heuristic (Kosicki, 1993) than as a theory in its most conventional sense. In an attempt to construct a more comprehensive theoretical model, Weaver, McCombs, and Shaw (1998) recently suggested that priming and framing should be viewed as natural extensions of agenda-setting. Priming is the impact that agenda-setting can have on the way individuals evaluate public officials by influencing the thematic areas or issues that individuals use to form these evaluations. Framing can be considered an extension of agenda-setting as it "is the selection of a restricted number of thematically related attributes for inclusion on the media agenda when a particular object is discussed" (McCombs, 1997, p. 6). In other words, whereas agenda-setting is concerned with the salience of issues, frame-setting, or second-level agenda-setting (McCombs, Llamas, Lopez-Escobar, & Rey, 1997) is concerned with the salience of issue attributes.

Empirical work, however, seems to contradict such theorizing, suggesting that although both are important, perceived importance of specific frames rather than salience is the key variable (Nelson, Clawson, & Oxley, 1997; Nelson & Kinder, 1996). In other words, "frames influence opinions by stressing specific values, facts, and other considerations, endowing them with greater apparent relevance to the issue than they might appear to have under an alternative frame" (Nelson et al., 1997, p. 569). In contrast to McCombs and his associates (McCombs, Llamas, Lopez-Escobar, & Rey, 1997), Nelson et al. directly operationalized salience of frames by measuring response latency (for an overview, see Bassili, 1995), and found support for their theorizing. Causal modeling revealed that various dimensions of perceived importance accounted for major proportions of the variance in framing effects, with salience or accessibility of frames playing only a minor role.

PARSIMONY VERSUS PRECISION: THE BENEFITS OF DIFFERENTIATING MODELS OF MEDIA EFFECTS

McCombs, Llamas et al. (1997) based their attempts to combine agenda-setting, priming, and framing into a single theoretical framework on the assumption that integrating theory is always desirable. However, if theories are based on distinctively different premises, and if they differ with respect to the empirical patterns observed, this strategy might in fact be counterproductive. As I argue in this article, agenda-setting and priming differ from framing with respect to their assumptions and premises. At the same time, they derive distinctively different theoretical statements and hypotheses from these premises. Consequently, these three approaches to media effects should be taken for what they are: related, yet different approaches to media effects that cannot be combined into a simple theory just for the sake of parsimony.

Thus, using consistent terminology for essentially incompatible theoretical models has done little to remedy the lack of conceptual clarity surrounding agenda-setting, priming, and framing in the area of media effects research (Entman, 1993; McNamara, 1992; Scheufele, 1999). Possibly as a result of the vagueness of the constructs and theoretical statements involved, the original authors admit, "evidence from ... agenda-setting studies is mixed" (Weaver et al., 1998, p. 1).

To provide a systematic overview of the different possible approaches to agenda-setting, priming, and framing in media effects research, it is necessary to develop clear conceptualizations of agenda-setting, priming, and framing based on their theoretical premises. This will allow researchers to define the role that the three concepts can play in media effects research and to determine if there are, in fact, theoretical overlaps. Based on these conceptual definitions, this article develops an analytic model incorporating all three theoretical approaches to develop strategies and recommendations for future research.

Theoretical Premises of Agenda-Setting, Priming, and Framing

As argued earlier, attempts to integrate agenda-setting, priming, and framing into a single model have largely ignored the differences between the premises underlying these three theoretical models. Agenda-setting, on the one hand, and priming as a direct extension or outcome of agenda-setting (e.g., Iyengar & Kinder, 1987), on the other hand, are based on the same assumptions or premises. Contrary to McCombs's (1997) theorizing, however, framing is based on premises that differ from those of agenda-setting or priming.

Salience: The theoretical premises of agenda-setting and priming. The theoretical foundation of agenda-setting and priming can be traced back to psychological concepts of priming in work on cognitive processing of semantic information (Collins & Loftus, 1975; Tulving & Watkins, 1975). By receiving and processing information, individuals develop memory traces (Tulving & Watkins, 1975) or activation tags (Collins & Loftus, 1975); that is, concepts or issues are primed and made more accessible in an individual's memory. Activation tags or memory traces, therefore, influence subsequent information processing (Salancik, 1974). "When a concept is primed, activation tags are spread. ... When another concept is subsequently presented, it has to make contact with one of the tags left earlier and find an intersection" (Collins & Loftus, 1975, p. 409).

The metaphor of activation tags or memory traces was later replaced by the construct of accessibility. The idea of accessibility is the foundation of a memory-based model of information processing, which assumes that individuals make judgments about other people or issues based on information easily available and retrievable from memory at the time the question is asked (Hastie & Park, 1986; Iyengar, 1990). According to a memory-based model, judgments and attitude formation are directly correlated with "the ease in which instances or associations could be brought to mind" (Tversky & Kahneman, 1973, p. 208).

Empirical work on accessibility generally falls into one of two categories. First, studies often test a memory-based model of information processing against a competing model of online processing, which sees attitudes as being formed when incoming information is initially processed (e.g., Hastie & Park, 1986; Moy, Scheufele, Eveland, & McLeod, in press). According to an online model, attitudes are stored in memory as what have been called summary or judgment tallies

(Lodge, McGraw, & Stroh, 1989), judgment operators (Hastie & Park, 1986), or information integrators (Wyer & Srull, 1986). New impressions are processed and integrated into a running tally, shaping one's current attitude (Tourangeau, 1984, 1987; Tourangeau & Rasinski, 1988). Although the attitude (or judgment tally) changes, the original cognition or argument that changed the attitude is eventually forgotten (Lodge et al., 1989). It is beyond the scope of this article to resolve this ongoing conflict. More recent research, however, has provided strong evidence for cognitive processes like rationalization (Rahn, Krosnick, & Breuning, 1994), priming (Petty & Jarvis, 1996; Sudman, Bradburn, & Schwarz, 1996), and affective priming (Moy et al., in press) that are all based on a memory-based model of information processing; that is, on the assumption of attitude accessibility. These operationalizations infer attitude accessibility as a construct from the behavioral or cognitive patterns observed.

Second, attempts have been made to measure attitude accessibility more directly. Bassili (1995) suggested an operationalization of attitude accessibility as a continuous variable that involves measuring the amount of time that it takes a respondent to answer a given question. The underlying rationale is that the longer it takes a respondent to answer a given question, the less accessible the evoked cognition. "Accessibility is conceived in terms of associational strength in memory and measured in the metric of response time" (Huckfeldt & Sprague, 1997, p. 6).

Both agenda-setting and priming are based on this assumption of attitude accessibility and, in particular, a memory-based model of information processing. Mass media can influence the salience of certain issues as perceived by the audience; that is, the ease with which these issues can be retrieved from memory. As hypothesized in the priming model, perceived issue salience becomes the independent variable and influences the role that these issues or considerations play when an individual makes a judgment about a political actor. Mass media, Iyengar and Kinder (1987) argued, affect "the standards by which governments, policies and candidates for public office are judged" (p. 63). Political issues that are most salient or accessible in a person's memory will most strongly influence perceptions of political actors and figures.

Attribution: The theoretical premises of framing. A macroscopic approach to framing that examines media frames as outcomes of journalistic norms or organizational constraints is based on what Pan and Kosicki (1993) called the sociological approach to framing research. This approach, although drawing on theoretical approaches in various fields and disciplines, is commonly linked to attribution theory (Heider, 1930, 1959, 1978; Heider & Simmel, 1944) and frame analysis (Goffman, 1974).

In his work on attribution theory, Heider (1930) assumed that human beings cannot understand the world in all its complexity. Therefore the individual tries to infer underlying causal relations from sensory information. These assumptions were supported by experimental evidence. A vast majority of individuals who were shown movies with abstract movements of geometrical shapes interpreted these movements as actions of human beings with a certain underlying motivation (Heider & Simmel, 1944). Based on these studies, Heider (1978) defined attribution as the link between an observed behavior and a person who is considered responsible for this action. In his later work, Heider (1959) expanded this definition of attribution to environmental factors; that is, an observed behavior can be attributed to both personal and societal or environmental factors. Drawing on Heider's distinction between societal and individual attributions of responsibility, Iyengar (1991) argued that people try to make sense of political issues by reducing them to questions of responsibility. In other words, responsibility for social issues or problems can be framed as individual responsibility or the responsibility of society at large.

Although he did not explicitly refer to Heider's (1959) findings, Goffman (1974) too assumed that individuals cannot understand the world fully and therefore actively classify and interpret their life experiences to make sense of the world around them. The individual's reaction to sensory information therefore depends on schemes of interpretation called "primary frameworks" (Goffman, 1974, p. 24). These frameworks or frames can be classified into natural and societal frames: Natural frames help to interpret events originating from natural and nonintentional causes, whereas societal frames help "to locate, perceive, identify, and label" (Goffman, 1974, p. 21) actions and events that stem from intentional human action. The most important implication for the field of mass communication research, then, is that there are various ways of looking at and depicting events in news media that depend on the framework employed by the journalists. Or as Goffman put it, "The type of framework we employ provides a way of describing the event to which it is applied" (p. 24).

Unlike the sociological approach, a microscopic or psychological approach (Fischer & Johnson, 1986) examines frames as individual means of processing and structuring incoming information. This psychological approach is summarized in work on frames of reference (Sherif, 1967) and prospect theory (Kahneman & Tversky, 1972, 1979, 1984; Quattrone & Tversky, 1988).

In his work on frames of reference, Sherif (1967) assumed that individual judgments and perceptions not only are influenced by cognitive or psychological factors but also occur within an appropriate frame of reference. Therefore, it is possible "to set up situations in which appraisal or evaluation of a social situation will be reflected in the perceptions and judgments of the individual" (p. 382).

Although this work does not suggest how mass media can influence individual judgments and perceptions, research on prospect theory (e.g., Quattrone & Tversky, 1988) points to a possible link between mass media coverage and the framework individuals employ to interpret events. Specifically, experimental research has shown that how a decision-making situation is framed will affect what people believe will be the outcome of selecting one option over the other

(Kahneman & Tversky, 1984). Edelman (1993) applied their findings to social settings: "The social world is ... a kaleidoscope of potential realities, any of which can be readily evoked by altering the way in which observations are framed and categorized" (p. 232).

EXPLICATING AGENDA-SETTING AND PRIMING

The interactive construction of reality by mass media and audiences as hypothesized by McQuail (1994) has important implications for the conceptualization of agenda-setting and priming as theories of media effects. An analysis of the roles of both audience members and mass media in this constructivist approach requires research on various levels of analysis.

Agenda-setting and priming, therefore, need to be conceptualized at two separate levels. On the macroscopic level, agenda-setting has to be examined based on the media agenda; that is, "the importance assigned to issues and personalities in the media" (Winter & Eyal, 1981, p. 376). Priming, an inherently individual psychological outcome of agenda-setting, does not operate at this level of analysis. Therefore, on the microscopic level, agenda-setting has to be examined based on the audience agenda or the salience or accessibility of certain issues in a person's memory, and, closely related, the priming of "criteria that citizens use to evaluate their leaders" (Behr & Iyengar, 1985, p. 38).

Research on agenda-setting and priming as media effects, therefore, can be classified along two dimensions. First, agenda-setting needs to be examined across levels of analysis; that is, both as media agendas and as audience agendas. Second, agenda-setting needs to be examined as both independent and dependent variables. Based on this distinction, three distinct processes can be differentiated: agenda-building, agenda-setting, and priming (see Figure 1).

Agenda-Building

Agenda-building as a term was introduced by Cobb and Elder (1971) who "are concerned with how issues are created and why some controversies or incipient

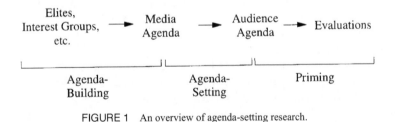

FIGURE 1   An overview of agenda-setting research.

issues come to command the attention and concern of decision makers, while others fail" (p. 905). In other words, in the process of agenda-building, the media agenda is considered the dependent variable. Rogers, Dearing, and Bregman (1993)—who used the term *media agenda-setting* instead of agenda-building—noted that agenda-setting research has widely accepted the media agenda as a given and only a few studies have considered the process by which it is constructed.

Without explicitly referring to agenda-building, Funkhouser (1973a) was one of the first researchers to examine the relation between real-world events and the amount of media coverage on these events. Assuming that "the contents of weekly news magazines would be a reasonable indicator of the contents of the news media nationwide" (p. 533), he compared the amount of media coverage—measured as the amount of coverage of a number of issues in news magazines between 1960 and 1970—to official statistics regarding these issues during the same time period. Overall, there was little support for the hypothesis that real-world events drive media coverage (Funkhouser, 1973a).

Explicitly referring to agenda-building, Lang and Lang (1981) conducted a case study of the Watergate scandal. They argued that previous research has largely ignored the question of how the public agenda is formed; that is, there is little or no "recognition of the process through which agendas are built or through which an object that has caught public attention, by being big news, gives rise to a political issue" (p. 448). Lang and Lang proposed a four-step model of agenda-building. In a first step, mass media highlight some events, activities, groups, or personalities. In a second step, these elements of a conflict are combined into a common frame or the description of some problem or concern. In a third step, the issue is linked "to secondary symbols, so that it becomes a part of the recognized political landscape" (p. 465). In a fourth and final step, spokesmen and spin masters play an important role in promoting issues and symbols and establishing a feedback loop to media coverage to increase issue coverage or at least to keep the issue alive. This formulation of the process of agenda-building, then, attributes a key role both to mass media for initially picking up an issue and to political actors for keeping an issue prominent in the media agenda or even increasing its prominence.

Without referring explicitly to the term agenda-building, Behr and Iyengar (1985) provided one of the few empirical examinations of the agenda-building process. To examine the impact of the media agenda on the audience agenda, they combined trend data from three national surveys with a content analysis of the *CBS Evening News*. They also collected a number of indicators of current conditions on all three issue areas under study. In addition, they recorded instances in which the president delivered speeches to the nation concerning any of these issues. Their analyses revealed that "television news coverage is at least partially determined by real-world conditions and events" (p. 47). Similarly, presidential addresses increased levels of news coverage for the respective issue for all issues under study. Finally, Behr and Iyengar (1985) found that levels of public concern were driven by television news coverage for two of the three issues under study. The reverse, however, was not true: "News coverage is for the most part unaffected by public opinion and the assumption that agenda-setting is a recursive process is on solid ground" (p. 47).

Agenda-Setting

A hypothesized positive relation between the media agenda as the independent variable and the audience agenda as the dependent variable was first examined empirically by McCombs and Shaw (1972). Their reasoning was based on earlier work by Cohen (1963), who argued that mass media "may not be successful much of the time in telling people what to think, but is stunningly successful in telling its readers what to think *about*" (p. 13). McCombs and Shaw examined the agenda-setting hypothesis during the 1968 presidential campaign. Employing a cross-sectional survey design, they compared 100 undecided voters' perceptions of issue salience with the amount of coverage of these issues, measured by a content analysis of television, newspaper, and magazine coverage. Based on zero-order correlations, they concluded "that media appear to have exerted a considerable impact on voters' judgments of what they considered the major issue of the campaign" (p. 180).

In 1996, Dearing and Rogers (1996) listed as many as 350 publications about the agenda-setting effect. It is therefore impossible to examine all or even a reasonable sample of studies. It is necessary, however, to summarize problematic areas common to a large number of studies in the area. All in all, criticisms of previous studies fall into one of two major categories.

First, agenda-setting is an inherently causal theory. Studies generally have found some form of positive association between the amount of mass media content devoted to an issue and the development of a place on the public agenda for that issue. The research designs and statistical methods employed, however, are in few cases suited to make causal inferences. As a result, "causal direction must remain an open question for now, at least in terms of most survey studies" (Kosicki, 1993, p. 106). Exceptions are experimental studies like Iyengar and Kinder's (1987) experimental research on agenda-setting and priming.

At least three conditions need to be fulfilled to infer some form of causal relation. First, some form of covariation needs to be identified between the two variables under study. Second, potential alternative explanations need to be ruled out. Third, a temporal order between independent and dependent variable has to be established, with the hypothesized cause preceding the effect (Lazarsfeld, 1957). Whereas the first condition (i.e., a covariation between media and audience agenda) is tested in most studies, third variable explanations and temporal order are controlled for in considerably fewer studies.

As far as third variable explanations are concerned, previous research has identified a number of them as well as contingent conditions under which agenda-setting effects will occur. Demers, Craff, Choi, and Pessin (1989), for example, identified issue obtrusiveness as a key contingency in the agenda-setting process. Findings on spurious explanations are, at best, mixed. Most important, the notion that real-world events rather than the portrayals of these events in mass media drives audience agendas is supported by few studies (Dearing & Rogers, 1996).

As far as the temporal order of variables is concerned, agenda-setting assumes that there is a process by which the media agenda influences the audience agenda over time. Across studies, however, the issue of time lag between media agenda-setting and audience effects "is insufficiently theorized and underspecified" (Kosicki, 1993, p. 107). Various researchers employed a combination of survey designs and content analytic designs with longer time lags (e.g., Allen, O'Loughlin, Jasperson, & Sullivan, 1994; Behr & Iyengar, 1985; Funkhouser, 1973b; Iyengar & Simon, 1993). Others used experimental designs with shorter periods of time between administration of the stimulus and measurement of agenda-setting effects (e.g., Iyengar & Kinder, 1987). Theoretical arguments typically are not the driving force behind the choice of the research design; rather, "time lags are tested in numerous ways until the optimal one is found" (Kosicki, 1993, p. 107).

The second area of criticism of previous agenda-setting research refers to the measurement of the criterion variable; that is, the perceptions of issue salience by the audience. In their seminal study, McCombs and Shaw (1972) operationalized issue salience among audience members as judgments about the perceived importance of issues. Later studies replaced perceptions of importance with terms such as *salience, awareness, attention,* or *concern* (Edelstein, 1993).

The conceptual difference between these concepts also has important operational consequences. If individual-level salience of issues is the key criterion variable, measures of perceptions of issue importance are inadequate indicators. Iyengar (1990), for example, described the power of television in the context of agenda-setting as the ability "to make information 'accessible' or more retrievable from memory" (p. 2). Measures of perceived importance, however, do not capture the ease with which considerations can be retrieved from memory. Rather, salience should be measured indirectly through variables like response latency (e.g., Bassili, 1995) or should be demonstrated in question order experiments (e.g., Zaller & Feldman, 1992).

Priming

The priming hypothesis states that mass media, by making some issues more salient than others, influence "the standards by which governments, presidents, policies, and candidates for public office are judged" (Iyengar & Kinder, 1987, p. 63). In this sense, studies testing priming effects examine agenda-setting as the independent variable and priming effects as outcomes of agenda-setting or as the dependent variable.

In a series of experiments, Iyengar and Kinder (1987) examined the impact of network newscasts on viewers' perceptions of issue salience on the criteria they use to make judgments about political candidates. They hypothesized that the salience of certain issues as portrayed in mass media influences individuals' perceptions of the president because respondents will use issues that they perceive as more salient as standards for evaluating the president. Even though they considered priming "a robust effect" (p. 72), they found mixed statistical support for their hypothesis. Strong priming effects emerged for only some issues and weak effects for others, such as unemployment. Iyengar and Kinder attributed this weak priming effect to the generally high salience of unemployment in American politics.

Finally, priming effects were studied during the Gulf War. Iyengar and Simon's (1993) combination of survey data and content analyses of network television news supported the basic priming hypothesis: Foreign policy issues that had been made more salient for individuals by intensive Gulf War coverage tended to override other issues as influences on assessments of presidential performance.

EXPLICATING FRAMING

Similar to agenda-setting and priming, framing has to be examined not only across levels of analysis but also as a dependent and independent variable. Two concepts of framing need to be specified: media frames and audience frames (Scheufele, 1999).

Media frames have been defined as "a central organizing idea or story line that provides meaning to an unfolding strip of events. ... The frame suggests what the controversy is about, the essence of the issue" (Gamson & Modigliani, 1987, p. 143). Media or news frames serve as working routines for journalists, allowing them to quickly identify and classify information and "to package it for efficient relay to their audiences" (Gitlin, 1980, p. 7). *Audience frames* are defined as "mentally stored clusters of ideas that guide individuals' processing of information" (Entman, 1993, p. 53).

A Typology of Framing

Similar to priming research, different approaches to framing can be classified along two dimensions. A *between-level* dimension conceptually defines media frames on a macroscopic level and audience frames on a microscopic level and hypothesizes potential relations between them. A *within-level* dimension conceptualizes media frames and audience frames separately as both independent and dependent variable. Similar to the research on agenda-building, agenda-setting, and priming, studies of framing commonly examine one of three distinct processes: frame-setting, frame-building, and individual-level outcomes of framing (see Figure 2).

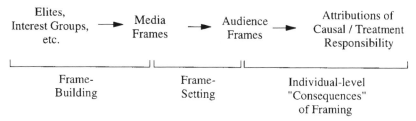

FIGURE 2 An overview of framing research.

Frame-building. Although studies have examined both extrinsic and intrinsic factors influencing the production and selection of news (e.g., Gans, 1979; Shoemaker & Reese, 1996; Tuchman, 1978), little evidence has yet been systematically collected on how various factors influence the structural qualities of news in terms of framing. Based on previous research (e.g., Shoemaker & Reese, 1996; Tuchman, 1978), at least five factors may potentially influence how journalists frame a given issue: social norms and values, organizational pressures and constraints, pressures of interest groups, journalistic routines, and ideological or political orientations of journalists.

Frame-setting. In many cases, studies examining media frames as the independent variable also examine audience frames as the dependent variable. Whereas some of this research experimentally manipulates media frames to examine their impact on audience frames, other studies include measures of both media and audience frames.

The most promising approach conceptualizing both media frames as the independent variable and audience frames as the dependent variable is reflected in the combination of content analytic data and survey data by Huang (1995, 1996). Using the Anita Hill–Clarence Thomas controversy as an exemplar, she analyzed "to what extent media frames are operative in audience frames" (Huang, 1996, p. 1). She measured frames on both a macro- and microlevel, comparing news frames, based on content analyses of how the network evening news and two local newspapers framed the controversy, and audience frames—based on coding answers to open-ended questions on the controversy. Her results (Huang, 1995) showed that media frames can find their way into audience frames. When media and audience frames overlap, however, the media and the audience accord different weights to those frames.

Other studies measure only the dependent variable and experimentally manipulate media frames as the independent variable. Iyengar's (1987) content analysis of network television newscasts showed that network newscasts are framed in episodic or thematic terms. Episodic newscasts depict public issues as concrete instances or specific events, whereas thematic newscasts report on a more abstract level in the form of general outcomes. Iyengar's (1991) analyses also indicated that networks rely extensively on episodic framing. He hypothesized that the type of media framing has an impact on the attribution of responsibility by audiences and differentiated two dimensions of attribution of responsibility: causal and treatment responsibility (Iyengar, 1987, 1991). Iyengar's results showed that a relation between media frames and audience frames is strongly contingent on the issue under study. An experimental manipulation of highly salient issues like unemployment, for instance, had little or no impact on individual attribution of responsibility.

Price, Tewksbury, and Powers (1995, 1997) offered the most elaborate approach to audience frames as dependent variable. Undergraduate students were asked to read news articles about possible cuts in state funding to the university that were experimentally prepared to manipulate various news frames. In a posttest questionnaire, the participants were asked to write down all thoughts and feelings they had while reading the news article, including those thoughts that were not necessarily directly relevant to the article. Coding of the open-ended question showed that issue frames of news stories had a significant influence on the respondents' cognitive responses. The most interesting finding was a phenomenon that Price et al. (1995) called "a kind of 'hydraulic' pattern, with thoughts of one kind, stimulated by the frame, driving out other possible responses" (p. 23).

Individual-level consequences of framing. To find an explicit and direct link between audience frames as independent variable and individual information processing or political action, one can turn to the social movements literature. Generally, the frames individuals use to interpret conflicts may have an impact on the "mobilization for collective action aimed at social change" (Gamson, 1985, p. 620). More specifically, other work has focused on how master frames invented by social movements can potentially influence the motivation for individuals to support these movements and to form consensus (Entman & Rojecki, 1993; Klandermans, 1988, 1992; Klandermans & Oegema, 1987). Gerhards and Rucht (1992) tried to synthesize the previous findings into a single model, differentiating three types of framing: diagnostic framing, or identifying a problem and attributing blame; prognostic framing, which specifies what needs to be done; and motivational framing, or the "call to arms for engaging in ameliorative or corrective action" (Snow & Benford, 1988, p. 199).

AGENDA-SETTING, PRIMING, AND FRAMING: MODELS FOR FUTURE RESEARCH

This article is concerned with agenda-setting, priming, and framing as distinctively different approaches to effects of political communication and argues for a more careful explication of the concepts and of their theoretical premises and roots in social and political psychology. I have shown that agenda-setting and priming, on the one hand, and framing, on the other hand, are, in fact, based on distinctively different assumptions and therefore translate into equally different theoretical statements.

Theoretical Differences

Agenda-setting and priming rely on the notion of attitude accessibility. Mass media have the power to increase levels of importance assigned to issues by audience members. They increase the salience of issues or the ease with which these considerations can be retrieved from memory if individuals have to make political judgments about political actors. In other words, media influence the standards by which audience members evaluate political figures. Framing, in contrast, is based on the concept of prospect theory; that is, on the assumption that subtle changes in the wording of the description of a situation might affect how audience members interpret this situation. In other words, framing influences how audiences think about issues, not by making aspects of the issue more salient, but by invoking interpretive schemas that influence the interpretation of incoming information. Although the process of issue selection or agenda-setting by mass media necessarily needs to be a conscious one, framing is based on subtle nuances in wording and syntax that have most likely unintentional effects or at least effects that are hard to predict and control by journalists.

An Analytic Model of Agenda-Setting, Priming, and Framing

This article has addressed McCombs, Shaw, and Weaver's (1997) proposition that priming and framing are extensions of agenda-setting from a largely theoretical perspective. The question that arises from this conceptual work, of course, concerns implications for research in these areas. More generally, testing these models of media effects requires linking macro- and microlevels of analysis. In other words, models of agenda-setting and framing link media content as the unit of observation to audience characteristics. This creates analytic and statistical problems when trying to assess the relation between media content and audience characteristics. Previous research has commonly addressed this issue in one of two ways.

First, researchers have compared aggregate measures of media content to aggregate measures of public opinion, either in cross-sectional designs (comparing the rank-orders of media and audience agendas) or in longitudinal designs (using time points as their unit of observation). In one of the earlier studies of agenda-setting, for example, Funkhouser (1973b) compared the average amount of issue coverage in mass media to the average importance attributed to these issues by the public. He found a rank-order correlation between media and audience agenda of .78. Studies like Funkhouser's (1973a, 1973b) have at least two inherent problems. First, relatively high rank-order correlations can be observed even if the actual ranking of issues differs substantially between media and audience agenda or if some issues covered in the media do not find their way onto the audience's agenda at all.

Second, studies examining audience and media agendas at the aggregate level potentially encounter ecological fallacy problems. It is possible that audience members who do not follow a given medium at all show the highest levels of congruency with the media agenda, whereas audience members who are highly exposed to the medium show only weak agenda-setting effects. Regardless of these differences, however, the rank-orders of media and audience agendas might be very similar.

These problems are addressed by the second approach to testing agenda-setting effects. McLeod, Becker, and Byrnes (1974), for example, suggested a microlevel approach to agenda-setting, comparing individual-level measures of perceived issue importance to a measure of media reliance weighted by the issue agenda predominant in that medium. Specifically, they examined the agenda-setting function of two competing community newspapers. Based on respondents' media reliance and the predominant agenda in the two local newspapers, they calculated a weighted index of received issue saliences that measured the weighted exposure to the agenda of one or both newspapers, depending on the media reliance patterns of each respondent. This analytic technique has the advantage that it allows for an individual-level estimation of agenda-setting effects.

The model outlined in Figure 3 is based on McLeod et al.'s (1974) core analytic model. It goes beyond their analyses, however, and applies their analytic strategies to the models of priming and framing. The goal of this model is to allow researchers to compare the distinctively different models of agenda-setting and priming, on the one hand, and framing, on the other hand. Specifically, it identifies the key differences between the respective models as far as content characteristics, audience variables, and media effects are concerned. To allow researchers to control for contingencies or third variable explanations, it also includes key controls identified in previous research (e.g., demographic controls, strength of partisanship, issue obtrusiveness, information processing strategies, etc.). Specifically, the models for agenda-setting and priming, on the one hand, and framing, on the other hand, include six blocks of key variables.

Demographic controls and preexposure orientations. In addition to standard demographic controls, previous research on agenda-setting, priming, and framing has identified a number of preexposure orientations that influence how audiences receive and process information and that might therefore influence agenda-setting, priming, or framing effects.

For example, the obtrusiveness of issues or other qualities might influence subsequent information seeking and processing. Wanta and Wu (1992) intro-

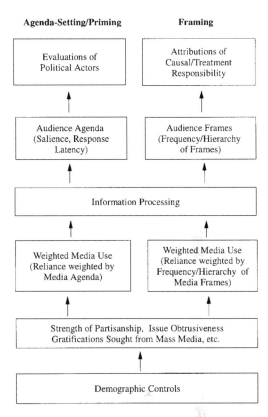

FIGURE 3 Analytic model of agenda-setting, priming, and framing.

duced the notion of interpersonal issues; that is, issues that are not covered in mass media. Interpersonal discussion with others, for these issues, is the main predictor of a person's individual agenda and "may interfere with media agenda-setting effects" (p. 850).

In addition to the quality of the issue, McLeod et al. (1974) identified four contingent or contributory audience orientations "under which the [agenda-setting] hypothesis holds in greater or lesser strength" (p. 55). The first orientation is the strength of partisan orientation (independent of its direction). Weaker partisans, McLeod et al. found, show significant agenda-setting effects, even after controlling for the direction general partisanship. The second orientation is the dependence on newspapers as information source. As can be expected, newspaper agenda-setting effects were more likely to occur for people who reported relying on newspapers than those who reported not relying on newspapers. The third orientation is political interest. Respondents who reported lower levels of political interest were more susceptible to agenda-setting effects. The fourth orientation is gratifications sought from newspapers. Specifically, older respondents who reported using newspapers to keep up with latest events showed strong agenda-setting effects.

Weighted media use. As argued earlier, indexes of weighted media use are a prerequisite for testing influences of media content on audience variables using individual-level data. As Figure 3 shows, however, different weighted indexes need to be calculated separately for agenda-setting and priming, on the one hand, and framing, on the other hand. Both indexes are based on respondents' reliance on a given medium for their political information. In most cases, the scope of the content analysis will make it unrealistic to include all print and broadcast media in a given market in the analyses. Rather, the predominant print and broadcast media should be selected. The content of each medium is then coded with respect to the frequency and hierarchy of issue frames or with respect to the salience attributed to different issues. Following McLeod et al. (1974), weighted indexes of exposure to media agendas or frames then are created based on a person's predominant media reliance.

Postexposure orientations: Information processing strategies. The individual-level effects of media agendas and news frames are very likely mediated by the way individuals process information they have gained from news media. Specifically, Kosicki and McLeod (1990) identified three dimensions of news processing. The first dimension refers to a respondent's tendency to scan media content for news of particular interest to him or her and not pay particular interest to or think about other stories. Framing and agenda-setting effects should be highest for this group. The second and third dimensions refer to a respondent's tendency to actively process and reflect on news content to get the real story behind the news. Reflecting on news content and pondering alternative frames and related issues can be expected to diminish the influences of media coverage on individual-level agendas and frames.

Audience agendas and audience frames. The final block of antecedent variables in the analytic model contains individual-level perceptions of salience and individual-level frames. These variables are the outcomes of agenda-setting or frame-setting processes, respectively. The theoretical differences between agenda-setting and priming, on the one hand, and framing, on the other hand, make it necessary to measure the two groups of variables in distinctively different ways. Individual-level salience of issues is ideally tapped indirectly through measures of response latency, whereas individual-level frames have mostly been measured by post hoc coding answers to open-ended survey questions or posttest questionnaires in experimental designs.

Outcomes: Evaluations versus attributions. As outlined earlier, previous research on priming has commonly examined evaluations of political actors as the final dependent variable. Framing research, in contrast, has focused on attributions of causal and treatment responsibility for social problems as the final dependent variable. To distinguish agenda-setting and priming from framing requires an assessment of discriminant validity. If agenda-setting, priming, and framing are related constructs, antecedents and outcomes of all three models should be similar. In other words, the blocks of antecedents outlined in Figure 3 should have a similar impact on individual-level perceptions of salience (i.e., on what people think about) and on the frequency and hierarchy of frames respondents invoke when they describe issues (i.e., on how they think about an issue). If priming and framing indeed differ from each other and from the concept of agenda-setting, they also should have different antecedents and outcomes. More important, each of the two models of media effects should have unique effects that remain significant, even if the other model is controlled for. For presidential evaluations as the dependent variable, for example, Iyengar and Kinder (1987) demonstrated significant influences of individual perceptions of issue salience. What remains unanswered is the question of whether the framing of an issue—regardless of its perceived salience—might have a significant effect on evaluations of political actors that goes above and beyond priming. This article has made a theory-driven argument in favor of precision rather than parsimony; that is, in favor of carefully distinguishing among agenda-setting, priming, and framing as different models of media effects. Following the analytic model outlined, future research will have to address this issue empirically.

ACKNOWLEDGMENTS

A previous version of this article was presented at the annual convention of the International Communication Association, San Francisco. I thank Patricia Moy, David Demers, Virginia Sapiro, and Zhongdang Pan for valuable comments on earlier versions of this article.

REFERENCES

Allen, B., O'Loughlin, P., Jasperson, A., & Sullivan, J. L. (1994). The media and the Gulf War: Framing, priming, and the spiral of silence. *Polity, 27,* 256–284.

Bassili, J. N. (1995). Response latency and the accessibility of voting intentions: What contributes to accessibility and how it affects vote choice. *Personal and Social Psychology Bulletin, 21,* 686–695.

Behr, R. L., & Iyengar, S. (1985). Television news, real-world cues, and changes in the public agenda. *Public Opinion Quarterly, 49,* 38–57.

Cobb, R. W., & Elder, C. (1971). The politics of agenda-building: An alternative perspective for modern democratic theory. *Journal of Politics, 33,* 892–915.

Cohen, B. C. (1963). *The press and foreign policy.* Princeton, NJ: Princeton University Press.

Collins, A. M., & Loftus, E. F. (1975). A spreading-activation theory of semantic processing. *Psychological Review, 82,* 407–428.

Dearing, J. W., & Rogers, E. M. (1996). *Agenda-setting.* Thousand Oaks, CA: Sage.

Demers, D. P., Craff, D., Choi, Y., & Pessin, B. M. (1989). Issue obtrusiveness and the agenda-setting effects of national network news. *Communication Research, 16,* 793–812.

Edelman, M. J. (1993). Contestable categories and public opinion. *Political Communication, 10,* 231–242.
Edelstein, A. S. (1993). Thinking about the criterion variable in agenda-setting research. *Journal of Communication, 43,* 85–99.
Entman, R. M. (1993). Framing: Towards clarification of a fractured paradigm. *Journal of Communication, 43,* 51–58.
Entman, R. M., & Rojecki, A. (1993). Freezing out the public: Elite and media framing of the U.S. anti-nuclear movement. *Political Communication, 10,* 155–173.
Fischer, G. W., & Johnson, E. J. (1986). Behavioral decision theory and political decision making. In R. R. Lau & D. O. Sears (Eds.), *Political cognition: The 19th annual Carnegie symposium on cognition* (pp. 55–65). Hillsdale, NJ: Lawrence Erlbaum Associates, Inc.
Funkhouser, G. R. (1973a). The issues of the sixties: An exploratory study in the dynamics of public opinion. *Public Opinion Quarterly, 37,* 62–75.
Funkhouser, G. R. (1973b). Trends in media coverage of the issues of the sixties. *Journalism Quarterly, 50,* 533–538.
Gamson, W. A. (1985). Goffman's legacy to political sociology. *Theory and Society, 14,* 605–621.
Gamson, W. A., & Modigliani, A. (1987). The changing culture of affirmative action. In R. G. Braungart & M. M. Braungart (Eds.), *Research in political sociology* (Vol. 3, pp. 137–177). Greenwich, CT: JAI.
Gans, H. (1979). *Deciding what's news.* New York: Pantheon.
Gerhards, J., & Rucht, D. (1992). Mesomobilization: Organizing and framing in two protest campaigns in West Germany. *American Journal of Sociology, 98,* 555–595.
Gitlin, T. (1980). *The whole world is watching: Mass media in the making & unmaking of the new left.* Berkeley: University of California Press.
Goffman, E. (1974). *Frame analysis: An essay on the organization of experience.* Cambridge, MA: Harvard University Press.
Hastie, R., & Park, B. (1986). The relationship between memory and judgment depends on whether the task is memory-based or on-line. *Psychological Review, 93,* 258–268.
Heider, F. (1930). Die Leistung des Wahnehmungssystems [The system of human perceptions]. *Zeitschrift für Psychologie, 114,* 371–394.
Heider, F. (1959). *The psychology of interpersonal relations* (2nd ed.). New York: Wiley.
Heider, F. (1978). Über balance und attribution [About balance and attribution]. In D. Görlitz, W.-U. Meyer, & B. Weiner (Eds.), *Bielefelder symposium über attribution* (pp. 19–28). Stuttgart, Germany: Klett.
Heider, F., & Simmel, M. (1944). An experimental study of apparent behavior. *American Journal of Psychology, 57,* 243–259.
Huckfeldt, R., & Sprague, J. (1997). *Accessibility and the political utility of partisan and ideological orientations* (Working paper). Bloomington: Indiana University.
Huang, K. S. (1995). *A comparison between media frames and audience frames: The case of the Hill–Thomas controversy.* Unpublished doctoral dissertation, University of Wisconsin, Madison.
Huang, K. S. (1996, May). *A comparison between media frames and audience frames: The case of the Hill–Thomas controversy.* Paper presented at the annual convention of the International Communication Association, Chicago.
Iyengar, S. (1987). Television news and citizens' explanations of national affairs. *American Political Science Review, 81,* 815–831.
Iyengar, S. (1990). The accessibility bias in politics: Television news and public opinion. *International Journal of Public Opinion Research, 2,* 1–15.
Iyengar, S. (1991). *Is anyone responsible? How television frames political issues.* Chicago: University of Chicago Press.
Iyengar, S., & Kinder, D. R. (1987). *News that matters: Television and American opinion.* Chicago: University of Chicago Press.
Iyengar, S., & Simon, A. (1993). News coverage of the Gulf crisis and public opinion: A study of agenda-setting, priming and framing. *Communication Research, 20,* 365–383.
Kahneman, D., & Tversky, A. (1972). Subjective probability: A judgment of representativeness. *Cognitive Psychology, 3,* 430–454.

Kahneman, D., & Tversky, A. (1979). Prospect theory: An analysis of decision under risk. *Econometrica, 47,* 263–291.

Kahneman, D., & Tversky, A. (1984). Choices, values and frames. *American Psychologist, 39,* 341–350.

Klandermans, B. (1988). The formation and mobilization of consensus. In B. Klandermans, H. Kriesi, & S. Tarrow (Eds.), *International social movement research: Vol. 1. From structure to action: Comparing social movement research across cultures* (pp. 173–196). Greenwich, CT: JAI.

Klandermans, B. (1992). The social construction of protest and multiorganizational fields. In A. D. Morris & C. McClurg Mueller (Eds.), *Frontiers in social movement theory* (pp. 77–103). New Haven, CT: Yale University Press.

Klandermans, B., & Oegema, D. (1987). Potentials, networks, motivations, and barriers: Steps towards participation in social movements. *American Sociological Review, 52,* 519–531.

Kosicki, G. M. (1993). Problems and opportunities in agenda-setting research. *Journal of Communication, 43,* 100–127.

Kosicki, G. M., & McLeod, J. M. (1990). Learning from political news: Effects of media images and information-processing strategies. In S. Kraus (Ed.), *Mass communication and political information processing* (pp. 69–83). Hillsdale, NJ: Lawrence Erlbaum Associates, Inc.

Lang, G. E., & Lang, K. (1981). Watergate: An exploration of the agenda-building process. In G. C. Wilhoit & H. de Bock (Eds.), *Mass communication review yearbook* (Vol. 2, pp. 447–468). Beverly Hills, CA: Sage.

Lazarsfeld, P. F. (1957). Interpretation of statistical relations as a research operation. In P. F. Lazarsfeld & M. Rosenberg (Eds.), *The language of social research* (pp. 115–125). Glencoe, IL: Free Press.

Lodge, M., McGraw, K. M., & Stroh, P. (1989). An impression-driven model of candidate evaluation. *American Political Science Review, 83,* 399–419.

McCombs, M. F. (1997, August). *New frontiers in agenda-setting: Agendas of attributes and frames.* Paper presented at the annual convention of the Association for Education in Journalism and Mass Communication, Chicago.

McCombs, M. F., Llamas, J. P., Lopez-Escobar, E., & Rey, F. (1997). Candidate images in Spanish elections: Second-level agenda-setting effects. *Journalism & Mass Communication Quarterly, 74,* 703–717.

McCombs, M. F., & Shaw, D. L. (1972). The agenda-setting function of mass media. *Public Opinion Quarterly, 36,* 176–187.

McCombs, M. F., Shaw, D. L., & Weaver, D. (1997). *Communication and democracy: Exploring the intellectual frontiers in agenda-setting theory.* Mahwah, NJ: Lawrence Erlbaum Associates, Inc.

McLeod, J. M., Becker, L. B., & Byrnes, J. E. (1974). Another look at the agenda-setting function of the press. *Communication Research, 1,* 131–166.

McNamara, T. P. (1992). Theories of priming. *Journal of Experimental Psychology, 18,* 1173–1190.

McQuail, D. (1994). *Mass communication theory: An introduction* (3rd ed.). Thousand Oaks, CA: Sage.

Moy, P., Scheufele, D. A., Eveland, W. P., Jr., & McLeod, J. M. (in press). Support for the death penalty and rehabilitation: Question artifact or communication effect? *Journal of Applied Social Psychology.*

Nelson, T. E., Clawson, R. A., & Oxley, Z. M. (1997). Media framing of a civil liberties conflict and its effect on tolerance. *American Political Science Review, 91,* 567–583.

Nelson, T. E., & Kinder, D. R. (1996). Issue framing and group-centrism in American public opinion. *Journal of Politics, 58,* 1055–1078.

Pan, Z., & Kosicki, G. M. (1993). Framing analysis: An approach to news discourse. *Political Communication, 10,* 55–75.

Petty, R. E., & Jarvis, W. B. G. (1996). An individual differences perspective on assessing cognitive processes. In N. Schwarz & S. Sudman (Eds.), *Answering questions: Methodology for determining cognitive and communicative processes in survey research* (pp. 221–257). San Francisco: Jossey-Bass.

Price, V., Tewksbury, D., & Powers, E. (1995, November). *Switching trains of thought: The impact of news frames on readers' cognitive responses.* Paper presented at the annual conference of the Midwest Association for Public Opinion Research, Chicago.

Price, V., Tewksbury, D., & Powers, E. (1997). Switching trains of thought: The impact of news frames on readers' cognitive responses. *Communication Research, 24,* 481–506.

Quattrone, G. A., & Tversky, A. (1988). Contrasting rational and psychological analyses of political choice. *American Political Science Review, 82,* 719–736.

Rahn, W. M., Krosnick, J. A., & Breuning, M. (1994). Rationalization and derivation processes in survey studies of political candidate evaluations. *American Journal of Political Science, 38,* 582–600.

Rogers, E. M., Dearing, J. W., & Bregman, D. (1993). The anatomy of agenda-setting research. *Journal of Communication, 43,* 68–84.

Salancik, J. R. (1974). Inference of one's attitude from behavior recalled under linguistically manipulated cognitive sets. *Journal of Experimental and Social Psychology, 10,* 415–427.

Scheufele, D. A. (1999). Framing as a theory of media effects. *Journal of Communication, 49,* 101–120.

Sherif, M. (1967). *Social interaction: Process and products.* Chicago: Aldine.

Shoemaker, P. J., & Reese, S. D. (1996). *Mediating the message* (2nd ed.). White Plains, NY: Longman.

Snow, D. A., & Benford, R. D. (1988). Ideology, frame resonance, and participant mobilization. In B. Klandermans, H. Kriesi, & S. Tarrow (Eds.), *International social movement research: Vol. 1. From structure to action: Comparing social movement research across cultures* (pp. 197–217). Greenwich, CT: JAI.

Sudman, S., Bradburn, N. N., & Schwarz, N. (1996). *Thinking about answers: The application of cognitive processes to survey methodology.* San Francisco: Jossey-Bass.

Tourangeau, R. (1984). Cognitive sciences and survey method. In T. B. Jabine, M. L. Straf, J. M. Tanur, & R. Tourangeau (Eds.), *Cognitive aspects of survey methodology: Building a bridge between disciplines* (pp. 73–100). Washington, DC: National Academy Press.

Tourangeau, R. (1987). Attitude measurement: A cognitive perspective. In H.-J. Hippler, N. Schwarz, & S. Sudman (Eds.), *Social information processing and survey methodology* (pp. 149–162). New York: Springer-Verlag.

Tourangeau, R., & Rasinski, K. A. (1988). Cognitive processes underlying context effects in attitude measurement. *Psychological Bulletin, 103,* 299–314.

Tuchman, G. (1978). *Making news: A study in the construction of reality.* New York: Free Press.

Tulving, E., & Watkins, M. J. (1975). Structure of memory traces. *Psychological Review, 82,* 261–275.

Tversky, A., & Kahneman, D. (1973). Availability: A heuristic for judging frequency and probability. *Cognitive Psychology, 5,* 207–222.

Wanta, W., & Wu, Y. (1992). Interpersonal communication and the agenda-setting process. *Journalism Quarterly, 69,* 847–855.

Weaver, D., McCombs, M., & Shaw, D. L. (1998, May). *Agenda-setting research: Recent developments in place and focus.* Paper presented at the annual convention of the World Association for Public Opinion Research, St. Louis, MO.

Winter, J. P., & Eyal, C. H. (1981), Agenda-setting for the civil rights issue. *Public Opinion Quarterly, 45,* 376–383.

Wyer, R. S., & Srull, T. K. (1986). Human cognition in its social context. *Psychological Review, 93,* 322–359.

Zaller, J. R., & Feldman, S. (1992). A simple theory of the survey response: Answering questions versus revealing preferences. *American Journal of Political Science, 36,* 579–616.

George Gallup and Ralph Nafziger: Pioneers of Audience Research

Steven H. Chaffee
Department of Communication
University of California, Santa Barbara

In keeping with end-of-century biographies of great leaders, this essay traces the careers of opinion pollster George Gallup and journalism educator Ralph Nafziger. They inadvertently overlapped in 1930, by publishing the first Journalism Quarterly articles on newspaper readers. Gallup became internationally recognized as creator of the Gallup Poll and other media audience enterprises. He invented some standard questions that are used in academic as well as commercial research today, and "a new form of journalism" built around public opinion on current events. Nafziger, as a professor and administrator, built research centers and graduate programs in 2 leading journalism schools. He was central to the establishment of research as an integral component within education for journalism and mass communication.

Empirical mass communication research departs from other scholarly traditions with its close examination of media audiences. Our self-imposed burden, before we venture conclusions about people's motives, attention, or reactions toward mass media content, is to gather evidence on these processes. When we do, we are following a path that was broken for us by George H. ("Ted") Gallup of Iowa (1901–1984) and Ralph O. Nafziger of Wisconsin (1896–1973).

In 1930 these two men, unlikely to be remembered together otherwise, introduced audience research into education for journalism by publishing two newspaper "reader-interest" field surveys of community residents (Gallup, 1930; Nafziger, 1930). Both authors circumspectly avoided tables of numbers, but their methodology represented a sharp departure for *Journalism Quarterly,* a journal that had in its first 6 years published teaching materials, musings on journalism as a profession, plus some occasional legal and historical scholarship.[1] I have chosen to devote my turn in this forum to these two pioneering authors because they had a formative influence on mass communication research as we practice it today. Their divergent careers offer very different role models, each estimable by its own lights, and a sense of our intellectual legacy.[2] In telling these parallel stories, I also note contributions of a few other leading social scientists, media professionals, and mass communication scholars of their era. I think of this essay as a matter of paying my respects.

THE ORIGINAL STUDIES

In 1930, Gallup, a graduate of the University of Iowa's first journalism class who had gone on to a PhD in applied psychology, was in his second year of teaching journalism at Drake University. Nafziger, a World War I Army combat veteran with 7 years of newspaper experience, was also teaching journalism while working on a PhD in political science at the University of Wisconsin. These two innovators were to become great institution builders in their respective spheres in the coming decades. Gallup literally created several commercial professions of mass communication, and Nafziger did somewhat the same thing, if less famously, within academics.

The first studies of each of them contained several hints of the very different futures that were in store for these two sons of the prairie. Gallup's (1930), which appeared first, was a methodological piece. He described his data collection procedure of an interviewer sitting down with the previous day's local newspaper and asking patiently how much of each item a person had read. His interviewers also asked whether the reader had liked or disliked each article. Gallup pointed his report toward management, arguing that his procedure produced much sounder information for editorial decisions than did such passive indicators as complaints, letters to the editor, circulation, or overheard conversations about the newspaper. His article said little about sampling or the communities his samples represented. Having completed surveys in a number of small Iowa towns, he offered summary conclusions about the newspaper in general, stressing soft news and features such as comics, which his interviews indicated were a major consideration "when a reader buys one newspaper rather than another" (p. 9).

Nafziger (1930), although his research was not dissimilar, was trying to get facts about a particular community (Madison, Wisconsin). The care he took in sampling followed his descriptive, journalistic approach to society. He was scrupulous about interviewing in every precinct of the city (stratifying for income), and proudly re-

---

[1] In its first 4 years, 1924 to 1927, the name of the quarterly had been *Journalism Bulletin.*

[2] Much of the information here on Nafziger is drawn from Rogers and Chaffee (1994, esp. pp. 25–29). The material on Gallup was mostly collected in the preparation of Chaffee (1999).

ported a response rate of 40% to 50% for his mailed questionnaire. Nafziger's questions were a bit more generic than Gallup's sit-down interview, even though his conclusions were more particularistic. In Madison, interviewers at the doorstep handed each respondent a list of regular features of the newspaper,[3] with instructions such as, "check comic strips you read." Gallup's interviewers would instead point to a specific strip on a particular day, implicitly assuming that generalization would be achieved by cumulating many readers' self-reports across a representative sample of days.

Like Gallup, Nafziger (1930) addressed his conclusions partly to management, which he was pleased to report had made several content changes based on his findings. However, he also chided the editorial side of the paper (and, in passing, of all newspapers) for not keeping up with their own advertising and circulation departments in use of new survey research techniques. Early on, then, we see Gallup approaching the newspaper as a problem in product design for the mass market, while Nafziger was thinking about it as a work institution, and its readership as reflecting a community in which he felt a personal stake.

"Gallup had a better questionnaire," Nafziger would recall later, "but we had a better sample" (personal communication, 1966).[4] This pithy contrast was prophetic, especially for Gallup, a master of the middle American vernacular who quickly established a national reputation in the polling industry through his keen sense of how to ask questions that people understood. Gallup developed what became the classic methods media industries use in their planning, and several of his standard opinion questions are to this day asked the way he drafted them. Gallup's sampling shortcuts, which were obvious to Nafziger if not to others, would not catch up with him for nearly two decades.

EARLY CAREERS

In 1931–32 Gallup moved to Northwestern University to teach advertising. After that year he left academics for the advertising industry itself, creating at Young & Rubicam (Y&R) in New York City the first ad agency research on radio's impact on consumers. Before leaving Iowa, however, he ran polls to support his mother-in-law's successful 1932 campaign for state office; this was his first and only foray into partisan politics.[5] His Gallup Poll, a side business at the time, made news in 1934 by successfully predicting that the Democrats would, contrary to expectations for an off-year election, gain seats in the House of Representatives even

---

[3]The newspaper in question was the *Wisconsin State Journal*.

[4]As a junior faculty member at the University of Wisconsin–Madison in the late 1960s, I heard this statement more than once, but did not understand it fully until I did the research reported here.

[5]Although the 1932 campaign was for a Democrat, as a matter of professionalism Gallup throughout his career refused to identify himself with any political party.

though they already held the White House. Two years later he (along with Elmo Roper and other survey exponents) won further recognition by predicting the landslide reelection victory of President Franklin D. Roosevelt. Y&R indulged him in building his own polling business, which added value to their commercial advice to clients; the advertising firm made him a vice president in 1937, and he remained with them at least part time for another 10 years.

Meanwhile, Nafziger left Madison (ABD) in 1935 to become an associate professor of journalism at the University of Minnesota. His dissertation, completed the following year, concerned the press and public opinion during what was then called, simply, the World War. Nafziger and the director of the Minnesota school, Ralph D. Casey, had been students together at Wisconsin, in the seminar where Professor Willard G. Bleyer prepared PhD candidates in social science fields for their journalism minor. Under Casey (a former *Seattle Post-Intelligencer* city editor who held a Phi Beta Kappa key), Nafziger became a standout on the all-star journalism faculty Minnesota assembled during the Great Depression. In 1937 he was promoted to professor, and in 1941 he won election as president of the American Association of Teachers of Journalism.[6]

Nafziger and a third alumnus of Bleyer's Wisconsin seminar, Chilton ("Chick") Bush of Stanford University, developed quantitative content analysis as a method of newspaper study alongside audience studies. (Content analysis became a more widespread form of scholarship in journalism schools than audience analysis.) Nafziger conducted comparative studies of newspapers, and in 1940 published an annotated bibliography on international journalism. Thus prepared, he scheduled a sabbatical leave to study the foreign press for the academic year 1941–42.

WAR AND INNOVATION

Nafziger was just getting started on his research at the Library of Congress in Washington, DC, in December 1941, when the bombing of Pearl Harbor abruptly ended his sabbatical. He volunteered to move his work over to the new Office of Facts and Figures (OFF),[7] where he began concentrating on the German press as part of the Allied counteroffensive against Nazi propaganda. This work brought him into contact with some of the most famous social scientists of the time, including some who were studying mass media in other ways. One was political scientist Harold D. Lasswell, considered the leading authority on propaganda analysis and a strong advocate of quantitative methods (Lasswell, 1950); Lasswell advised on the content analyses Nafziger was doing and on the design of Allied propaganda as

---

[6]The American Association of Teachers of Journalism later became the Association for Education in Journalism, and today is the Association for Education in Journalism and Mass Communication.

[7]Within a year, the OFF's name was changed to the Office of War Information. After the war it was changed to today's U.S. Information Agency.

well. Another wartime government consultant Nafziger met was Paul F. Lazarsfeld of Columbia University, whose Office of Radio Research contracted with the Columbia Broadcasting System to do audience studies (Lazarsfeld & Kendall, 1948). Nafziger's erstwhile statistics professor, Samuel Stouffer, had relocated to Washington, on leave from Harvard University, to head up the Army's American Soldier studies that included innovative field experiments on troop "orientation" films (Hovland, Lumsdaine, & Sheffield, 1949).

Also in the nation's capital to help at OFF was Wilbur Schramm, a University of Iowa professor of literature and creative writing. Nafziger and Schramm, whose paths would often cross professionally after the war, took note of the way the entrepreneurial Lazarsfeld ran a collaborative media–university research shop. When their work at OFF was downsized in 1943, Nafziger and Schramm returned to their home universities with expanded visions. At Minnesota, Nafziger established the first journalism school research center, built around audience studies. Soon after being appointed director of the journalism school at Iowa, Schramm followed Nafziger's example, adding to his audience research center the first PhD program in mass communication.[8] It was in this way that Gallup's home institution eventually built on the approach to research he had introduced there as a graduate student some two decades earlier.

As the Depression ended and the war began, Gallup had ideas of his own. He hit on the idea of selling to newspapers a column under his byline (originally called "America Speaks") based on what survey data showed people were thinking about current issues. He called this, not hyperbolically, "a new form of journalism." Gallup was not literally the inventor of opinion surveys, but the phrase *Gallup poll* became eponymous and he was often treated as the spokesman for the industry. He established similar survey research firms in Great Britain, Canada, Australia, and Sweden by 1940, and at the end of the war in 1945 newspapers in all four countries were subscribing to his columns (Gallup, 1942).

Eventually Gallup's news releases were run as conventional articles with their own headlines over Gallup's byline. In the 1930s he moved his survey research headquarters, which he called the American Institute of Public Opinion (AIPO), to Princeton, New Jersey. (The marketing office remained in New York City.) The firm's survey questionnaires consisted mostly of commercial marketing research, which kept the ledgers balanced. AIPO itself often showed an operating loss (despite many subscribing newspapers), but the poll's publicity was effective advertising for Gallup's other businesses.

AIPO reported opinions on such varied topics as religion, alcoholism, and attitudes toward women, but politics was always a mainstay. Gallup was the first to ask people to rate "the job the president is doing," a question that became a standard by

---

[8]Schramm's contributions as the founder of mass communication study are outlined in Rogers and Chaffee (1994).

which journalists and historians judge presidential performance. In time, presidential job ratings even became a kind of political capital; a U.S. president can get his way with Congress much more readily if he stands high in "the polls."

Gallup also began asking what people thought was "the most important problem" facing the country, thereby earning the gratitude of future generations of agenda-setting scholars. He recognized the value of keeping question wording constant over the years so that results could later be utilized by historians in search of reliable indicators of shifting American social values.

Another Gallup business was the Audience Research Institute (ARI), which he created for radio and motion picture clients. One of his methodological innovations was the coincidental method of measuring the radio audience, by contacting people at home and asking what they were listening to at the moment. In the film industry, one of ARI's first contracts was with the Selznick Organization, on the marketing campaign for *Gone With The Wind*. Based on audience comments collected after a sneak preview in a California town, Gallup advised them to sell it as a love story, not a war movie. Thus promoted, it became the most profitable film of its era.

In the 1940s, ARI survey results led to modified movie titles, promotion strategies, casting, and plots, leading writers and actors to complain about Gallup's artless advice. To "do an ARI" became Hollywood talk for any sort of market testing, and Gallup was often blamed for the notorious sugar-coated "Hollywood endings" that were imposed on novels and plays over the protests of their authors. Producers, though, capitalized on Gallup's reputation for scientific methods to reassure potential investors who might be wary of business judgment in flaky, scandal-ridden Hollywood.

CHALLENGE AND RESPONSE

For all his skills at writing questions, formatting interviews, and forming new businesses, Gallup's basic sampling method in the 1940s remained crude by scientific standards. Instead of random selection he relied on "barometer counties" and quota sampling methods, procedures that are cited in today's textbooks as how not to do it. To hold down field costs, for example, Gallup interviewers did not make callbacks (i.e., a second attempt to contact a home after the first visit failed to yield an interview). Such economies got AIPO by for some years, and Gallup's descriptions of his demographic sampling probably sounded quite scientific to the statistically unlettered public, journalists, and politicians of the time. In 1936, for instance, when the *Literary Digest* prominently mispredicted that President Franklin D. Roosevelt would lose to Republican challenger Alfred E. Landon, Gallup accurately predicted the election correctly based on a sample that, he bragged, was only 6% the size of the *Digest*'s—a "mere" 125,000 interviews by AIPO.

It was not until after the great debacle of 1948, when Gallup and other pollsters incorrectly predicted that Thomas E. Dewey would defeat President Harry S. Truman, that AIPO began to modernize its data collection techniques to match those of rival firms. Meanwhile, the embarrassment of 1948 cost ARI most of its Hollywood contracts, and survey research firms in general fell into a depression of their own. Gallup's prestige forever tarnished, AIPO became dependent on earnings from his other market research enterprises.

In his 1972 book *The Sophisticated Poll Watcher's Guide,* Gallup drew back from promoting his services on the basis of prediction, asserting that his purpose in comparing polls with election results was merely to validate the sample-survey method. This was disingenuous considering that he had built his businesses on the promise that he knew how to predict what the public would do. However, prediction is a bit more than a survey can tell us, and Gallup's newly modest claims helped educate people about the limitations of the tools he had created.

Nafziger's career trajectory was more consistently upward, although as a professor he could never achieve the fame or fortune that Gallup enjoyed. After the war, he poured his energies into teaching reporting of public affairs and developing the research division of the Minnesota journalism school. Working with the *Minneapolis Star and Tribune,* he created the nationally respected Minnesota Poll, a statewide service noted for its penetrating questions on current public issues. Nafziger's graduate students conducted survey interviews for the Poll, and the newspaper firm in turn subsidized his research center and published his students' stories. This nonprofit arrangement was modeled to an extent on Gallup's commercial example, except its underlying purpose was educational. Nafziger's students learned social research methods as well as Gallup's new form of journalism, and some used Minnesota Poll data for their graduate theses.

For Nafziger 1948 was pivotal in more positive ways than for Gallup. He spearheaded creation of the emerging research field's first methods textbook, entitled *Introduction to Journalism Research* (Nafziger & Wilkerson, 1949). A decade later he would do the same for a revised volume, modernizing the term *journalism* to *mass communication* (Nafziger & White, 1963). In this same period, Schramm moved from Iowa to the University of Illinois, where as head of the University of Illinois Press he published several collections of papers that included journalism professors like Nafziger and Casey, alongside prominent social scientists such as Lasswell, Lazarsfeld, and Hovland (Schramm, 1948, 1949). As Schramm's books became our first theory texts, Nafziger's played the same role on the research methods side of the embryonic doctoral curricula in mass communication.[9]

Even more important for Nafziger in 1948–49 was a decisive change in his institution and his job. The journalism faculty at Wisconsin had grown dissatisfied with the leadership of Bleyer's successor as director, Grant Hyde, complaining that he

---

[9]It was no coincidence that leading early doctoral programs in empirical research on mass communication were established at Schramm and Nafziger's schools: Iowa, Minnesota, Wisconsin, and Illinois (along with Stanford, Schramm's next destination after Illinois).

showed little research leadership. Their search for a new director soon focused on Nafziger, and in 1949, at age 53, he decided to make the move. He brought with him from Minneapolis to Madison not only his accumulated research expertise and vision, but also a prominent newspaper columnist, Graham Hovey of the *Star and Tribune,* to teach reporting and interpretation of public affairs. Student journalists at Wisconsin were overjoyed at this indication that their school was catching up with "modern" trends in the professional field.[10]

GOLDEN YEARS

Deftly intertwining his two professional loves, journalism and research, Nafziger served as director at Wisconsin for 17 years until he reached mandatory retirement age at 70. In that time, he built a journalism school the equal of those at Minnesota and Iowa—and anywhere else. Soon after retirement he was selected to become the first executive secretary of the Association for Education in Journalism (AEJ). Running this academic society was a half-time job, and he continued to work with international journalism agencies including the Berlin Institute, the Asian Foundation, United Nations Educational, Scientific, and Cultural Organization, and the East–West Center. He kept regular work hours until a few months before he died from complications of surgery in 1973.

The journalism school that Nafziger put together at Madison included, as at Minnesota, a research center and a PhD program. He first appointed Malcolm S. MacLean, Jr., an innovative young scholar from Minnesota, to direct these activities. After MacLean left Wisconsin, Nafziger hired Percy H. Tannenbaum, an experimentalist from Schramm's new doctoral program at the University of Illinois, to head the center, and Minnesota's first mass communication PhD, Harold L. ("Bud") Nelson, to build a parallel doctoral track in media law and history. Nafziger also supported his energetic editing instructors, Scott Cutlip and Bruce Westley, in taking advanced graduate work to upgrade their research skills. All these people were to make important contributions to journalism and mass communication research in the coming decades.

Nelson eventually succeeded Nafziger as director, presiding over an era in which Wisconsin reigned as the most productive mass communication research institution in the country. A survey of research articles in journals in the period from 1962 to 1971 (Cole & Bowers, 1973), for example, generated the following 1 to 2 aggregate scores by institution: on an index of faculty journal article productivity, Wisconsin (4.6) and Stanford (3.0); on a weighted index adjusted for faculty size, Wisconsin (11.9) and North Carolina (6.9); based on PhD school, the top two were

---

[10]According to Randall Harrison, editor of the student newspaper *The Daily Cardinal* at the time Nafziger returned to Wisconsin as director (personal communication, May 31, 1993).

Wisconsin (90.8) and Minnesota (68.9). In other words, no matter how one counted, the faculty and doctoral program Nafziger created stood head and shoulders above its rival institutions. Those other programs and faculties, by the way, included many Wisconsin people. Not surprisingly, the second AEJ Deutschmann Award for career contributions to research was given in 1972 to Nafziger; he followed his graduate school colleague Bush and preceded Schramm in this distinguished progression.

Gallup did not vanish from the scene, nor want for career recognition, after his embarrassment of 1948, of course. He became in time the senior voice of the entire public opinion research profession, speaking out on occasion as he was awarded a long stream of honorary degrees and other prestigious citations. Through his leadership of the American Association for Public Opinion Research and other professional organizations he pressed for self-policing and reporting standards in the polling field. He also advocated electoral reforms to counteract the influence of special interests against majority opinion, which was in a way his own special interest. Following the Vietnam War Gallup wrote that "the collective judgment of the people is amazingly sound, even in the complex area of foreign policy" (as cited in Chaffee, 1999, p. 660), echoing a view he had originally expressed on the eve of World War II.[11] He never fully retired from professional activity. When he died of a heart attack at 83, he held the titles of chairman of the board and chief executive officer of the Gallup Organization, and Gallup polls were being published in some 50 countries.

Neither Gallup nor Nafziger would have considered himself a theorist of mass communication. They were methodologists in 1930, and they certainly remained that in their different ways. Epistemologically, it would be fair to characterize them both as positivists. That is, they considered the results of their research, including the numbers they produced from their surveys, as facts that carried their own messages. When they sampled, they of course generalized from the sample to the population from which it was drawn, but they took care not to extend their conclusions too far. It was left to others, building on their methods and data, to develop and systematically test theories of public opinion and of mass communication processes and effects. Gallup and Nafziger were, though, visionaries of a rare order.

It would be shortsighted to conclude that Gallup only built businesses while Nafziger built schools and research centers and faculties. Gallup, for instance, helped establish the national journalistic honor society Quill and Scroll while he was still in high school. In the late 1960s the Quill and Scroll Foundation recognized this accomplishment by endowing a professorship in his honor at the Univer-

---

[11]Gallup's polls showed that most Americans favored entry into World War II, but in the case of Vietnam, predominant public sentiment moved against the war. Those were also Gallup's expressed views at those times.

sity of Iowa.[12] It is a rough indicator of the difference between their two careers that the original endowment for the Gallup chair was alone more than double the annual salary Nafziger was receiving when he retired from Wisconsin at about the same time.

Nafziger, too, is memorialized, albeit not in the highly public way that Gallup's name lives on. In Vilas Hall at the University of Wisconsin–Madison, the journalism faculty holds major events in its Nafziger Conference Room, and a Nafziger Award is given each year to a recent graduate who has achieved early distinction as a journalist. The Association for Education in Journalism and Mass Communication confers its Nafziger–White award on the new PhD whom its research committee deems to have produced the nation's best dissertation each year.[13] In these ways, his half-century of work on behalf of journalism and mass communication research is extended for future generations.

Nafziger's greater monument, though, is the institution of empirical research on mass communication within American schools of journalism and mass communication. And Gallup, although he is remembered more for the imprint of polling on 20th-century society than for his academic contributions, should share some of the credit (or blame, as you will) for these developments. It is unlikely that this journal, the authors who appear in it, the research they do, or the institutions where they work would exist with their present vigor and sense of purpose had it not been for these two men who gave us new ways of studying mass communication seven decades ago.

ACKNOWLEDGMENTS

I thank Jack M. McLeod, Paul Mark Wadleigh, and Bryant Paul for their thoughtful comments on an earlier draft of this essay.

REFERENCES

Chaffee, S. H. (1999). George Horace Gallup. In J. Garraty & M. Carnes (Eds.), *American national biography* (Vol. 8, pp. 659–660). New York: Oxford University Press.

---

[12]Gallup Professors at Iowa have over the years included Malcolm S. MacLean, Jr., James Carey, Lee Thayer, and Gil Cranberg.

[13]The Nafziger and White (1963) methods book was produced as a group project by the AEJ council on communication research, which Nafziger chaired. He and White elected not to take any royalties for this service contribution, so the proceeds went to the committee. Some years later, its successor body, the AEJ elected standing committee on research, decided to use these funds to establish an annual dissertation competition in the names of the co-editors of the book that had generated the funds.

Cole, R. R., & Bowers, T. A. (1973). Research article productivity of U.S. jouralism faculties. *Journalism Quarterly, 50,* 246–254.

Gallup, G. H. (1930). A scientific method for determining reader-interest. *Journalism Quarterly, 7,* 1–13.

Gallup, G. H. (1942). Reporting public opinion in five nations. *Public Opinion Quarterly, 6,* 429–436.

Gallup, G. H. (1972). *The sophisticated poll watcher's guide.* Princeton, NJ: Princeton University Press.

Hovland, C. I., Lumsdaine, A. A., & Sheffield, F. D. (1949). *Experiments on mass communication: Studies in social psychology in World War II.* New Haven, CT: Yale University Press.

Lasswell, H. D. (1950). Why be quantitative? In B. Berelson & M. Janowitz (Eds.), *Reader in public opinion and communication* (Rev. ed., pp. 265–277). Glencoe, IL: Free Press.

Lazarsfeld, P. F., & Kendall, P. (1948). *Radio listening in America.* Englewood Cliffs, NJ: Prentice-Hall.

Nafziger, R. O. (1930). A reader-interest survey of Madison, Wisconsin. *Journalism Quarterly, 7,* 128–141.

Nafziger, R. O., & White, D. M. (Eds.). (1963). *Introduction to mass communications research.* Baton Rouge: Louisiana State University Press.

Nafziger, R. O., & Wilkerson, M. W. (Eds.). (1949). *An introduction to journalism research.* Baton Rouge: Louisiana State University Press.

Rogers, E. M., & Chaffee, S. H. (1994). Communication and journalism from "Daddy" Bleyer to Wilbur Schramm: A palimpsest. *Journalism Monographs, 148,* 1–50.

Schramm, W. (Ed.). (1948). *Communications in modern society.* Urbana: University of Illinois Press.

Schramm, W. (Ed.). (1949). *Mass communications.* Urbana: University of Illinois Press.

The Politics of Studying Media Violence: Reflections 30 Years After The Violence Commission

Sandra J. Ball-Rokeach
Annenberg School for Communication
University of Southern California

This article is designed to fill a void in the analysis of political forces operative in the study of media effects, generally, and of mediated violence in particular (e.g., Bogart, 1972; Einsiedel, 1988; Paletz, 1988; Rowland, 1983; Wilcox, 1987). Its distinctive aspect is my personal involvement in the political struggles that surrounded the work of the 1968–69 Commission on the Causes and Prevention of Violence (the Eisenhower Commission) in my role as Codirector of the Media and Violence Task Force. The first sections are written from my perspective after the fact, and the middle sections are written more to communicate the specific ways in which political forces intrude on the process of writing commission reports. The concluding sections raise questions about the questions that have driven inquiry into media and violence.

This assessment of the relationship between mediated violence and social action is situated within the political context in which violence is defined and media effects are researched. Weber (1958) assumed a fundamental relationship between violence and power when he defined power as the ability to get others to do what they would not otherwise do, and observed that the state has a monopoly on violence as a legitimate means of sustaining its power. Consistent with Weber, violence is situated within the context of conflict wherein violence is one form of manifest conflict. Violence is defined as the threat or exertion of physical force that may cause bodily harm. This definition is normatively neutral; that is, the use of physical force may be legitimate or illegitimate, legal or illegal.

By and large, the question of media and violence has been researched from a normatively biased position that limits attention to the violence of actors unprotected by the semantic shield of legitimacy. Government commissions and academic research have not addressed the role of media violence in the promotion of legitimated uses of physical force. The most basic reason is that the relatively powerful can define the violence out of their uses of physical force. The judge who sentences a person to death, the parent who spanks a child, the husband who beats his wife, the police officer who clubs a violator, or the president who declares war occupies a position that carries the semantic power to label such uses of physical force so as to disassociate them from the realm of violence. It would seem strange to speak of a judge using violence instead of capital punishment, unless, of course, you are opposed to this use of physical force. Similarly, the parent speaks of discipline, the husband speaks of keeping his wife in line, the police officer speaks of law and order, and the president speaks of defending national interests. Violence has thus become a distorted linguistic category that conceals the essential sameness of the uses of physical force by the relatively powerful and powerless. Both employ violence as one way to resolve or win conflicts over scarce resources.

Thus, this discussion begins with the semantic politics of how violence has been defined and how such a definition affects the questions that have and have not been asked. Gone unasked are questions about the effects of media storytelling on the probability of legitimate or legal violence, on people's willingness to legitimate certain uses of physical force, and the probability of physical force being employed as the preferred mode of social control. The most common questions that have been asked pertain to a limited set of actors and media stories. Far and away the most common questions concern the effects of television entertainment stories on children, male adolescents, and male college students. There are a number of excellent reviews of the relevant research literatures (see, e.g., Donnerstein, Slaby, & Eron, 1994; Geen, 1994). Although the primary conclusions of the Violence Media Task Force are noted, more attention is given in this article to a critical analysis of the question-asking process and its effects on public understandings of the issue and government regulatory policies (e.g., the V-chip and recent rating schemes).

THE QUESTION-ASKING CONTEXT AND PATERNALISTIC SOCIAL CONTROL

Since the age of print, political philosophers have been concerned about the capacities of mass media to serve as either demagogic tools of mass manipulation or as precipitants of "the most base features of human nature," violence and sex. The Judeo-Christian assumption that humans, by nature, are predisposed to violence as a means of obtaining their selfish sexual and economic interests pervades the litany of investigations into the medi–violence connection. A related assumption is that certain individuals are more vulnerable than others to media stimulation; namely, not-yet-civilized children and undercivilized adults (e.g., the uneducated, oversexed, or poorly socialized).

These assumptions parallel those underlying mainstream theories of illegitimate or illegal violence (for a review and challenge to these assumptions, see Ball-Rokeach, 1980). It has been assumed that males, by nature or biogenetic makeup, are more aggressive than females, and are therefore more likely to employ physical force. Illegitimate or deviant violence is assumed to be an outcome of a psychological, social, cultural, economic, genetic, or biochemical deficit. The most common deficits include inadequate socialization into nonviolent means of resolving conflict (e.g., low internal or impulse control), economic (e.g., relative deprivation), membership in a subculture that endorses violence (e.g., machismo), chromosome deformity (e.g., an extra X chromosome), or biochemical imbalance (e.g., an abnormally high testosterone level).

Taken together, these assumptions produce a "paternalistic social control" perspective on the media and violence problem. The susceptible child and the easily provoked male cannot be expected to be exposed to media violence without increasing the probability that they will be stimulated or influenced to act violently; therefore, "normal" adults and their representatives must take action either to make violent media stimuli unavailable or to inoculate against stimulus effects. Real-world deviant violence, in other words, is an accident waiting to happen. The proposition that the causes of legitimate normative violence are the same as the causes of illegitimate deviant violence remains an anathema to the paternalistic social control orientation. In contemporary terms, deviant violence is a "public health" problem, a disease that requires control and treatment. The media thus take on a disease-carrier status. The term *antisocial media effects* is introduced to make it clear that the disease is disruptive of social order.

A consistent aspect of the public health approach is a preference for a psychological level of analysis in which the individual is the affected (infected) unit. Of the thousands of media and violence studies that have been conducted over the last half-century, most operate from a psychological perspective in which researchers look to characteristics of individuals to explain why some are encouraged to antisocial behavior and others are not. Public discourse around the media and violence issue is thus dominated by questions of what is wrong with that type of individual, not what is wrong with that person's group or society. Only rarely, such as in the aftermath of a political assassination, does the question of a "sick society" get asked. Instead, the presumed treatment goal is to construct restraints on the disease carrier or to immunize the vulnerable individual against the disease.

THE POLITICS OF STUDYING MEDIA VIOLENCE: THE VIOLENCE COMMISSION

The research literature on media and violence has been produced largely by social scientists funded by governmental agencies or commissions. As with any other area of inquiry, fluctuations in funding levels reflect a larger political context. In the case of media and violence, the issue usually gains funding priority status when events occur that place illegitimate or antisocial violence high on the public and thus policymaker agenda. I had an opportunity to observe this process directly as a brand new sociology PhD assuming the role of Codirector of the Media and Violence Task Force of the National Commission on the Causes and Prevention of Violence. The Violence Commission was appointed by President Lyndon B. Johnson in July 1968.

With 30 years of hindsight, it is easy to see that the basic approach and research conclusions have not changed all that much, but the importance of the issue-framing process is more clear. Reviews of media and violence research rarely, if ever, speak to the reasons the literature addresses certain questions and not others. It is, nonetheless, important to examine the process that constrains the question of media and violence to the realm of the abnormal and the individual level of analysis, because the questions that have gone unasked have at least as much theoretical and social significance as those that have been addressed. After reviewing the process as it took shape in the case of The Violence Commission, and, then, reviewing its research and policy conclusions, I return to discuss why it is time to broaden our inquiry to include new questions and new perspectives on the problem.

The Violence Commission Context

Those were bloody years that led to the establishment of The Violence Commission. The nonviolent civil rights movement had been displaced by urban riots following the April 1968 assassination of Dr. Martin Luther King; the anti-civil-rights movement had continued its periodic terrorism; the Vietnamese War had escalated to dominate the nightly news with stories of dead or maimed soldiers and civilians; the antiwar movement had taken on some violence of its own and had been violently dealt with on some college campuses; and President Johnson was under siege from the right to win the violent conflicts abroad and at home, and from the left to resolve those conflicts nonviolently. The President was further pressed by low favorability ratings to announce that he would not seek another term. On the night of June 5, 1968, he had to face the California Democratic Party primary victory of his nemesis, Senator Robert Kennedy, and then deal with Kennedy's victory night assassination. This context merged with earlier traumas, especially the 1963 assassination of President John F. Kennedy. The seeming tumble of America into uncontrollable violence provoked the question of whether America had become a sick, violent society.

Five days after Senator Kennedy's assassination President Johnson announced the formation of a blue-ribbon commission whose charge was to inquire into the causes of the violence that pervaded the scene and to propose ways that it could be stopped or prevented. The Commission Chair was Dr. Milton Eisenhower, brother of former President Dwight D. Eisenhower and a political scientist who was the president of Johns Hopkins University at the time. Lloyd Cutler, a Washington, DC, corporate lawyer and Democratic Party power player, who subsequently became General Counsel to President Jimmy Carter, was appointed to the all-important position of Executive Director. Among the 12 Commission members were representatives of almost every possible political stripe (read designed for stalemate). These included the brilliant Senator Philip Hart; distinguished Philadelphia Court of Appeals Judge Leon Higgenbothem; soon-to-be Platform Committee Chair of the fateful 1968 Democratic Party convention, Congressperson Hale Boggs; the savvy Republican and Supreme Court want-to-be Albert Jenner; the powerful Cardinal Cooke of New York; and maverick social analyst, Eric Hoffer. Although these and other commissioners played important roles at various points, the key players in this, as in most commissions, were the chair and the Commission staff.

Eisenhower did not follow the usual course of abdicating the investigatory report-writing role to the politically positioned corporate lawyer working in a "player" firm or government agency. Instead, he innovated the first and only (as far as I know) strategy of hiring academic research directors (sociologists Dr. James F. Short, Jr., and Dr. Marvin E. Wolfgang) and pairing a lawyer with an academic as codirectors of the six Commission task forces. In addition to the Violence and Media Task Force, there were task forces examining the history of violence in America, individual acts of violence, assassinations, firearms, social protest, and several investigative reports concerning urban and protest violence.

The Political Context of the Violence and Media Task Force

Throughout the 18-month life of the Commission, this task force, codirected by the author and Robert K. Baker (a young Justice Department lawyer), received understandable press scrutiny and, therefore, particularly close scrutiny of the Commission executive staff. Of the 7-day work week, typical of these types of politically charged endeavors, we spent more time negotiating the political terrain than conducting an inquiry. Resident Commission staff were housed in the New Executive Office Building, replete with trappings of importance; for example, daily paper shredding, FBI security checks of all consultants and staff, and suspension of important conversation when riding the elevator. Two operative social facts undermined Eisenhower's efforts to equalize the academic and lawyer roles. First, lawyers are more invested in the long-term political process because their positions ultimately depend on it in a way that is not true for the social scientist. Second, the lawyer's case-mounting epistemology dominated the process. The lawyer codirector, for example, proposed that we start writing the task force report before surveying the research literature and hold public hearings to prove a case, rather than air varying positions.

The media were hardly uninterested parties. For example, Drew Pearson, one of the most powerful newspaper columnists of the era, wrote a column attacking the Task Force social science codirector as a "foreigner" who could not possibly understand American media (this despite her U.S. citizenship and residence from the age of 10 months, but Canadian birth and contemporaneous employment at a Canadian university). The heart of his attack was the charge that President Johnson was out to "whitewash" the media due to his (and his wife's) ownership of television and radio stations in Texas, and to the fact that the law firms of both the Executive and Deputy Directors (Cutler and Thomas Barr) represented major television networks. This column provoked a strange FBI investigation into the background of the "foreigner" task force codirector. The culmination of this and related events came when I used the bugging of staff phone lines to indicate that I was considering holding a press conference to resign in protest to political interference. This threat, combined with the valiant efforts of Research Codirector Short, produced a number of high-level meetings designed to "cool the mark out" or to contain the situation (i.e., no public resignation) through guarantees of no White House or other interference with the task force's inquiry. Both Cutler and Barr formally exempted themselves from further participation in the task force's activities.

This anecdote, combined with the lawyer codirector's proposal to take a case-proving approach, serves to illustrate two generally applicable social facts: (a) the media system not only has a vested interest in what research and commissions have to say about its impact on social behavior, but also has the preemptive power to frame inquiries into its role; and (b) the social scientist, even when given a privileged codirector position, is operating in a world dominated by political lawyering and media epistemologies that generally disregard the social science commitment to discovery of media effects through unbiased research. The second point is further illustrated by the discourse style characteristic of both Commission hearings and media stories, namely, a dichotomous yes–no formulation that leaves no room for the carefully qualified social science style (e.g., Do the media cause real-world violence, yes or no? vs. For some people under some conditions, media violence is one of many causes of real-world violence). The fact that major media organizations have their own research departments mobilized to take on claims of antisocial media effects only adds to the imbalance.

These political context factors have important constraints on the question-asking and answering process, but the more general constraint of limiting question-asking to individuals' illegitimate violence has more far-reaching consequences. These usually go unnoticed and uncontested, but did not in the case of The Violence Commission. As noted earlier, the era of the 1960s was marked by challenges to established conceptual parameters of violence. War protest had successfully penetrated the semantic shield of labeling American uses of physical force in war as matters of patriotic courage and skill. The civil rights movement similarly penetrated the conventional law-and-order label applied to the use of physical force to maintain racism. The semantic contours of violence now included the Vietnamese War and attacks on civil rights protesters. The discourse could not be contained to individual acts of violence (e.g., assassinations and other violent crimes), but had to be extended to include state violence (the war and racism) and the collective violence of urban riots and some antiwar protests. The Commission's task force reports reflected the broken frame (see especially Gerome Skolnik's 1969 report, *Politics of Protest*).

Adding to the frame-busting impetus of the times, the collective violence of the August 1968 Chicago Democratic Party convention occurred shortly after the Commission's formation. When the Chicago police were ordered to clear a park full of thousands of antiwar protesters, the violence that ensued was covered by the huge media presence assembled in Chicago. A special investigative team headed by Edward Walker, a Chicago lawyer, was formed and its report became hotly contested. The title of Walker's (1968) report, *The Chicago National Convention: A Police Riot,* communicated its conclusion. The Media and Violence Task Force was instructed to undertake a special inquiry into the possible bias of media coverage of the violence that occurred in the park and in the streets of Chicago. Thus, the Task Force was compelled to move away from its given mission of inquiring into the effects of media violence on individuals to address a real-world case of collective violence involving protesters and police. The highly unusual examination of network outtakes that followed revealed no support for the allegation that the media had focused only on the most egregious instances of police violence.

Task Force Conclusions About Violence and the Media

The Task Force's research-related activities included reviewing the research literature and the history of inquiry into the issue, commissioning original papers, and conducting original research. Our reviews of the research literature and the history of inquiry led to three summary conclusions. The first was that the research literature was largely about the effects of violent media entertainment on the antisocial violent behavior of children, male adolescents, and male college students. As such, this literature had little to tell us about the extent to which media news or entertainment stories about violence (legitimate or illegitimate) contributed to the war, collective protest, or social control violence of the 1960s. The second conclusion was that the research literature, up to the time of our inquiry, had not been interpreted as providing a clear judgment about the effects of media violence. Prior to our inquiry, there had been several decades of investigation into the role of media violence in juvenile delinquency (e.g., the Kefauver Commission), child and adolescent violence (e.g., several Senate inquires led by Senator Pastori), and in civil disorders (e.g., the McCone Commission and the 1967 Kerner Commission). The third conclusion was that there was a discernible pattern of media response to governmental inquiries into the media and violence issue. For a short period (i.e., 1 to 2 years) following public inquiry, there was a reduction in the level of violent media content, but this was followed by a stair-step-like increase such that the next level was higher than the level at the time of the previous inquiry. By the time we began our investigation in 1968, approximately 82% of prime-time television programming contained violence as a major component of the program (see chapter 15 of the *Violence and the Media Task Force Report;* Baker & Ball, 1969).

Our review of the research literature, when combined with the thrust of the commissioned papers that detailed the latest thinking and research evidence (see Task Force Report appendices for papers by Blumenthal, Catton, Feshbach, Goranson, Greenberg, and Haskins; Baker & Ball, 1969), led to what became a most controversial conclusion. The major effects hypothesis at the time was the social learning hypothesis advanced by Albert Bandura and his colleagues (for a revised version of this approach, see Bandura, 1994). The essential logic was that individuals, and especially children, can learn violent behavior by observing what happens to media models who engage in violent acts. In much the same modeling process that occurs in direct observation, the important issue is whether or not media models are rewarded or punished for their use of violence. The probability of learning the violent act and of performing it after media exposure is heightened by media models being rewarded. Similarity between the media portrayal situation and the situation actually encountered postexposure and audience member identification with the media model also increase the likelihood of modeling effects. These effects were observed for both boys and girls. The presence of an adult coviewer who voices disapproval of media models' violence reduces the probability of cognitive and behavioral effects.

Aggressive cues was the next most common hypothesis. It is based in the classical frustration–aggression model and is generally associated with the work of Leonard Berkowitz and his colleagues (for how this approach has been revised, see Jo & Berkowitz, 1994). Its basic logic was that film or television portrayals of violent acts serve as aggressive cues or stimuli that may trigger inherent aggressive drives. Because males are thought to have stronger aggressive drives, the research focuses on male viewers. The probability that viewers will engage in violent acts postexposure is increased by being in a state of frustration at the time of exposure, by similarity between the characteristics of the source of the viewer's frustration and violent media actors, by the media violence being portrayed as justified, and by failure to show the painful consequences of violence in the media portrayal.

The third hypothesis holding sway at that time was catharsis. This hypothesis, advanced especially by Feshbach and Singer (1971), draws on the classical Aristotelian notions of catharsis wherein the opportunity to vicariously participate in another's violence (or other extreme emotional situations) serves as a safety valve that reduces the need of the observer to engage in actual violence (for a revised statement of this approach, see Gunter, 1994). This hydraulic model holds that people build up frustration to the point where they explode in aggressive behavior. Media portrayals of violence thus afford an opportunity for viewers (and especially males assumed to have more intense aggressive drives) to cathart or lower their frustration level via vicarious participation in the actor's aggression.

After reviewing the research literature and the commissioned papers, we reached our conclusions: (a) Exposure to media and especially television violence did increase the probability of viewers (especially children and young males) engaging in antisocial violence, and (b) the evidence suggested that catharsis was not a viable account of the effects process. We noted the properties of television that make it a particularly potent effects agent, including the implicit authenticity of its audiovisual stimulation and home-viewing environment, its pervasive use, and its centrality in the everyday lives of people and society. The vast majority of studies addressed only short-term effects (e.g., hours postexposure), and there was less conclusive evidence of long-term effects: Greater degrees of exposure during childhood were associated with higher levels of violence in young adulthood.

These conclusions represented the first time that a governmental inquiry had moved off the fence to come down on one side of the media and violence issue. This fact, combined with the hotly contested political context of our inquiry, produced considerable internal negotiation and external reaction. Internal meetings held to discuss our conclusions produced a compromise whereby the Violence and the Media Task Force report findings (Baker & Ball, 1969) would be uncoupled from the less conclusive stance taken in the overall report of The Violence Commission (1969). Subsequent characterizations of the Task Force Report (e.g., Gunter, 1994) confuse its conclusions with the obfuscated conclusions presented in the report of the full Commission.

Also included in the Task Force Report were summaries of the findings of two original research efforts. Both projects employed a normatively neutral definition of violence, the threat or exertion of physical force that could cause bodily injury. The first effort was the founding study in George Gerbner and colleagues' Cultural Indicators project (see Baker & Ball, 1969, chapter 15, pp. 311–340), which became well known for its yearly report of the level and nature of violence in prime-time television entertainment programming. Over and above the conclusion that violence pervaded prime-time television programming, Gerbner and his colleagues found that violence was the dominant way in which conflict was expressed and resolved in television stories. The dominantly male, middle-class, White "good guy" characters employed as much violence as the usually male, lower class, non-White "bad guys." The major difference between good guys and bad guys was that good guys used violence and won, while bad guys used violence and lost. An important aspect of this line of research is that it locates the analysis of media violence in the context of social power and conflict, and asks what can audiences learn about violent behavior, about norms for violence (when is it legitimate or illegitimate?), and about the world around them (e.g., how violent is that world?). From this early inquiry, Gerbner and his colleagues went on to develop cultivation theory (for a review, see Gerbner, Gross, Morgan, & Signorielli, 1994).

The second project was a national survey of American adult and teenage self-reports of their experience with violence as assailants, victims, or observers, and their norms for violence—the conditions under which they would approve of the use of low- or high-severity violence by people occupying state (e.g., police and judges) and nonstate roles (e.g., parents or teens). There are many interesting findings (Baker & Ball, 1969, chapters 16, 17), but the most relevant findings for present purposes were that (a) a majority of adults and teens reported experience with low-level violence as a victim or observer, but only a small percentage reported experience with the kind of severe violence that is commonplace in television stories; and (b) most adults and teens were willing to approve the use of violence only when there was serious provocation and only when the user had legal authority. The implications we drew from comparing the "real" and "television" worlds of violence were that (a) television entertainment programming afforded a unique opportunity for most viewers to learn severe violence acts, (b) the norms for violence that television viewers may learn endorse violence as the most effective path to individual success, and (c) television stories give a distorted picture of the world as a place where violence reigns as the way to solve conflicts, a world where the admired employ violent over nonviolent strategies and gain status and pleasure as a result. There was some indication in the findings that people who prefer and are most exposed to violent media content also have higher levels of violence experiences and have norms that are more supportive of the use of violence. The issue of causality is better addressed in the controlled experimental studies that formed the basis of our effects conclusion; however, subsequent longitudinal survey research has afforded stronger evidence (see Donnerstein et al., 1994).

Another social fact that emerged out of our original research was that any attempt to translate the negotiation of established assumptions about violence that pervaded the context of The Violence Commission into formal task force questioning was summarily rejected. For example, probably the most significant finding that came out of our adult and teen survey was that when a neutral definition of violence was employed, self-reported experience with violence and norms for violence did not substantially differ across levels of income and education. This finding indicated that theories of deviant violence based on economic or educational deficit notions (i.e., most social theories) may not be valid accounts of the threat or exertion of physical force irrespective of its normative status. Government commissions are not usually in the business of giving a stamp of approval to such paradigm subversive findings.

VIOLENCE AND MEDIA TASK FORCE CONCLUSIONS IN CONTEXT OF SUBSEQUENT INQUIRIES

Shortly after President Johnson left office in January 1969, President Richard Nixon appointed the Surgeon General's Scientific Advisory Panel to initiate an inquiry into television violence. One reason for this seemingly redundant action was resistance to our conclusions. In analyzing the conclusions reached in the first 1972 Surgeon General's Report, Bogart (1972) noted that they were essentially the same as those reached by the Violence and Media Task Force. By the 1982 10-year follow-up Surgeon General's Report, the conclusion that television violence was one cause of individuals' antisocial violence had become widely accepted among scholars and policymakers. Attention shifted to specification and elaboration of the effects process. For example, more complicated cognitive processing and viewer–media interactions are detailed in Huesmann's (1986) reciprocal effects developmental model. Our recommendation to expand attention beyond the learning of violent acts to the learning of violent attitudes and norms for violence was reflected in subsequent research (e.g., the notion that people learn violent "scripts").

While studies of the effects of television violence continued, the issues of pornography and violence had been joined in another commission appointed by President Nixon in the early 1970s, The Commission on Pornography and Obscenity. This hotly contested Commission and report suggested that exposure to pornography might be serving the catharsis safety-valve function that had been rejected with respect to exposure to violence. The ensuing debate produced among researchers a series of studies that sought to sort out the effects of "erotica" from the effects of the "sexual violence" contained in pornographic films and videos. By the early 1990s, the research literature (see especially the work of Bryant, Donnerstein, and Malamuth, as well as Zillmann as reviewed in Harris, 1994), lent support to the conclusion that prolonged exposure to sexual violence also had undesirable effects, including emotional densensitization to violence and its victims and encouragement of the rape myth, or the idea that women really want to be raped. It is particularly interesting that some pornography researchers have moved to consider the potential effects of erotica for undermining commitment to the family institution (e.g., Zillmann, 1994) because it shifts the focus away from exclusive concern for effects on the behavior of the poorly socialized or otherwise deficit male to effects on "normal" adults.

THE MOVE TO REGULATION

With respect to media violence, the broad consensus reached, especially with respect to its antisocial effects on children, turned the attention of scholars and policymakers to how the historical pattern of media nonresponsiveness could be countered through the development of public pressure and regulatory policies.

For example, Donnerstein et al. (1994) stated in their report to the American Psychological Association's Commission on Youth and Violence that "the mass media are significant contributors to the aggressive behavior and aggression related attitudes of many children, adolescents, and adults" (p. 1). These frequent participants in congressional investigations went on to argue for regulatory action: "We call upon the Federal Communications Commission to review, as a condition for license renewal, the programming and outreach efforts and accomplishments of television stations in helping to solve the problem of youth violence in America" (p. 21).

We have come full circle from allegations that the media powerfully affect especially child audiences, through decades of research contesting the issue, to the Violence and Media Task Force Report conclusions (Baker & Ball, 1969) and their buttressing through other investigatory commissions and agencies, to the government regulatory policies of the 1990s. The culmination of this movement is evident in President Bill Clinton's October 11, 1997 statement: "We know that the media can powerfully affect our children for good or for evil." Similarly, Title I of the Children's Television Act states "It has been clearly demonstrated that television can assist children to learn important information, skills, values and behavior." Comparable statements and assumptions are contained in other acts, especially the 1990 Television Program Improvement Act (Television Violence Act) and the 1996 Telecommunications Act's V-chip and rating system provision. It was not social science evidence per se that fueled the move to regulation; rather, such evidence was effectively employed by citizen action groups willing to invest in long-term political struggle to achieve regulatory action, primarily with respect to children's television (e.g., Action for Children's Television, National Association for Better Broadcasting, Media Action Research Center, Coalition for Better TV, and the Center for Media Education).

Regulatory action was achieved (for better or worse) through a process of agenda setting wherein pressure groups seek to get the issue on the public agenda so that it generates a place on the policymaker agenda. The process is not linear, in that it takes repeated and tenacious mobilization cycles. The media, of course, are a fundamental part of the agenda-setting process, such that change agents usually must attain a position on the media agenda to gain a position on either the public or the policymaker agenda. Given the vested interest of the media in this issue and very real First Amendment considerations raised by regulatory action, the struggle is immense. Nonetheless, pressure groups armed with social science research and political savvy have succeeded in framing the issue in the paternalistic social control or public health terms that require regulatory action.

The struggle is not over, nor is the role of social science research. For example, two major research efforts are underway to further specify the issue and its policy implications. One is being conducted at the Center for Communication Policy at the University of California at Los Angeles and was commissioned by the television industry in response to congressional inquiries into how to implement the V-chip and rating system. The other is being conducted in the Department of Communication at the University of California at Santa Barbara and is geared to specification of the kinds of television content that are particularly problematic with regard to violence effects.

WHAT NOW? UNASKED QUESTIONS

Each era has focused on the dominant or newest mass medium of the day. The early violence and media research concerned print media, particularly comic books. This was replaced by a focus on film, which, in turn, was replaced by a focus on television. Of course, the growth of the cable and video industries means that the television of today is a different medium from what it was 30 years ago. With the rise of computer-based media, such as video games and the Internet, we see another shift to the latest technology of the day. A problem with this shifting focus is that research evidence across mass media does not cumulate over time. For example, with the exception of research on sexual violence, we have little contemporary research on one of the most popular media among adolescents, film. Perhaps it is time to redirect effects studies to consider the effects of the media system, rather than one or another mass medium. People consume one medium in tandem with all the other media with which they establish dependency relationships. Thus, the effects process may be better conceived in terms of the media system that people construct in their everyday lives.

If the issue remains largely constrained to the effects of media (television) portrayals of antisocial violence on the probability of antisocial violence effects (behaviors and attitudes) on children, it is hard to see why we need more research to document the conclusions reached in the 1970s and 1980s. However, the redirection of such research to policy-related concerns is likely to continue as the regulatory struggle continues. Research to evaluate the effectiveness of the 1990s regulations, with respect to both media implementation and amelioration of the effects problem, may develop as a new research direction.

The near-exclusive focus on entertainment programming that continues to characterize social science inquiry is less and less defensible given the blurring of the distinction between entertainment and news genres. While debate continues as to whether audiences make the news–entertainment distinction and if that distinction matters with regard to effects (e.g., Cantor, 1994), the outcome of the debate becomes less consequential as media production structures and processes continue to merge the two genres. As a result, it would seem desirable to broaden the inquiry to media violence that is framed or advertised as news. This is not likely to happen, however, as long as the underlying assumptions that have guided inquiry into violence and media effects persist.

As long as the normative definition of violence determines the field of concern, and as long as it is assumed that children and "deficit males" are most at risk of media effects, the paternalistic social control perspective will continue to rule out of consideration what may be even more important effects concerns. The paternalistic social control perspective is likely to persist, not because it has unassailable validity, but because it is politically viable. The intensity of struggles surrounding past inquiry and present regulatory debate pale in comparison to the conflicts that would emerge if the media and violence issue were reframed to consider the effects of news and entertainment violence on the legitimate as well as illegitimate behavior and attitudes of "normal" adults as well as children at both the individual and group level of analysis. To treat all violence as problematic with respect to legitimacy or as a problem that needs to be addressed is to challenge all authority structures that rely on the threat or exertion of physical force as one important basis of their power. These include most importantly the state, but also gender, age, and race dominance structures.

It is no accident that my first publication after my Violence Commission experience was titled "The Legitimation of Violence" (Ball-Rokeach, 1971). The experience of working on the media and violence issue as it had been defined traditionally, while in the midst of the legitimate and illegitimate violence of the late 1960s, produced a deep frustration with the limits of the extant research literature. With the questions motivating that literature now more or less asked and answered, it seems a propitious time to step back to consider other questions about the relationship between media violence stories and real-world violence. The plea made in the 1971 paper was to consider the media's role in legitimating (or delegitimating) violent social control and social change strategies. This move requires a shift from uncritical acceptance of normative definitions to treating the legitimacy of violence as a variable, and setting the analysis of both the media and violence within the social dynamics of conflict. The perspective that comes closest to this concern is Gerbner's cultivation approach (see Gerbner et al., 1994), which posits that the television world of violence leads people to believe that the world is a more violent place than it is, a distorted view that tends to promote a willingness to legitimate increasingly violent means of social control. Even this research tradition, however, tends to focus on entertainment programming, when it would be equally fruitful to consider news as well.

Whereas social science research warrants the conclusion that media violence is *one* cause, not *the* cause of child and "deficit male" violence, the importance of media violence stories for questions of legitimation may be much greater. For example, children have many influences operating on them, but the media stand out as the best resource for surveying and understanding the larger social environment, its threats, and its opportunities. The media system has a central role in public opinion and agenda setting, and these processes are fundamentally involved in changing parameters of legitimate and illegitimate violence. Contemporary social issues where such legitimacy questions have important relevance include law enforcement policies and practices, sexual harassment, terrorism, prison management, parent treatment of children, interethnic and intergang conflict, racism, and homophobia. It would be highly productive for society if the media and violence research literature had something substantial to say about these issues.

REFERENCES

Baker, R. K., & Ball, S. J. (1969). *Violence and the media: A report of the Violence and Media Task Force to the National Commission on the Causes and Prevention of Violence.* Washington, DC: U.S. Government Printing Office.

Ball-Rokeach, S. J. (1971). The legitimation of violence. In J. F. Short, Jr. & M. E. Wolfgang (Eds.), *Collective violence* (pp. 100–111). Chicago: Aldine.

Ball-Rokeach, S. J. (1980). Normative and deviant violence from a conflict perspective. *Social Problems, 28,* 45–62.

Bandura, A. (1994). Social cognitive theory of mass communication. In J. Bryant & D. Zillmann (Eds.), *Media effects: Advances in theory and research* (pp. 61–90). Hillsdale, NJ: Lawrence Erlbaum Associates, Inc.

Bogart, L. (1972). Warning: The Surgeon General has determined that TV violence is moderately dangerous to your child's mental health. *Public Opinion Quarterly, 36,* 491–521.

Cantor, J. (1994). Fright reactions to mass media. In J. Bryant & D. Zillmann (Eds.), *Media effects: Advances in theory and research* (pp. 213–246). Hillsdale, NJ: Lawrence Erlbaum Associates, Inc.

Donnerstein, E., Slaby, R., & Eron, L. (1994). The mass media and youth aggression. In L. E. Eron, J. H. Gentry, & P. Sohlegel (Eds.), *Reason to hope: A psycho social perspective on violence and youth* (pp. 219–250). Washington, DC: American Psychological Association.

Einsiedel, E. F. (1988). The British, Canadian, and U.S. pornography commissions and their use of social science research. *Journal of Communication, 38,* 108–121.

Feshbach, N., & Singer, R. (1971). *Television and agression.* San Francisco: Jossey-Bass.

Geen, R. G. (1994). Television and aggression: Recent developments in research and theory. In D. Zillmann, J. Bryant, & A. C. Huston (Eds.), *Media, children, and the family* (pp. 151–162). Hillsdale, NJ: Lawrence Erlbaum Associates, Inc.

Gerbner, G., Gross, L., Morgan, M., & Signorielli, N. (1994). Growing up with television: The cultivation perspective. In J. Bryant & D. Zillmann (Eds.), *Media effects: Advances in theory and research* (pp. 17–42). Hillsdale, NJ: Lawrence Erlbaum Associates, Inc.

Gunter, B. (1994). The question of media violence. In J. Bryant & D. Zillmann (Eds.), *Media effects: Advances in theory and research* (pp. 163–212). Hillsdale, NJ: Lawrence Erlbaum Associates, Inc.

Harris, R. J. (1994). The impact of sexually explicit media. In J. Bryant & D. Zillmann (Eds.), *Media effects: Advances in theory and research* (pp. 247–272). Hillsdale, NJ: Lawrence Erlbaum Associates, Inc.

Huesmann, L. R. (1986). Psychological processes promoting the relation between exposure to media violence and aggressive behavior by the viewer. *Journal of Social Issues, 42,* 125–139.

Jo, E., & Berkowitz, L. (1994). A priming effect analysis of media influences: An update. In J. Bryant & D. Zillmann (Eds.), *Media effects: Advances in theory and research* (pp. 43–60). Hillsdale, NJ: Lawrence Erlbaum Associates, Inc.

Paletz, D. L. (1988). Pornography, politics, and the press: The U.S. Attorney General's Commission on Pornography. *Journal of Communication, 38,* 122–136.

The report of the National Commission on the Causes and Prevention of Violence, to establish justice, to ensure domestic tranquility. Washington, DC: U.S. Government Printing Office.

Rowland, W. D. (1983). *The politics of TV violence: Policy uses of communication research.* Beverly Hills, CA: Sage.

Skolnick, J. (1969). *The politics of protest: Violent aspects of protest and confrontation.* Washington, DC: U.S. Government Printing Office.

Walker, D. (1968). *The Chicago national convention: A police riot.* Washington, DC: U.S. Government Printing Office.

Weber, M. (1958). Politics as a vocation. In H. Gerth & C. W. Mills (Eds. and Trans.), *From Max Weber: Essays in sociology* (pp. 77–128). New York: Oxford University Press.

Wilcox, B. L. (1987). Pornography, social science, and politics: When research and ideology collide. *American Psychologist, 42,* 941–943.

Zillmann, D. (1994). Erotica and family values. In D. Zillmann, J. Bryant, & A. C. Huston (Eds.), *Media, children, and the family* (pp. 199–214). Hillsdale, NJ: Lawrence Erlbaum Associates, Inc.

Children and Media: On Growth and Gaps

Ellen Wartella
College of Communication
University of Texas, Austin

This essay argues that there is far too little research on the effects of new types of media programming and formats on children. In fact, the gap between the research base and production and policy issues appears to be widening. The essay advocates use of the developmental research model to study media effects on children. More specifically, researchers should focus more on the neuropsychological effects of format characteristics and viewing styles of children.

In December 1997, international attention was riveted on an event not yet adequately accounted for: Approximately 700 Japanese children were sent to hospitals with apparent seizures after watching an episode of the Japanese animated cartoon show *Pokemon*, which included strobe-like special effects. What became apparent in the press reports and subsequently is the inadequate research base available on the effects of audiovisual format features on the neuropsychology of child viewers. While an extreme example, this case illustrates the ongoing public concerns about television's role in the lives of children, a concern that has not abated over the more than 50 years of television. I return to this example later.

Let me get to my major point. While there is public interest in children's television, there is far too little ongoing research on the consequences of such media use for children. Over the last decade we have seen (a) continued public interest and public concerns about children and television issues; (b) the development of new, plentiful, and sometimes even good quality children's television; and (c) attempts to establish national and international policies on children's television. However, there has not been a corresponding growth in research on the consequences of such media use for children and, in particular, the consequences of new types of programming and formats. Indeed, from my vantage, the gap between the research base of our understanding of television's effects on children, on the one hand, and the list of production and policy issues, on the other, seems to be widening.

Evidence for continued public interest in children and television issues can be found both anecdotally and statistically. Consider, for example, the public discussions of television violence over the past 4 or 5 years (Center for Communication and Social Policy, 1996, 1997, 1998) that centered on how violence is portrayed on television and the creation of violence ratings. Evidence of the effects of violent television programming on children formed the basis of the government policy requiring ratings. Parents should be able to use these ratings to guide their children away from potentially harmful content. Similarly, the information/ educational rating system now attached to children's programs to identify quality children's television programming is based on research demonstrating that children can and do learn from appropriately designed television.

Aside from such observations, though, one can look for evidence of how the press covers the issue of children's television. A LEXIS/NEXIS search of the top 66 newspapers in the country and abroad between 1993 and 1998 shows the number of stories about children and television increasing over that time from 1,585 in 1993 to 1,741 stories in 1998, with more than 1,500 stories appearing every year. Moreover, the topic of children and television still outweighs other media and children concerns. Only 6 stories about children and the Internet were cited in 1993, while 719 were found in 1998 demonstrating increasing public and news interest in this new medium and its relationship to children's development. A search of stories about children and computers found an increasing number here as well, from 452 in 1993 to 984 in 1998. However, neither the Internet nor computers were of as much interest in the press as television and children issues.

Furthermore, since the passage of the Children's Television Act in 1990, there has been considerable increase in the number of children's programs on American television, and this corresponds with the growth of independent stations and cable television. The success of Nickelodeon, the children's channel, has spawned blocks of children's programming on The WB, UPN, and Fox broadcast networks. These have been added to the traditional programming for children found on public television and on Saturday mornings on at least ABC and CBS. (NBC now focuses primarily on teen programming on Saturdays.) More television shows are produced for children today than 10 years ago, and there is data to support this. When my colleagues and I conducted an analysis of children's media in one community in the Midwest, we found 258 hours of children's television (defined as programs aimed at children age 12 and under) based on a content analysis of 1 week's worth of programming in November 1987 in Champaign-Urbana, Illinois (Wartella, Heintz, Aidman, & Mazzarella, 1990). The *National Television Violence Study*, in conducting its content analysis of a constructed week's worth of programming across the 1996 to 1997 television season, found nearly twice the number of children's programs on broadcast, basic cable and premium cable television—479 hours of programs. While this latter estimate was based on sampling programs from the Los Angeles area compared to a Midwest community, the national nature of cable television suggests that this is a reasonably fair comparison. In short, the number of programs for children has increased and any perusal of these titles demonstrates that there is diversity in the program genres, including news, science, dramas, cartoons, educational fare, game shows, and preschool programs.

National policy interest in children's television has not diminished since the passage of the 1990 Children's Television Act. Congress required that broadcasters provide 3 hours a week of educational/informational programs. Furthermore, since the mid-1990s, at least two major annual conferences on children and television policy issues are held nationally at the Annenberg Policy Center and the Children Now conference on the west coast. Furthermore, the 1990s brought the Center for Media Education into existence to continue the policy advocacy work of Action for Children's Television. Just this year, the National Communication Association established national standards for communication and media literacy to be promoted in America's public schools.

In addition to the national activities, international interest in more quality children's television and strong public policies to support such programs has been demonstrated in recent years. In 1995, the first World Summit on Children and Television was held in Melbourne, Australia. This event brought together children's television producers, researchers, educators, and policy experts to promote world-wide dissemination and growth in children's television. The Second World Summit was held in London in March 1998. At both of these summits, a world community of advocates for children's television promoted the development of a Children's Television Charter, a global consensus on quality children's television. It is clear that summits will become biennial international meetings to share intellectual and financial resources to be devoted to the development of more children's television around the world. How to reach, teach, and delight children through television is the focus of such summits.

But has our field kept pace with the public interest? I fear not. For instance, a search of *Social Science Abstracts* and *Humanities Abstracts* for five of the top television research journals in our field (*Journal of Communication, Journal of Broadcasting and Electronic Media, Communication Research, Human Communication Research*, and *Critical Studies in Mass Communication*) found only 26 articles (including book reviews) during the 5 years of 1993 to 1998, and while edited and scholarly books were published during this period, this is a good estimate of the relative paucity of recent research studies on children and television in our journals. Indeed, in the most recent book reviewing the children and television literature, Judith Van Evra's *Television and Child Development*, published in 1998, almost two-thirds of the references (65%) are from the 1980s and only 30% are from the 1990s.

That is not to say research is not being conducted. It has been, and it is. One of the interesting characteristics of children's television production in the United States (and increasingly around the world) is the use of research in its production. It is standard practice for children's television producers to engage in watching and talking with children about what they like and what they say television provides them by way of engagement, education, and entertainment (Wartella, 1994; Palmer, 1987). There has been a proliferation of such studies to "gain the child's perspective" in hopes of either better satisfying children's wants and consumption desires or to insure that they've interpreted the television messages in the intended fashion.

Such research on children's use of television, whether conducted for commercial or public television production, has tended to emphasize an *empowered child research* orientation. I choose this frame instead of others (such as a market orientation) to highlight one aspect of this way of "knowing child audiences." The assumption here is that children are competent, self-aware users of television who can reliably report to us about their consumption and the influence television has in their lives. Such information, I might add, is also most useful when trying to develop media products children are most likely to want to use. Such research has proliferated over the past decade as the number of children's television shows has increased. However, such research is often program specific and often proprietary. Here, Linda Kahn, at the time Vice President for Production for Nickelodeon, comments on the use of research at the children's channel (as cited in Wartella, 1994):

> We don't buy the series unless we go out and test it with kids . . . We talk about them on a lot of levels, just on the shows themselves, on the characters, on what happened, on what they think might happen in other episodes, on things they might like to see happen . . . And being in touch with the constituency is the key in anything that we do. (p. 49)

The increased use of research in commercial television production for children appears to parallel that in the production of children's educational television, which has, at least since the development of *Sesame Street* in the late 1960s, been identified with extensive use of research in the production of the educational curriculum and programming format (see Johnston & Ettema, 1982; Lesser, 1974; Palmer, 1987). However, there is a major difference between the commercial model and the educational or public broadcasting model of producing educational television both in what research is used and in how it is used. In the educational television model, research is often used both to aid in the production of the programs (much like in the commercial arena) and to ascertain the effects of the program on child audiences and whether the educational goals of the program were met.

These examples from the world of production illustrate that research with children is used to understand more about the desires and likes of child audiences. There are similar illustrations of empowered child audiences in more recent academic research which examines how children use television as well as other, new media. In *Playing with Power in Movies, Television, and Video Games* (1991), Kinder talks about the "challenging and empowering" aspects of children's media use. Both Kinder and Seiter (1993) in *Sold Separately* have similar arguments about the ways in which various television and other new media cultural products empower children by providing among other things freedom from adult authority and creative outlets. Seiter noted that television, advertising, and the toy culture they spawn foster social relationships and the building of peer cultures. Indeed, their work and others, which offer a more qualitative, cultural analysis of children's interactions with television, provide important information on children's cultural life in late 20th-century America. The dominating role of television and other media products in children's culture is often richly described.

While the empowered child research paradigm has many uses and clearly has given children a voice as fans, users, and even sometimes creators of media products, such research tends to emphasize the positive aspects of children's engagement with television. Less emphasis in such studies is placed on questions of the consequences of media use for children's health and welfare, in particular, their cognitive, emotional, and physical development. It is the *developmental research model* which addresses questions of the consequences of television use for children's development. This model has had a strong tradition in U.S. child and television research since the 1970s and has been influential in examining public policy questions about television's influence on children (Wartella, 1993). It certainly has focused attention on age-related differences in children's abilities to make sense of television content and the potentially harmful consequences of such exposure. This model highlights how children differ from adult television viewers and the implications of that difference. While the developmental model has been important in many of the violence effects studies (Center for Communication and Social Policy, 1996), it is also the tradition of research which led to the development of *Sesame Street* and other age-targeted programs. Such research tries to utilize a variety of methods, often quantitative and experimental social science methods, for examining how media products may influence children's knowledge, attitudes, or behaviors as well as their physical reactions. Such research is in far less favor today than it was 10 or even 20 years ago, and such research has been the basis, at least in the United States, for a variety of government rules and policies regulating media practices for children. The current television ratings system, as well as regulations governing advertising to children, are all consequences of research demonstrating the impact of certain television content or formats on child users. Also, many of these studies try to examine television's effects on children within a wider understanding of child development.

My concern is that there is far too little of this latter research which examines the consequences of children's television use for their development, just at the time when new views of child development are gaining ground (Flavell, 1992), when new television forms and formats are developing, and when new public concerns about the consequences of children's use of television are being raised.

First, Flavell's (1992) review of the field of cognitive development research demonstrated that the developmental paradigm has been a productive one in demonstrating that children undergo "extensive and varied cognitive growth between birth and adulthood... that is extremely rich, complex and multifaceted." (p. 998). Recent additions to the researchers armamentarium of methods that are less reliant on observational and highly verbal testing procedures (procedures involving modeling, imitation of others' actions, studying eye movements, among others) has led to revised estimates of children's competencies as compared to those of Piaget (1955). For instance, recent studies have led to new views of infants' cognitive ability, which suggest more abilities than Piaget theorized. Most importantly, the years from birth to age three are seen as crucial for development to proceed. Second, there has been a movement away from belief in general stages of development towards examination of the "powerful effects of well-organized content knowledge or expertise on the child's cognitive level within specific content areas" (Flavell, 1992, p. 1000) Third, new work studying sociocultural influences on development suggests that the ways in which children participate in structured social activities with their families, other adults, and children influence the rate and sorts of domain specific developmental progressions that occur. In short, developmentalists are revising their views of children's development to note that development proceeds in knowledge domain-specific ways and that one can talk about the things that develop such as basic processes, strategies, metacognitions, and content knowledge. Younger children are viewed as more competent than thought earlier this century, and developmental growth is seen as more varied and less uniform.

This new orientation toward developmental theorizing, which recognizes the importance of the child's social and cultural environment, clearly resonates with new work on children and television. Child developmentalists are reconsidering previous research, such as Piaget's (1955) universal stages through which all children must pass, and are now specifying both individual- domain-specific developmental patterns and the cultural factors which may influence development. This would suggest that perhaps we need to reconsider our previous television and child research in order to address these issues as well.

Furthermore, there are several areas where we have an inadequate research base to understand television's influences on children. For instance, changes in television forms and formats, too, may influence children's development in ways different than previous research in the area would suggest. Within the next few years, high-definition television will elicit a different psychological experience from current analog television. How might child viewers react to such a format? We need more research on the neuropsychological effects of format characteristics and viewing styles of children. In particular, in the wake of the Japanese *Pokemon* event in 1997, what we don't know about format effects may be harmful to children.

Or consider the current status and interest in media literacy programs in American schools (see Rubin, 1998). There is heightened interest in teaching media and television literacy in public schools, and while program materials are proliferating, we still lack empirical research on the effectiveness of these programs. We have inadequate evidence of how these programs influence children's understanding of television or its influence on them.

The controversy surrounding the PBS program *Teletubbies* has centered on the old issues of commercialization and marketing spin-offs of this preschool program and the appropriateness of targeting young children for television shows. While I personally believe the show is developmentally appropriate for its very young viewers (that is, children under two), I have a nagging concern that we have no research base from which to estimate the long-term consequences on children's development of very early television watching.

A review of the research literature on the effects of sexual messages in entertainment television on children and adolescents also found a few dozen content analyses of how sex is portrayed in television, film, and magazines (Huston, Wartella, Donnerstein, Scantlin, & Kotler, 1998). However, even in this time of unwanted teenage pregnancies, AIDS, and other sexually transmitted diseases, the review found only 15 studies in the entire literature on media effects that examined the question of the effects of sexual messages on children.

In short, there are decided and important gaps in the research literature about television's influence on children. I have tried to demonstrate that these gaps are important to us as communication researchers, to us as citizens, to our children, and to our future. Without an adequate, objective, social science research base to guide public policy and media practice, media issues are subject to political and economic pressures only. The lack of ongoing research on these important children and television issues is considerable. There is much we could know but do not know.

REFERENCES

Center for Communication and Social Policy, University of California, Santa Barbara. (Ed.). (1996). *National Television Violence Study (1994–1995)*. Thousand Oaks, CA: Sage.

Center for Communication and Social Policy, University of California, Santa Barbara. (Ed.). (1997). *National Television Violence Study (1995–1996)*. Thousand Oaks, CA: Sage.

Center for Communication and Social Policy, University of California, Santa Barbara. (Ed.). (1998). *National Television Violence Study (1996–1997)*. Thousand Oaks, CA: Sage.

Flavell, J. H. (1992). Cognitive development: Past, present, and future. *Developmental Psychology, 28,* 998–1005.

Huston, A., Wartella, E., Donnerstein, E., Scantlin, R., & Kotler, J. (1998). *Measuring the effects of sexual content in the media: A report to the Kaiser Family Foundation* (Rep. No. 1839). Menlo Park, CA: Kaiser Family Foundation.

Johnston, J., & Ettema, J. S. (1982). *Positive images: Breaking stereotypes with children's television.* Beverly Hills, CA: Sage.

Kinder, M. (1991). *Playing with power in movies, television, and video games: From Muppet Babies to Teenage Mutant Ninja Turtles.* Berkeley: University of California Press.

Lesser, G. S. (1974). *Children and television: Lessons from Sesame Street.* New York: Vintage.

Palmer, E. (1987). *Children in the cradle of television.* Lexington, MA: Lexington.

Piaget, J. (1955). *The language and thought of the child.* New York: World.

Rubin, A. M. (Ed.). (1998). Media literacy symposium. *Journal of Communication, 48*(1).

Seiter, E. (1993). *Sold separately: Children and parents in consumer culture.* New Brunswick, NJ: Rutgers University Press.

Van Evra, J. (1998). *Television and child development.* Mahwah, NJ: Lawrence Erlbaum Associates, Inc.

Wartella, E. (1993). Communication research on children and public policy. In P. Gaunt (Ed.), *Beyond agendas: New directions in communication research* (pp. 137–148). Westport, CT: Greenwood.

Wartella, E. (1994). Producing children's television programs. In J. Ettema & D. C. Whitney (Eds.), *Audiencemaking* (pp. 38–56). Beverly Hills, CA: Sage.

Wartella, E., Heintz, K., Aidman, A., & Mazzarella, S. (1990). Television and beyond: Children's video market in one community. *Communication Research, 17,* 45–64.

Where Have All the Milestones Gone? The Decline of Significant Research on the Process and Effects of Mass Communication

Melvin L. DeFleur
College of Communication
Boston University

Between about 1930 and the early 1980s, a number of seminal research studies yielded most of today's theories of the process and effects of mass communication. Since that time, few studies have made significant theoretical contributions. This apparent slowdown is inconsistent with certain trends in the media industries and in the academy that logically should result in greater production of seminal studies. The question is why so few milestones have been produced in recent years? A possible answer is that certain trends are taking place in U.S. society that tend to reduce the number of ground-breaking studies that will be produced by contemporary academics. Specifically, social scientists have turned from media studies to their more traditional research agenda; increasing attention is being paid to qualitative analysis by today's media scholars, and many are now preoccupied with critical perspectives rather than research. Additionally, higher pay in applied research may be drawing bright doctors of philosophy away from basic studies; heavy use of part-time instructors increases the workload of full-time faculty; and, finally, funding for basic research in mass communication is increasingly difficult to find.

Between about 1930 and the early 1980s, a number of studies were published that led to significant advances in understanding the process and effects of mass communication. Sometimes referred to as *milestones*, these were well-funded, large-scale efforts, conducted with important objectives in mind, and based on standards of methodology respected in their time (Lowery & DeFleur, 1995). A few were much more modest in scale, but whether large or small, they yielded important concepts, generalizations, and theories that are now part of the accumulated knowledge of how the U.S. media function and the kinds of influences that they have on individuals and society.

Since that period, there has not been a similar level of production of such seminal studies. No widely heralded investigation has been produced in nearly two decades—one that provoked wide discussion and changed the way scholars think about the mass communication process. Many noteworthy studies, even hundreds of well-conducted and interesting investigations, have been reported. However, most focus on restricted topics or hypotheses, or are efforts to explore issues raised by the earlier milestones. When asked by my publisher to revise a book summarizing the existing milestones and adding new ones, I could not identify even one that fit the same criteria as the earlier investigations (Lowery & DeFleur, 1995).

It is the purpose of this essay to suggest some of the reasons why the field of mass communication has changed in this respect. The reasons advanced include a change in the agendas of the social sciences, a lack of a programmatic approach by media scholars, a shift to nonquantitative and critical modes of analysis by many writers, and changes in the work conditions of the professorate.

THE CHANGING RELATION BETWEEN THE MEDIA AND THE ACADEMY

A number of trends in U.S. society would seem logically to lead to a prediction that important research on the process and influences of mass communication would have increased, rather than decreased. Specifically, the media have expanded and become more complex; their labor force has grown considerably; and colleges and universities now offer far more instruction related to work in the media labor force than ever before. Yet, as already mentioned, there has been no corresponding increase in the production of ground-breaking studies.

The Growth of the Media Labor Force

It is now widely understood that over the last half-century the United States increasingly became an information society. In the older manufacturing-based economy, blue-collar employees worked on factory floors producing things with their hands and machines. However, after midcentury, more than half of our workers were manipulating words and numbers to provide both products and services. With the coming of the computer revolution and the increasing globalization of the economy, the pace of that change has accelerated.

One reason that the percentage of the workforce manipulating symbols, as opposed to things, has increased greatly is that our media system has continued to expand. Before midcentury that system included only telegraph, telephone, print, radio, and film. Today, it includes not only all of the earlier media, but also fax, cellular phones, video-cassette recorders, television, cable, satellite television delivery, and the Internet—with its e-mail, local networks, and World Wide Web. As the media system expanded, a corresponding need for communication specialists and practitioners grew. This, in turn, increased the need for media-related education and has expanded the number of communication professors, scholars, and researchers.

The Growth of Media-Related Curricula

Preparing a well-educated labor force for the media industries posed a new challenge for colleges and universities. At the close of World War II, there was a very limited relation between the mass media and the U.S. academy. Journalists had been educated on campus for decades, but that was not the case for other media professionals. Only a limited number of fledgling programs existed to prepare students for careers in movie making and radio broadcasting or other media employment. No degree programs existed in such fields as advertising or public relations.[1] As television usage spread, a similar situation prevailed. Institutions were slow to offer industry-related curricula. In the more general field of mass communication studies, there certainly were no advanced academic programs designed around studies of research and theory development.

The 1960s saw the beginnings of a gradual and long-term expansion in the number of programs, departments, schools, and other academic units with curricula focused specifically on the mass media. Some were theory- and research-based programs. Others were professionally oriented, providing for media-related career training. At present, undergraduate, master's, and doctoral degree programs in mass communication exist on many campuses. Professional programs prepare students with the skills needed in such fields as advertising, public relations, film production, and broadcast news. Some programs remain theory oriented, preparing students to conduct basic research on mass communication. In the professional schools, in particular, many of the courses are now taught by part-time professors, often brought in from the media. In such settings, the study of research methods and theory development may be marginal at best or simply ignored.

Today, students can graduate with a degree in, or at least a major in, media-related communication at the majority of U.S. institutions of higher learning. The numbers rise or fall from time to time, but somewhere between 5% and 10% of all undergraduate and graduate degrees now granted in the United States are in various fields of media-related communication.

---

[1] The first bachelor's degree program in public relations was established at Boston University in 1947.

That change has not always been a smooth one. Media-related studies are still regarded with suspicion by many traditionalists on campus. They are not always respected by professors, or even administrators, from the physical, biological, and social sciences. Nevertheless, course work in such fields as advertising, public relations, marketing communication, magazine publishing, film and television production, broadcast journalism, and the use of the Internet as a medium for public communication are now providing an annual pool of college graduates that can be hired to exercise the many specialized skills that are at the heart of those industries.

THE DECLINE IN THE PRODUCTION OF RESEARCH MILESTONES

From these three trends one might logically predict that there would be a corresponding increase in significant research on the process and effects of mass communication. Few would disagree with the conclusion that the growing presence and importance of mass communication in the lives of individuals has increased the need to understand their nature and influences. It follows, then, that scholars in the communications disciplines should now be formulating and testing more and better theories, many with practical importance, to explain how the media function and how they influence people, both individually and collectively.

However, in fact, that has not been the case. The development of media theory seems stalled. For a time, earlier in the 20th century, scholarly inquiry and the development of research-based theories to explain the process and effects of mass communication did increase at a rapid rate. Starting even before World War II, and continuing until the early 1980s, scholars conducted a number of seminal studies aimed at understanding the nature, functions, and consequences of mass communication.

As the scientific study of media influences got underway, it was psychologists and sociologists who provided leadership. Some of the Payne Fund studies concluded that movies had powerful influences on children (Blumer, 1933). Later, in 1938, a quantitative study reported that a radio program prompted millions of people to panic (Cantril, 1940). These findings reinforced beliefs in the *magic bullet* theory, an earlier and now discredited formulation explaining that the media had immediate, uniform, and powerful effects on all who were exposed to their messages. Later, as additional studies were reported, the concept of powerful media began to be questioned (DeFleur & Ball-Rokeach, 1989). The results from studies of the influences of training films by the U.S. Army led to a new formulation, now termed the *selective and limited influence theory*. It explained that the media could change beliefs, opinions, attitudes, or behavior for only some people under some circumstances (Hovland, Lumsdaine, & Sheffield, 1949). The classic

Erie County study of media influences on a presidential election campaign showed that belief in powerful, immediate, uniform, and widespread effects was no longer tenable. This milestone also led to important theoretical concepts, such as the two-step flow of communication and personal influence (Lazarsfeld, Berelson, & Gaudet, 1944). Clearly, empirical research was beginning to reveal with greater accuracy the complex relation between the mass media and their audiences.

Additional milestone research revealed that the media were not particularly powerful, that the audience was highly selective, and that the process of shaping people's beliefs, attitudes, and behavior with mass communications is very complex. Studies now regarded as classics yielded such insights as the *uses and gratifications theory*, explaining that audiences used content from the media as guides for their personal choices and derived many psychological rewards from exposure to mass communications (Herzog, 1944). Another modest experiment led to *modeling theory*, which explained the influence of media-depicted models of actions or situations on acquiring new forms of behavior (Bandura, 1965). A study of Iowa farmers in a relatively obscure journal provided the foundation for *adoption of innovation theory*, describing the pattern followed when people begin using new products or processes after obtaining information from the media (Ryan & Gross, 1943). Other classic research yielded theories of persuasion, explaining how the structure and other features of a message were related to changing beliefs, attitudes, and behavior (Hovland, Janis, & Kelly, 1953). A study of a small community showed how personal influence was exercised in the two-step flow of communication from the media to opinion leaders, and from them to others who did not attend directly (Katz & Lazarsfeld, 1955). More recently, *agenda-setting theory* was formulated to explain how levels of prominence selected by the media in forming their agenda play a part in setting personal agendas among their audiences (McCombs & Shaw, 1972).

At one point, attention to television almost crowded out research on other media. Its influences on individuals and society were addressed in literally thousands of studies (Pearl, Bouthilet, & Lazar, 1982). A major focus was on the relation between portrayed violence on TV and aggressive conduct in children and youth. This issue was a special focus for psychologists. Their interest was not so much on the process of mass communication, as such, but on media-provided stimulus factors that produce aggressive or violent behavior. By the end of the 1970s, it seemed clear that under certain circumstances, the portrayal of violence in television content could increase somewhat the probability of aggressive behavior in some kinds of children. That generalization still represents what we now know about that issue.

In retrospect, then, the decades from the 1930s to the early 1980s, appear to have been a kind of golden age of research on mass communication. During that period a significant number of studies had especially high theoretical yield. Some were large-scale efforts like the massive Payne Fund studies (Charters, 1933);

others were methodological masterpieces, like the Erie County investigation (Lazarsfeld et al., 1944). Few were programmatic—an exception being the Yale studies of persuasion (Hovland et al., 1949). Others were small in scope, but theoretically important.

Early in the 1980s, however, the golden age all but came to an end. That is not to imply that research on mass communication ceased. During the last two decades thousands of studies have been published. However, most explored very specific issues or narrowly focused hypotheses; some retested or studied extensions of ideas generated by the original milestones. Perhaps many scholars will challenge these conclusions, or claim that their personal research, or their favorite recent study, should be regarded as truly seminal. Perhaps they would be right. Overall, however, there has been a conspicuous decline in theoretical advances in the study of mass communication compared to the earlier period.

A major question is, Why? Are today's researchers less creative? Are the questions of media functioning and influences any less important? Are members of the public apathetic and uninterested in how mass communications influence them and their children? Is research on mass communications unrewarding, either in terms of personal interest or academic advancement? The answers to all of these questions seem to be a resounding "no." Today's researchers are equally smart and energetic; they have research methods and computer tools at their command that the older generation lacked; the public is still concerned; scholars still need research to develop reputations for career advancement. Where, then, have all the milestones gone?

The answer to why there has been a decline in theoretical productivity in the study of the mass media has no easy answer, but a case can be made that it lies in a complex set of changes that have taken place, both in society as a whole, and in the academy more directly. The sections that follow discuss those changes in an attempt to provide an explanation of why the production of influential research has slowed, or even stopped.

One factor has been the withdrawal of social scientists—who conducted most of the early milestones—from the mainstream of media research. A second is the failure to develop and establish a programmatic approach to the investigation of media processes and influences. A third is the shift away from science to qualitative studies and a focus on criticism within the communication disciplines. A fourth factor is the loss of talented researchers who leave the low pay of the academy to earn high salaries elsewhere. A fifth is that funds for studies of mass communication, especially from federal sources, are more difficult to obtain at present than was the case during the golden age of media research. Sixth, and finally, there have been changes in the work environment of college and university professors in the field of mass communication that may limit their ability to conduct research resulting in significant scholarly publication. Each of these factors can be discussed more fully.

THE SHIFTING AGENDA OF THE SOCIAL SCIENCES

At present, the study of mass communication and its influences on individuals and society is not at center stage in the social and behavioral sciences. It was at an earlier time. After pioneering the investigation of the influences of mass communications, such fields as social psychology and sociology went on to pursue other agendas. To illustrate, between 1940 and the end of the 1950s, among the most respected media scholars were sociologists Lazarsfeld and Merton. Both of these world-class researchers made the study of mass media central to their discipline. Similarly, in social psychology, Hovland was conducting his classic experiments on communication and persuasion. During the 1960s, many psychologists were focusing intensely on the relation between television and violence. By the 1970s, however, their participation declined and their influence waned. Other kinds of scholars were undertaking media studies and distinguished sociologists and psychologists were no longer the central figures pushing forward the cutting edge. That does not mean that research on mass communication ceased. For a time, the issue of violence and children continued to be almost a one-dimensional concern.

What happened was that the social science agenda changed. For many in those disciplines, the level of importance assigned to the study of media effects was reduced by attention to other concerns. As the late 1960s and early 1970s came, sociologists and psychologists turned to studies of deviant behavior, such as the causes of the rising crime rate, youthful violence, drug use, the influences of the counterculture, the roots and consequences of social inequalities, such as racial and ethnic discrimination, and the unequal status of woman in society. The study of deviant behavior and the problems of disadvantaged people have always been central in social science. Even many of the early studies of mass communications were conducted as a means of furthering these objectives. In other words, social scientists who had conducted media studies earlier returned to their traditional concerns, leaving basic research on the process and influences of mass communication to others.

THE LACK OF A PROGRAMMATIC APPROACH

Even during the golden age, when a series of well-known studies yielded significant theoretical advances, mass communication research was never conducted programmatically. With few exceptions, each study was a one-shot enterprise, done independently for its own sponsor's reasons. Such research sought short-term objectives that were deemed important at the time. There was no theoretical trail being followed, or accumulative refinement of concepts leading from the results of one study to the design of the next. In contrast, programmatic research and concept refinement is often the case in the physical and biological sciences, where one investigator's results yield insights or theoretical advances that open pathways taken by subsequent researchers. Even today, mass communication research seldom follows a programmatic approach, holding back the pace of theoretical development.

The lack of integration between studies is also reflected in the methodology employed in mass communication research. For example, concepts are often defined in a multiplicity of ways from one study to the next, with each researcher conceptualizing variables differently from the definitions of previous investigators. Such basic procedures as measurement, sample selection, and statistical analysis are conducted differently from one investigator to the next, even when researchers are studying essentially the same phenomena. Such a lack of methodological standardization makes it difficult to replicate studies of a particular process or effect, reducing the ability of investigators to accumulate evidence related to specific generalizations, hypotheses, or theories. It seems likely that this unintegrated approach will continue to be a handicap to the development of future milestones.

THE SHIFT TO NONQUANTITATIVE AND CRITICAL MODES OF ANALYSIS

In earlier years, when social scientists managed the research agenda of mass communication, the accepted epistemology for research was defined by the rules of natural science. Empirical observation of independent and dependent variables within a system of controls was required. Evidence was gathered within well-understood requirements for valid and reliable measurement. Quantitative analysis of data was assumed. Statistical probability provided the accepted criterion for making decisions about results. As social scientists began to turn to different agendas, other kinds of investigators, using other approaches to the accumulation of knowledge about the media, took their place. Today, many media scholars are not well-trained in, are not committed to—or indeed are openly critical of—the postulates, procedures, and requirements of science. Such scholars often use a qualitative and intuitive approach to describe the nature of various features and processes of mass communication. Although such an approach has merit in many cases, it is not likely to produce significant milestones in research that will provide a foundation for theoretical breakthroughs or definitive assessments of existing formulations.

The reasons for that pessimistic conclusion are not complex. Whatever the merits of qualitative research, it lacks some of the features of science that for centuries made it the acceptable mode of analysis employed to advance knowledge in a multitude of disciplines. Specifically, qualitative research is limited in rigor in that it does not use control procedures to identify and limit the influence of extraneous variables. It does not provide for tests of validity and reliability in measurement, or other forms of observation. It lacks clear criteria for accepting or rejecting conclusions and does not provide for assessments of generalizability of findings. Thus, qualitative investigation is unable to provide for effective replication, and it does not make use of systematic criteria for deciding when propositions are, or are not, supported by evidence. Therefore, although qualitative studies can be interesting, insightful, and useful, especially as a means of first exploring some new research domain, they are not likely to yield major milestones in research that advance theories in the field of mass communication.

Another problem is the number of scholars who engage mainly in criticism of the media and their content. These writers make use of ideological, as opposed to scientific, perspectives to reach conclusions about the process and effects of mass communication. They are committed to various forms of critical analysis, whether from a so-called cultural perspective, from an ideology derived from Marxism, or from convictions about hegemony said to be exercised by some broad conspiracy of owners, exporters, the government, or others seeking to exploit audiences. Such scholars provide interesting interpretations of what is wrong with our media and their content, or how someone is improperly using audiences to gain political power or profit. However, they seem to produce little in the way of systematic, empirically verified conclusions of how mass communication takes place, or how the media influence individuals and society.

There are several reasons why the current growth in the numbers of academics committed to critical analysis of the media is unlikely to produce seminal findings that push forward the envelope of understanding. For one thing, critical analysis rests on very different assumptions than science. Essentially the "postulates" of science assume (a) that there is order or patterns in the phenomena under study, (b) that patterned relations between variables can best be detected through controlled empirical observation, (c) that relations of cause and effect between variables can be identified through such study, and (d) any conclusions reached are tentative and subject to modification, or even rejection, as a result of further observation (DeFleur & Dennis, 1996).

In contrast, critical cultural analysis, or related perspectives based on assumptions of hegemony, are based on a different epistemology shared among those who study the media with these perspectives. Conclusions and interpretations are already decided on before the analysis begins. They are derived a priori from the ideology rather than from unbiased and systematic empirical observation. This is a problem with all politically or religiously derived ideologies. Proof—in the form of empirical evidence obtained from unbiased observation—is not needed. The prior convictions of the already converted provide sufficient verification for whatever conclusions are advanced or claims are made. Such exercises may train students for jobs in a nonexistent critical cultural industry, but they contribute little to the development of a tested body of explanations of the process and effects of mass communication.

That is not to say that the voices of those specializing in critical cultural perspectives should not be heard. Robust discussion of claims and conclusions is one of the great strengths of the American universities. John Milton (1644/1965) said it well in *Aeropagitica*, his treatise on freedom to publish without prior consent by the Crown: "Let Truth and Falsehood grapple; whoever knew Truth put to the worse, in a free and open encounter" (p. 409). Thus, the marketplace of ideas seems likely to allow those who rely on the scientific method to prevail. Those who limit their analyses of the media to ideological criticism are likely in the long run to be relegated to the sidelines. The bottom line, then, is that the milestones of the future will be products of carefully conducted scientific research, as opposed to qualitative writings or ideological criticism.

CHANGING WORK CONDITIONS OF ACADEMICS

Three additional factors have appeared in recent decades that seem likely to limit progress in understanding the nature of mass communication. One is that many of the bright young people who do attain a mastery of the scientific method in doctoral programs may never use it to conduct basic studies of the influences and functioning of the media. Another is that since the period in which the last milestones were produced, funding for research on mass communication has become increasingly difficult to obtain. Still another is that the academy itself is changing in ways that may discourage rather than encourage difficult and large-scale investigations.

The Movement of Capable Researchers From the Academy to Industry

A clear trend among media-related industries is that they have discovered research. This happened because clients who hire advertising firms, public relations agencies, or other groups that offer services or consulting on communication problems want to see what kind of results they are getting for the fees that they pay. Promotional efforts are expensive, whether for selling a product, improving an image, or getting elected. Earlier, practitioners would show their clients that they had placed their ads, public relations messages, or election campaign announcements in various media. Both parties would then assume that lots of people would be exposed to the messages and would thereby be influenced by them.

Today, no such assumptions are entertained. Research milestones, produced over the decades discussed earlier, have shown that achieving effects through mass communication is not that simple. Clients want empirical evidence that people are not only aware of their ads or campaigns, but also that they have been influenced by them. This means that they want research to be conducted to provide a factual basis for claims made by communications practitioners. For this reason, an applied communication research industry is growing in the business, industrial, and commercial world. Surveys, focus group studies, content analyses, and opinion polls are now routinely conducted to provide answers to practical problems and to assess potential outcomes. These may be as mundane as what is the best color for a package of cereal, or as complex as deciding what attack ads are most likely to provide an edge in an election without backfiring on the candidate who uses them.

One of the most difficult aspects of conducting such research is locating and hiring research specialists who are fully trained in the techniques that are required for planning studies, gathering the needed data, performing the appropriate statistical analyses, and preparing reports that can be understood by clients who are not sophisticated in research methods. There is, in any realistic sense, only one category of persons who can provide effective leadership to a team that does these things. That person is a talented product of a doctor of philosophy (PhD) program, preferably in mass communication, who has mastered the mysteries of quantitative research methodology and who has the writing and speaking skills required. Those who take such employment, as opposed to toiling in the vineyards of academe, are likely to make salaries that make the pay of an assistant professor seem like a begrudged welfare check. Pay levels that are double, or often triple, those paid to PhDs who elect to teach are not at all uncommon. For this reason, a mini-brain-drain appears to be starting—a drain that channels capable researchers out of the professorate. If this continues, many of the brightest and best scholars—PhDs who might have produced the next milestones—will be drawn away to the more practical and more lucrative world of applied communication research.

Declining Funding for Basic Mass Communication Research

During the 1960s and 1970s, public interest in the effects of mass communication was at an all-time high. Massive funding became available from such federal agencies as the National Institutes of Mental Health after Congress identified the issue of violence and the media as one that deeply concerned parents. Moreover, rising rates of crime, delinquency, civil disturbances, substance abuse, and other forms of deviant behavior were widely attributed to media influences.

Since that time of abundant government funding, however, the amount of financial support for media-related research has clearly declined. There has long been some funding available from private foundations, but even here there is a decreasing interest in supporting basic research on the process and effects of mass communication. The limited support that exists tends to be in areas where the media are thought to play a role in promoting behavior that poses a public health hazard. For example, studies of such issues as the influence of liquor advertising on the consumption habits of youth, or the role of media models in prompting children to begin smoking, are projects that have recently been funded.[2] Theoretical research,

---

[2] As an example, see Requests for Proposals, National Institutes of Alcohol and Alcohol Abuse, "Effects of Alcohol Advertising on Underage Drinking," February 2, 1998 (RFA: AA-98–002).

focusing on the ways in which media content is shaping nonproblem behavior or central values in the U.S. culture would be difficult to fund.

Changes in The Work Environment of College and University Teachers

Finally, current changes within the academy itself seem designed to limit the interest of the bright young people who might think about entering the teaching profession. This may place limits on the prospects for the future production of truly significant research milestones. One ominous situation is the great increase in the number of part-time instructors that are now offering courses to communication students. According to Walker (1998), this is a national trend that is by no means limited to the communication disciplines. Although part-time instructors are often wonderful people, they do not spend the time on campus required to advise students, serve on departmental committees, help students plan and conduct theses or dissertations, participate in student organizations, and all the rest. Typically, the part-timer arrives at his or her class, offers a lecture, chats briefly with students for a short time, and then departs.

A related trend is that undergraduate enrollments are rising and are predicted to soar in the years ahead as a result of earlier changes in the birthrate (Zuniga, 1998). With more part-timers and fewer full-time faculty available to take care of non-teaching duties, and more students to deal with, less and less time will be available to plan and conduct research.

Challenges to tenure offer another ominous situation. Professional schools, in particular, are easy targets for legislators and administrators who seek to abolish this traditional protection for academics. Some opponents see tenure mainly as a matter of undeserved job security for professors, but there are abundant cases every year to show that instructors are at risk in some institutions if they speak out or publish facts, state views, or reach conclusions that are not approved—either by central administration, by some large donor to the institution, or by a controlling political figure. Moreover, tenure offers not only protection in the area of academic freedom, but also the ability to pursue a long-range project—such as a milestone in mass communication research—that may have no tangible results for several years. In a situation where some sort of scholarly product has to be produced every year to gain extension of a short-term contract, abolishing the protection of tenure may very well inhibit a researcher from undertaking the kind of time commitment required to produce a major contribution.

SUMMARY AND CONCLUSIONS

A golden age of research productivity in the study of the processes and effects of mass communication appears to have existed from the decade just before World

War II until the early 1980s. During that time a number of studies yielded most of the theoretical perspectives explaining the influences on individuals and society that are at the heart of our understanding of the process and effects of mass communication. Since that time, milestone studies have not been produced at the same rate. This slowdown seems inconsistent with the increase in the number and reach of media, the growth of their labor force, and the expansion of media-related curricula on U.S. campuses. Those trends would seem to predict a corresponding increase in significant media research and further theory development.

There appear to be a number of complex reasons why the development of knowledge about the process and influences of mass communication has stalled. For one thing, social scientists, who were responsible in large part for the earlier surge in media research, have returned to their traditional agendas and media research is no longer at center stage in either psychology or sociology as once was the case. Among those who continue to study mass communication, new epistemologies have in part replaced those central to science. Qualitative research is now a more accepted strategy than it was earlier, even though this approach is not likely to produce additional milestones. Furthermore, many media scholars have little interest in—or indeed are openly hostile to—the methods and epistemology of science. Instead, they are committed to criticism of the media, following the dictates of an ideology rather than the implications of findings based on empirical data. These writers are quite unlikely to produce additional milestones.

In addition, the conditions of work in the academy are undergoing change. Those who become well-trained in quantitative research now have opportunities open to them for well-paid employment in nonacademic and applied settings. In such roles they are unlikely to produce milestones yielding additional theories. Another limiting situation is that sources of funding for many of the milestone studies are not now supporting media-related research. Finally, part-time instructors teach many courses, leaving an additional workload of advising, departmental chores, and other responsibilities to those who teach on a full-time basis. With rising enrollments ahead, this will limit the time that professors have for research. All of these factors, taken together, are likely to slow rather than promote additional milestone investigations that will advance theoretical understanding of mass communication and its influences.

REFERENCES

Bandura, A. (1965). Influence of models: Reinforcement contingencies on the acquisition of imitative responses. *Journal of Personality and Social Psychology, 2,* 589–595.
Blumer, H. (1933). *The movies and conduct.* New York: Macmillan.
Cantril, H. (1940). *The invasion from mars: A study in the psychology of panic.* Princeton, NJ: Princeton University Press.
Charters, W. (1933). *Motion pictures and youth: A summary.* New York: Macmillan.
DeFleur, M., & Ball-Rokeach, S. (1989). *Theories of mass communication.* White Plains, NY: Longman.

DeFleur, M., & Dennis, E. (1996). The assumptions of science and the goals of media research. In *Understanding mass communication* (5th ed., pp. 500–503). Boston: Houghton Mifflia.

Herzog, H. (1944). What do we really know about daytime serial listeners? In P. Laxarsfeld & F. Stanton (Eds.), *Radio research, 1942–43* (pp. 3–33). New York: Duel, Sloan & Pierce.

Hovland, C., Janis, I., & Kelley, H. (1953). *Communication and persuasion.* New Haven, CT: Yale University Press.

Hovland, C., Lumadaine, A., & Sheffield, F. (1949). *Experiments on mass communication.* Princeton, NJ: Princeton University Press.

Katz, E., & Lazarsfeld, P. (1955). *Personal influence: The part played by people in the flow of mass communication.* Glencoe, IL: Free Press.

Lazarsfeld, P., Berelson, B., & Gaudet, H. (1944). *The people's choice.* New York: Duel, Sloan & Pierce.

Lowery, S. A., & DeFleur, M. L. (1995). *Milestones in mass communication research* (3rd ed.). White Plains, NY: Longman.

McCombs, M., & Shaw, D. (1972). The agenda-setting function of the mass media. *Public Opinion Quarterly, 36,* 176–177.

Milton, J. (1965). Aeropagitica: A speech of Mr. John Milton/for the liberty of unlicenced printing/to the Parliament of England. In D. Masson, *The life of Milton* (p. 409). Gloucester, MA: Peter Smith. (Original work published 1644).

Pearl, D., Bouthilet, L., & Lazar, J. (1982). *Television and behavior: Ten years of scientific progress and implications for the eighties* (Vol. 1). Washington, DC: U.S. Government Printing Office.

Ryan, B., & Gross, N. (1943). The diffusion of hybrid seed corn in two Iowa communities. *Rural Sociology, 8,* 10–23.

Walker, P. (1998, May 29). The economic imperitives for using more full-time and fewer adjunct professors. *Chronicle of Higher Education, XLIV*(31), p. B6.

Zuniga, R. (1998). *Knocking at the college door: Projections of high school graduates by state and race/ethnicity 1996–2012.* Boulder, CO: Western Interstate Commission for Higher Education.

The End of Mass Communication?

Steven H. Chaffee and Miriam J. Metzger
Department of Communication
University of California–Santa Barbara

Many people no longer consider the term *mass communication* to be an accurate descriptor of what it is that some communication scholars study. Developments in computing and information technologies over the last 2 decades have blurred the boundaries between the forms of communicating around which the academic field of communication was developed. Consequently, and as media convergence proceeds, some have suggested that the word *mass* in mass communication should be replaced with the term *media* (see Turow, 1992).[1] This change in terminology is not insignificant, as it implies a shift toward the view that media communication, rather than mass communication, is our focal topic of study. Further, it forces us to question whether mass communication is a fleeting idea, a purely 20th-century phenomenon. This notion is certainly shocking, but could it be true? What is the future of mass communication in the new media environment?

WHAT IS MASS COMMUNICATION?

Before evaluating the future of mass communication, we need to begin with a definition of what we are talking about, which is more difficult than it might first appear. Mass communication means different things to different people. For some, the core concept lies in the first word, *mass*. That is, the mass-ness of mass communication sets it apart from other forms of communication in human history in that it allows a communicator to reach a much larger and more geographically dispersed audience than ever before. T. S. Eliot's famous quip about how television allows us

---

[1]The recent change in the title of the National Communication Association's flagship journal in mass communication from *Critical Studies in Mass Communication* to *Critical Studies in Media Communication* is another example of this movement.

all to "laugh at the same joke at the same time" captures nicely this aspect of mass communication.

For others, the term *mass communication* is an oxymoron. These people tend to focus on the second word, *communication*. Because traditional definitions of communication are based on the idea of exchange, and because the technologies for mass communication (until recently) only allowed information to flow in one direction, true communication on a mass scale was impossible, according to this view. Most of us, however, think of mass communication in one or more of three ways: as a set of media institutions, as a societal problem, or as an academic field of study. We begin, then, with a brief historical overview of these three widely held conceptualizations of mass communication.

Mass communication as a set of media institutions. A common view of mass communication is as a set of media institutions—the organizations that send mediated messages through various channels. In fact, most college-level introductory texts on the subject of mass communication are organized according to this view, with a chapter devoted to each of the mass media industries, including newspapers, magazines, books, film, radio, television, and their "support" industries, advertising and public relations.

The defining feature of these media institutions is their capacity for mass production and dissemination of messages. As Schramm (1954) and others have argued, the technologies powering the mass media unshackled communication from the bounds of time and space, thereby enabling for the first time in history instant communication with a large and largely anonymous audience. Media institutions such as film studios and television networks crystallized quickly to capitalize on and profit from the new opportunity for communication on a massive scale. These organizations were wildly successful, which enabled them to grow large, although the technologies themselves kept entry costs high, allowing only a few companies to dominate each media industry. Thus, by the middle of the 20th century, the mass media could be characterized by their "bigness and fewness" (Schramm, 1957).

Mass communication as a societal problem. The bigness and fewness of the mass media meant that only a handful of gatekeepers made decisions about what media content would be distributed widely to the population. This situation elicited fear from social critics and gave rise to another view of mass communication: mass communication as a societal problem. This view was fueled by the realization that along with mass production came the possibility for mass persuasion. Seen as good at first, especially by companies that realized they could use the media to hock their products, by World War II, the idea that single individuals or companies could bend the entire world to their will using mass communication became a widespread concern. From this perspective, the defining feature of mass communication was that the media had grown too big and powerful for society to control.

Fear of being unable to control the media stems in part from early assumptions about the vulnerability of the audience. A product of industrialization, mass communication emerged as urbanization was reaching new heights in American society and as those migrating to urban centers found themselves without their familiar social networks (e.g., Lasswell, 1930). The fact that the first audiences for mass media formed just as the social fabric was supposedly unraveling gave rise to the notion of audience members as socially and psychologically isolated, with few resources to resist media messages. For example, in popular writing of the time, audience members were often portrayed as atomized and helpless in the face of the powerful mass media's efforts to exploit them (Chaffee & Hochheimer, 1985; Katz, 1960).

Furthermore, it was in this milieu that media owners were consolidating their power, making efforts to control them increasingly difficult. Trends toward monopolization of the film and television industries began almost immediately, with the creation of the studio system and the rise of radio and television networks as examples. Centralized control of media content by professional and typically wealthy gatekeepers quickly characterized most mass communication. Given the financial barriers to entry and the physical scarcity of the airwaves, the average person had almost no opportunity for personal expression to reach a mass audience.

Also early on in the rise of the mass media, the industry's view of the audience shifted from an anonymous mass to a market that was both quantifiable and extremely profitable. Profit maximization in the production of mass communication meant aiming content at the lowest common denominator. Precise ways of monitoring the popularity of particular content became available from ratings services such as Arbitron and Nielsen, allowing the popular to be identified and repeated. The ultimate effect of these occurrences was a homogenization of media content that amused media audiences rather than enlightened them (Adorno & Horkheimer, 1972).

Mass communication was perceived to be uncontrollable for another reason as well. The mass media, particularly radio and television, were obtrusive in an unprecedented way. This perception was largely the result of the pervasive nature of the broadcast media. The fact that television came directly into the home and that viewers were to some extent a captive audience led people to feel that they were being stripped of the power to control their own living rooms. This was seen as especially problematic when violent and sexual content appeared in the media, and the official response to these concerns was to protect public morality and safety from the potential evil influence of the mass media (particularly broadcasting) through legislation. Policies such as licensing in the public interest, equal opportunities for political candidates, safe harbor, and the fairness doctrine were developed to ensure that single individuals could not bend the world to their will or corrupt children with prurient and/or dangerous ideas.

Mass communication as an academic field. Another view of mass communication is as a field of academic study. The defining feature of this conceptualization of mass communication is that it has knowable boundaries that are open to research. Early on, the study of mass communication focused primarily on applied problems, partly in response to the view of mass communication as a societal problem. Paul Lazarsfeld's Bureau of Applied Social Research at Columbia University, with its emphasis on radio and other mass media effects, was a direct result of this focus (Schramm, 1997). The emergence of mass communication as an academic discipline came in the 1950s and has had three strands: basic education in mass communication practice, empirical research of mass communication processes and effects, and critical and cultural studies of the mass media.

Schools of broadcast, journalism, and film have been the primary training ground for media workers. There, such vocational skills as writing, reporting, editing, design, and production are taught to those who will then employ them in the media industries. Although most of these programs were once located in some of the largest universities in the United States, that is less true today. After World War II, many universities shifted their emphasis toward empirical research rather than vocational training in communication (Delia, 1987).

Over the last 50 years, thousands of empirical studies of mass communication have investigated aspects of mass communication, including the content, audience, and effects of the media, as well as evaluation research (e.g., the effectiveness of communication campaigns) and legal and policy issues surrounding the mass media (e.g., the impact of TV program ratings on viewing behavior). What these studies have in common is the application of behavioral science to perceived social problems or benefits that may be caused by the mass media, and the use of quantitative methods such as content analyses, surveys, and experiments to test hypotheses. Early researchers expected to prove that mass communication had significant effects on audiences, but their studies did not confirm this conclusion consistently. Instead, Bauer (1964) said that "the model that ought to be inferred from research is of communication as a transactional process of equitable exchange" (p. 319), rather than a model of exploitation and one-way influence.

Quantitative research was not the only academic approach to mass communication, however. Scholars researching the mass media from the perspective of critical theory and cultural studies have used mostly qualitative methods to study how the media are used to maintain power relationships in society or how media texts are consumed by individuals and groups in society, for example. For many of them, the media are ideological and, as such, research in this area has focused on such themes as elite domination of the media industries, reproduction of the status quo via the mass media, and issues of democratizing access to the mass media, especially for oppressed groups such as women and minorities, to name a few examples.

The preceding three views lay out the defining features of mass communication as it has been conceived since the early 20th century: mass production, lack of individual control, and finite in available channels. The remainder of this article argues that these fundamentals of mass communication are not as true today as they once were, and that this is due to the emergence of new media for human communication. In short, the argument to be made is that contemporary media are "demassifying" mass communication. Some examples of today's new demassifying technologies include handheld devices such as cell phones or video games, but most important, Internet-based communication, including e-mail and the World Wide Web. This does not imply, however, that all demassified technologies are new. In fact, many older technologies allowed for narrowcasting to specific audiences and user control of content to some extent. In radio, FM and audiotape serve as examples; in television, UHF, cable, satellite, and videocassettes illustrate this point. What *is* different about the new media is a matter of degree, as we argue in the next section.

THE NEW MEDIA AND THE END OF MASS COMMUNICATION

More than any other technologies for mass communication, contemporary media allow for a greater quantity of information transmission and retrieval, place more control over both content creation and selection in the hands of their users, and do so with less cost to the average consumer. The Internet serves as the best example and, through digital convergence, will form the backbone of most future mediated communication. The Internet was designed to be decentralized, meaning that control is distributed to all users who have relatively equal opportunity to contribute content. The increased bandwidth of the Internet further enhances users' ability to become content producers and to produce material that is fairly sophisticated at low cost. In addition, many of the new technologies are more portable and, therefore, more convenient to use compared with older mass media.

These characteristics of the new media are cracking the foundations of our conception of mass communication. Today, media institutions are changing such that mass production is less mass. The explosion of available channels afforded by the new technologies contributes to the demassification of the media by diffusing the audience for any particular media product. This has resulted in channel specialization, and the old model of broadcasting to the masses has given way to market segmentation and targeting to niche audiences. Although existing media institutions are well positioned to adapt to these changing conditions, the fact that the new media shrink the size of the audience for any particular channel is likely to create opportunities for others. That is, if smaller audiences mean reduced costs of production and distribution, then more content producers will be able to enter the media market. In the near future, the issue may be less about what media companies are doing *to* people and more about what people are doing *with* the media.

The notion of the media as a social problem because of their unchecked power over the means of mass expression is also breaking down with the emergence of the new media. As described earlier, this idea rested on mass society theory and particularly on the notion of a passive, atomized audience. Although the idea of an atomized society has never really been correct (a more accurate descriptor, both then and now, is a "molecular society" where individuals are embedded in small interpersonal networks), it is even more far fetched today as new technologies extend our networks across the globe and blur the boundaries between mass and interpersonal communication.

Furthermore, tight control over access to the media by elites and professional gatekeepers is waning as individuals and organizations of modest means become content selectors and editors in their own right. Opportunities for self-expression once denied by the old media are celebrated by the new media. This idea is encapsulated in the now well-worn phrase "on the Internet anyone can be an author." The threat of homogenized media content is diminished as new technologies enable many millions of individuals to become content producers and as audiences are reconceptualized as smaller and discrete "taste cultures," rather than as an amorphous mass.

Also, the trend toward redistribution of power over the media from elites to users makes obsolete the idea of a small handful of willful individuals attempting to impart a dominant ideology to maintain the status quo. For example, in addition to allowing a greater variety of voices and views into public discourse, the interactive capacity of the new media creates new ways of grassroots organizing and coalition building. Also along with media elites, the government is losing its power to control media content. The rationale for regulating the broadcast media, namely scarcity of the electromagnetic spectrum, is largely irrelevant with the new media and, consequently, the government's legal basis for protecting public morals and safety through content regulation is not easily applicable to this domain. In summary, as the mass-ness of the media declines and as new technologies continue to empower individuals, social control by elite groups in society may become more difficult.

The academic study of mass communication must also change as a result of new technologies, and not simply in name. However, this is less true for some aspects of the discipline than for others. The study and use of practical skills in the preparation of students to enter jobs in the media sector will continue as new media develop. Skills such as writing, editing, and production may be slightly different, but they are just as useful in the new media environment as they were in the old. The new media do, however, seriously challenge the core assumptions of traditional empirical and critical mass communication research.

One of the assumptions of empirical studies of media content has been that the media are limited, identifiable, and, therefore, knowable through quantitative research. This is changing. An example of two content analyses of media violence serves to illustrate the point. The first report was commissioned by the Surgeon General in the early 1970s and involved researchers at several major universities around the country (Comstock & Rubinstein, 1971). To get a clear picture of the amount of violence in the media, a viewer survey was used to ascertain the most popular programs on television. Sixty-five program series were mentioned, all from the three major networks. Weekday prime-time and Saturday morning network television programs were then recorded for 1 week and analyzed to determine the amount of violence in each show.

In contrast to this, as part of the National Television Violence Study (1997), researchers at the University of California–Santa Barbara performed a content analysis in 1996–1997 with goals similar to the earlier report. However, the proliferation of television and cable channels quickly proved this task to be much more complex than it was in the early 1970s. For example, the researchers determined that 23 channels had to be included in the content analysis to capture the shows that the public was watching and, therefore, provide a realistic picture of the amount of violence that viewers were exposed to in the media. These channels are listed in Table 1. A viewer survey like the one done for the Surgeon General was not feasible in this study because the number of shows that viewers could select from would be overwhelming.

TABLE 1
Comparison of Studies of Media Violence

1971 *(Surgeon General's Report)*	1996–1997 *(National Television Violence Study)*		
Broadcast	*Broadcast*	*Cable*	*Premium*
ABC	ABC	A&E	Cinemax
NBC	NBC	AMC	HBO
CBS	CBS	Black Entertainment	Showtime
	Fox	Cartoon Network	
	KCAL	Disney	
	KTLA	Family	
	KCET	Lifetime	
		MTV	
		Nickelodeon	
		TNT	
		USA	
		VH1	

MILESTONE MASS COMMUNICATIONS THEORIES

This example illustrates that the amount of material available from the new media is vast, which makes studies of media content much more difficult than ever before. In fact, Internet content is literally unbounded, and when traditional media migrate online (e.g., Web-based digital television), comprehensive analyses of content may be all but impossible. To exacerbate this problem, each individual user's experience with content may differ in the new media environment, as interactive technologies allow for users to select a subset of the available content on, for example, an entire Web site or follow different hyperlinks from page to page. Unlike most traditional media texts, researchers cannot assume that because two people visited the same Web site, they were exposed to the same content. On the other hand, network technologies will allow researchers to record with absolute accuracy the programs each user has accessed, at what time, and for how long. As Web content becomes tagged with descriptors in its markup programming language, it will be possible to ascertain the specific content the user has accessed in the future.

Studies of media audiences may suffer the same fate as audiences become harder to identify and monitor in the new media environment. Already, services that provide demographic profiles of Web site visitors have been launched, but problems of online privacy and user deception have prevented their widespread use, at least as of yet. Media effects studies, too, may be more difficult with audiences that are not as well assembled or accessible to researchers as they once were. In addition, mass communication law and policy will have to change dramatically given that the basis for media regulation is inapplicable to new technologies that do not rely on scarce resources and, thus, provide increasingly abundant opportunities for self-expression.

Finally, critical and cultural approaches to the study of mass communication will have to adapt as well. Many of the themes in this research, such as the focus on elite domination of the media, may not fit very well if the new media are able to upend traditional power structures in society. At the very least, scholars in this branch of the field will need to reassess the ways in which the most dominant media corporations exercise their economic power and how they try to maintain dominance through the marketing and distribution of their media products in the new media environment.

In summary, the mass media are changing in important and radical ways, as summarized in Table 2. Several of these changes have been mentioned already, for example, the number of channels going from few to many; the conception of the audience shifting from a unified mass of millions who "consume" messages to a diffuse group of even more millions, each of whom can, if desired, produce their own messages; the transfer of control from senders to users; and the model of transmission going from time-specific, one-way communication to two-way, interactive exchange. Also, as discussed earlier, traditional research on media content and its effects on audiences will become more complex because of the

TABLE 2
Summary of Differences Between "Mass" and "Media" Communication

	Mass Communication	*Media Communication*
Channels	Few	Many
Audience	Unified	Diverse
Control	Sender	User
Transmission	One-way, time-specific	Interactive, at convenience
Research paradigms	Content analysis, effects on audience	Interface design, information search
Typification	Television	Video games, Web sites
Motivation	Arousal	Need satisfaction
Ego concept	Identification	Self-actualization
Social control	Laws, professional ethics, public education	Technical devices, monitoring
Learning	Social modeling	Experiential
Scare statistic	Number of murders a child sees by age 18	Number of murders a child commits by age 18

vastness of media communication and the dispersion of the mass media audience. In its place will likely be studies of user interface design and information search strategies.

Other important differences are apparent as well. For example, mass communication is typified by television, whereas video games and Web sites may be considered the archetypes of media communication. User motivation also changes as communication moves from mass to media. If a major motivation for using mass communication was arousal regulation, as some have claimed (e.g., Zillmann & Bryant, 1985), in an environment that enables people to locate information easily and efficiently, users' motives may shift instead to more specific need satisfaction. Motivation is tied to the ego concept, and the process by which the ego concept is developed may change as well. With mass communication, the ego concept is developed through identification with attractive others, for example, television characters or celebrities. With media communication, it is likely to develop through self-actualization, as the ability to connect with people who share our personal interests and ideas is enhanced through the new technologies.

In the mass communication environment, social control is maintained through laws (e.g., content regulation), professional ethics, and public education. In the new media environment, technical devices and monitoring are used to keep people in line (e.g., software that prevents access to certain Web sites or removes offensive language from chat groups). The method of learning via mass communication was assumed to occur through social modeling (Bandura, 1986, 1994), but with the increased interactivity and user control of media communication, learning will be more experiential (Lieberman, 2001). Finally, the scare statistic with traditional mass communication was how many murders a child *sees* by the age of 18; with the interactive media experiences afforded by new technologies, particularly video games, it is how many virtual murders a child *commits* by the age of 18.

THE END OF MASS COMMUNICATION THEORY?

Although some of these prophesies have yet to realize their full potential in today's media environment, many will come to fruition in the next 5 to 10 years. As these changes in the media environment challenge our long-standing conceptions of mass communication, many of our theoretical models will have to be reevaluated. For example, how will such core mass communication theories as agenda-setting, cultivation, and critical theory, all of which assume a centralized mass media system, work in the new decentralized and demassified media environment? Albeit a risky endeavor, some speculation is in order.

Agenda-Setting

A fundamental assumption of agenda-setting theory is that people get their news from a finite number of news sources or outlets. Furthermore, because news is selected by professional gatekeepers who operate under similar news values, the media agenda is thought to be uniform across those few outlets, at least on the national level. However, as the number of news outlets increases and the number of news consumers for any particular outlet decreases, the idea of a unified media agenda becomes problematic. Some have suggested that in place of a collectively shared agenda, fragmented and competing media agendas, and therefore public agendas, will emerge (Shaw & Hamm, 1997).

One result is that agenda-setting research will become a much more difficult enterprise. For example, measuring the media agenda, which is now accomplished through content analyses of major news outlets, will become particularly challenging as the available sources of news expand. Measuring the public agenda will be equally problematic as people filter and personalize their news using new media technologies. For example, Negroponte's (1995) idea of the "daily me," whereby new technologies are programmed to automatically select news and other media content that fit individual users' tastes and political perspectives, will make agreement among respondents' answers to the pollsters' "most important problem" question extremely unlikely.

Shaw and Hamm (1997) pointed out that this is bad news for the positive aspects of the media setting public and policy agendas, such as when the media help to achieve a critical mass of people who mobilize to solve some social problem. The outcry and subsequent assistance to millions of people starving in Africa during the 1980s as a result of media coverage is an example of the positive effect of agenda-setting (Bosso, 1989). Through the daily me concept, the new media will allow people to isolate themselves from the larger public discourse and, in the process, undermine the very notion of a larger public discourse. The result may be that the kind of widespread collective action seen in the past may not be possible in the future. The problem is that the public will not be able to come together over common issues because there will not be any issues that they share in common. Of course, the extent to which audiences will prefer customizing their own news to news that has been preselected by expert news editors is an interesting question that will have to be addressed in future agenda-setting research.

New communication technologies may be good news, however, in combating the negative aspects of agenda-setting. Specifically, the interactive or two-way communication capacity and overall increased information flow associated with new technologies may give more power to people whose agendas would not normally be reported in the major mass media. Also, media communication enables people to not only set their own media agendas but to influence others' issue agendas by helping them locate and contact people who care about similar issues. The new media may also give people more power to set the policy agenda through direct electronic access to their political representatives and, particularly, through new opportunities for grassroots organizing with interested others. In addition, the availability of competing news interpretations or frames on the Internet may help audiences better understand issues, although this will depend on their motivation to seek out multiple sources of news, which may be low (Neuman, 1991). However, if these possibilities are realized, the key problem for agenda-setting theory will change from what issues the media tell people to think about to what issues people tell the media they want to think about.

Cultivation

Cultivation theory rests on the assumption that mass media content forms a coherent system, a worldview that is limited to certain themes (e.g., violence) due to economic constraints, such as the use of lowest common denominator programming to appeal to a mass audience (e.g., Gerbner & Gross, 1976). However, this assumption may break down with the new media as scarcity disappears and as content becomes increasingly diversified, and when mass audiences shrink in size for any given channel and become more selective. In cultivation terms, the ability of the media to homogenize or mainstream viewers to a single worldview may decline because so many different worldviews are increasingly available.

Some scholars have argued that the greater diversity of content and the user control afforded by new communication technologies spell the end of cultivation theory (e.g., Bryant, 1986). In fact, there is some evidence for this conclusion. Perse, Ferguson, and McLeod (1994), for example, found diminished cultivation effects among owners of VCRs and other "new" technologies (i.e., cable television) that increase television viewers' channel repertoire. To the extent that the new media facilitate exposure to a multiplicity of truly diverse content, rather than simply extend the reach of traditional media messages, they will likely lead to reduced cultivation effects.

However, the end of the media's ability to mainstream audiences to a common symbolic environment does not necessarily mean the end of cultivation theory. Instead, as many worldviews are disseminated through the new media, cultivation theory may shift toward a vision in which individuals are cultivated to specialized worldviews of their own choosing. The new media's power to cultivate these self-selected worlds may be stronger because of *resonance,* which is the idea that cultivation effects may be boosted for those whose everyday reality matches the mediated reality to which they are exposed. That is, with narrowcasting and better ability to select and filter content, audiences for new media will likely opt for content that is consistent with their preexisting ideas and prejudices, thus allowing them to match their media experience to their own views with greater precision than ever before possible. Because of this, people will be able to live in a cocoon of self-reinforcing media, enhanced by like-minded others who they have found online.

Although the idea of media users being cultivated to the specific worldviews that they choose for themselves is not inherently dangerous, some of those views may be even scarier and more violent than that of broadcast television. Extreme perspectives, from hate groups to pedophilia, are thriving on the Internet where conventional social restraints on the expression of unpopular opinions are eliminated (for this reason, it has been suggested that the new media are bringing the end of the spiral of silence as well). These conditions give new opportunities for once disparate groups to grow into "loud minorities" who may feel empowered by the social support of extreme, but similarly inclined others (Sunstein, 2000).

Critical Theory and Cultural Studies

The implications of the new media for critical theory were touched on earlier. If new technologies shift power from elite groups to a greater proportion of media users, and particularly if media producers and receivers do become interchangeable, problems such as media-induced hegemony and democratic access to the media will be less pressing. Also, as opportunities for media audiences to define their own social reality and challenge the status quo are facilitated and even invigorated by the new media, ideological control by elite-owned media may become anachronistic.

However, critical theorists may point out that the history of every technology is toward greater centralized control by groups who are already in power, and the Internet is no exception (Beniger, 1996). Companies with familiar logos, large employee rolls, and profuse computing power are already lining up to take control of cyberspace, as the recent AOL–Time Warner merger illustrates. The real problem for anyone producing content in the new media environment will be in figuring out how to capture people's attention amid the plethora of competing options. Well-known companies with deep pockets and decades of experience honing their skills at attracting audiences may have the edge in the future in this regard, just as they have had in the past.

Critical theorists might also point out that although democratic access to the new media may be true in theory, it is far from what is happening in practice. The problem of the "digital divide" has received a great deal of attention in both the scholarly literature and popular press. The fear is that less privileged groups in society will be left behind during the information revolution because of their impaired economic ability to access new technologies. If past research on the diffusion of media technologies serves as a guide, this fear is well founded, although there is already some evidence that the digital divide might be decreasing, at least in the United States (Pew Research Center for the People and the Press, 1999).

The new media do present opportunities for cultural studies theorists, with their emphasis on audience reception research. Theories of how users create, interpret, and appropriate content will likely become central in the new media environment. For example, studies of fan cultures will be needed by media scholars and practitioners to understand how, in a situation of abundant choice, certain media texts can gain and hold people's attention. Also, insights gained from these theorists may help empower those who want to use the new media to subjugate the dominant ideology by offering alternative perspectives.

CONCLUSION

Thus, is this the end of mass communication? Should we abandon the term as well as our existing theoretical models? In some respects, the answer is yes. Certainly, people's everyday mass media experience will become more individualized as the new media continue to evolve and diffuse throughout society. Media producers will develop products tailored to smaller but more homogeneous audiences rather than to an undifferentiated mass. However, in other ways, the answer is no. First, according to Turow (1992), the "mass media are a part of the process of creating meanings *about* society *for* the members of society" (p. 107). In this way, mass communication serves an important and unique function in society, one that is unlikely to diminish in the future. For example, there is reason to believe that "media events" such as live war footage or the Olympics will continue to unite audiences on a mass scale, just as they have always done (Dayan & Katz, 1992). Second, although smaller than in the past, audiences for many of the new media channels will still be massive, numbering in the millions. As a result, what we have learned by studying the techniques and effects of mass communication will continue to be applicable in the new media environment.

Furthermore, although some long-standing theories will become less relevant or at the very least will have to change their focus as mass becomes media communication, others will likely increase their stature in the field. For example, in addition to theories of audience reception, uses and gratifications approaches to new media, with their focus on audience motivations for media use, will probably become more important as audience members are more active, either instrumentally or ritualistically, in selecting and producing content for themselves (Morris & Ogan, 1996). In fact, any theories in which selective exposure plays a central part are likely to be reinvigorated in the new media environment.

More important, however, researchers need to resist the temptation to simply apply old models of mass communication to the new media. Because of fundamental differences between the old and new technologies that have been discussed in this article, new theories of media uses and impacts must be developed and tested. The new media bring challenges to our old models, as well as the occasion to reevaluate, extend, and perhaps even supercede them. Steve Chaffee began that task with his ideas in this article, and now he leaves it up to the rest of us to continue.

ACKNOWLEDGMENTS

I am indebted to several people who assisted in the preparation and publication of this article. First, I wish to thank Carol Pardun who provided the opportunity for me to write this tribute to Steve Chaffee. Second, Dale Kunkel and Debra Lieberman, Steve's wife, both helped to refine and improve the article with their valuable feedback. Most of all, I am grateful to have benefited directly from Steve's wisdom in the short time that he was my friend and colleague at the University of California–Santa Barbara, and I feel privileged to be able to honor his memory with this article.

REFERENCES

Adorno, T., & Horkheimer, M. (1972). *The dialectic of enlightenment.* New York: Herder & Herder.

Bandura, A. (1986). *Social foundations of thought and action: A social cognitive theory.* Englewood Cliffs, NJ: Prentice Hall.

Bandura, A. (1994). Social cognitive theory of mass communication. In J. Bryant & D. Zillmann (Eds.), *Media effects: Advances in theory and research* (pp. 61–90). Hillsdale, NJ: Lawrence Erlbaum Associates, Inc.

Bauer, R. A. (1964). The obstinate audience. *American Psychologist, 19,* 319–328.

Beniger, J. R. (1996). Who shall control cyberspace? In L. Strate, R. Jacobson, & S. B. Gibson (Eds.), *Communication and cyberspace: Social interaction in an electronic environment* (pp. 49–58). Cresskill, NJ: Hampton.

Bosso, C. J. (1989). Setting the agenda: Mass media and the discovery of famine in Ethiopia. In M. Margolis & G. A. Mauser (Eds.), *Manipulating public opinion: Essays on public opinion as a dependent variable* (pp. 153–174). Pacific Grove, CA: Brooks/Cole.

Bryant, J. (1986). The road most traveled: Yet another cultivation critique. *Journal of Broadcasting & Electronic Media, 30,* 231–244.

Chaffee, S. H., & Hochheimer, J. L. (1985). The beginnings of political communication research in the United States: Origins of the "limited effects" model. In E. M. Rogers & F. Balle (Eds.), *The media revolution in America and in Western Europe* (pp. 267–296). Norwood, NJ: Ablex.

Comstock, G. A., & Rubinstein, E. A. (Eds.). (1971). *Television and social behavior* (Vols. 1–4). Washington, DC: U.S. Government Printing Office.

Dayan, D., & Katz, E. (1992). *Media events: The live broadcasting of history.* Cambridge, MA: Harvard University Press.

Delia, J. (1987). Communication research: A history. In C. R. Berger & S. H. Chaffee (Eds.), *Handbook of communication science* (pp. 20–98). Beverly Hills, CA: Sage.

Gerbner, G., & Gross, L. (1976). Living with television: The violence profile. *Journal of Communication, 26,* 173–199.

Katz, E. (1960). Communication research and the image of society: Convergence of two traditions. *American Journal of Sociology, 65,* 435–440.

Lasswell, H. D. (1930). *Psychopathology and politics.* Chicago: University of Chicago Press.

Lieberman, D. A. (2001). Using interactive media in communication campaigns for children and adolescents. In R. Rice & C. Atkin (Eds.), *Public communication campaigns* (3rd ed., pp. 373–388). Newbury Park, CA: Sage.

Morris, M., & Ogan, C. (1996). The Internet as mass medium. *Journal of Communication, 46,* 39–49.

National television violence study. (1997). Thousand Oaks, CA: Sage.

Negroponte, N. (1995). *Being digital.* New York: Knopf.

Neuman, W. R. (1991). *The future of the mass audience.* Cambridge, MA: Cambridge University Press.

Perse, E. M., Ferguson, D. A., & McLeod, D. M. (1994). Cultivation in the newer media environment. *Communication Research, 21,* 79–104.

Pew Research Center for the People and the Press. (1999, January 14). The Internet news audience goes ordinary [Online]. Retrieved July 2, 1999 from the World Wide Web: http://www.people-press.org/tech98sum.htm.

Schramm, W. (1954). *Process and effects of mass communication.* New York: Basic.

Schramm, W. (1957). *Responsibility in mass communication.* New York: Harper & Brothers.

Schramm, W. (1997). *The beginnings of communication study in America: A personal memoir.* Thousand Oaks, CA: Sage.

Shaw, D. L., & Hamm, B. J. (1997). Agendas for a public union or for private communities? How individuals are using media to reshape American society. In M. McCombs, D. L. Shaw, & D. Weaver (Eds.), *Communication and democracy: Exploring the intellectual frontiers in agenda-setting theory* (pp. 209–230). Mahwah, NJ: Lawrence Erlbaum Associates, Inc.

Sunstein, C. (2000). *Republic.com.* Princeton, NJ: Princeton University Press.

Turow, J. (1992). On reconceptualizing "mass communication." *Journal of Broadcasting & Electronic Media, 36,* 105–110.

Zillmann, D., & Bryant, J. (Eds.). (1985). *Selective exposure to communication.* Hillsdale, NJ: Lawrence Erlbaum Associates, Inc.

Reevaluating "The End of Mass Communication?"

Gabriel Weimann, Nirit Weiss-Blatt, Germaw Mengistu, Maya Mazor Tregerman, and Ravid Oren

Department of Communication
University of Haifa, Israel

It is hard to imagine a more challenging arena for communication research than that presented by new media and their impact on our society. We have witnessed the fastest evolution in communication technology in human history and, along with it, the evolution of communication conceptions and theories used to assess its impact. More than a decade has passed since Chaffee and Metzger first published their intriguing article "The End of Mass Communication?" and suggested that the new media will change the notions of mass communication and, as a result, the theories used in communication research. Today, we know more about new media and its effect on communication, society, and communication theories. The present article, therefore, sets out to reassess Chaffee and Metzger's claim by describing the development of several core theories of communication research, namely the agenda-setting theory and the notions of media audiences and the Digital Divide, in light of the new media. Our review shows that the role played by communication technologies in social, cultural, political, and economic processes is as central and influential in the new media era as it was in traditional media environment and that, although theories may change to accommodate the changes of the new media environment, researchers are still dealing with the "old" issues of power and resistance, and structure and ownership.

INTRODUCTION

More than a decade has passed since Chaffee and Metzger (2001) published their intriguing and challenging article "The End of Mass Communication?" At the time of publication, they could present only some speculative evaluations of the impact of the new media on the notion of mass communication, its features, and its audience. The Internet, they noted, was designed to be decentralized, meaning that control is distributed to all users who have relatively equal opportunity to contribute content. They even argued that "these characteristics of the new media are cracking the foundations of our conception of mass communication" (p. 369). Thus, they suggested that core mass communication theories need to be reevaluated due to the emergence of new communication platforms.

Today, we know more about the new media and its impact on communication, society, and communication theories. Since the publication of the "The End of Mass Communication?," numerous studies have examined the communicative, political, social, cultural, and economic aspects of the new media environment (reviewed in articles collected by Lievrouw & Livingstone, 2006, 2009; Wellman & Haythornthwaite, 2002; and by Holmes, 2005; J. E. Katz & Rice, 2002). The cumulative data not only provide an empirical documentation of the changes but also highlight some of the theoretical implications of these changes. There have been very few attempts to reassess mass communication concepts in light of the changes introduced by new media technologies (e.g., Handayani, 2011; Lorimer, 2002; Metzger, 2009, 2013; Napoli, 2010). However, as Napoli (2010) noted, "No such reassessments have been conducted recently enough to fully consider the implications of recent developments such as the rise of Web 2.0 platforms and user-generated content" (p. 506). Because Chaffee and Metzger suggested several core theories as "test cases," we decided to examine their assumptions regarding the predicted changes in these theories, namely, the concept of media audiences, the agenda-setting theory, and the notion of the Digital Divide. We begin by reviewing the changing conceptions of the media audience in light of new media technologies; then, we review the theoretical implications of these changes in the core theories suggested by Chaffee and Metzger, and we conclude by revaluating the shifting power relations between the media and its audience, and their overall implications on communication theories.

Two concerns should be stated here in relation to the scope of this review: (a) There is a wide range of new media, online platforms, and communication technologies. Being unable to distinguish among them and relate each one separately to the theoretical and empirical traditions, we preferred to use the broad category of "new media" without subdivisions or subcategories. (b) Our scan of the literature revealed hundreds of relevant studies. We preferred to highlight the dominant trends emerging from these studies and so to reflect the "state of the art" rather than present a detailed list of all the studies. Thus, the studies cited here represent only a small sample of the entire body of research reviewed for this report (more than 450 studies).

CHANGING THE CONCEPT OF "MEDIA AUDIENCE"

One of the issues raised by Chaffee and Metzger concerns the concept of "audience." They suggested that in contrast to the conception of the audience as a unified, mainly passive mass, the new media audience is viewed as a diffused group, people who produce and disseminate messages as well as consume them. Therefore, this new notion of the audience, according to them, presents new opportunities to explore the ways in which audiences interpret and create content and calls for a reevaluation of theories used in audience research. To this end, we examine three different, yet interrelated, changes in the conceptual terms used in communication research to describe the audience.

From Users to Multitaskers

As new media technologies presented people with more media choices and possibilities, practices of use, motivation and satisfaction became more central as components of audience analysis (LaRose & Eastin, 2004; Livingstone, 2003, 2008). In fact, the gradual substitution of the "old" term, "audience," with the "new" term, "users," reflects a growing interest in the diversified and complex ways people engage with today's saturated and convergent media environment. Indeed, empirical evidence suggests a change or an expansion of the ways people engage with media due to the new media development. Uses and gratification research, for example, show an expansion of the gratifications supplied by the media due to the unique facets of Internet use (LaRose & Eastin, 2004). On the same note, the growing body of literature on media multitasking, that is, the engagement in two or more activities at once, also points the new technologies as causing a sharp increase in media multitasking behavior, especially among younger audiences (Rideout, Foehr, & Roberts, 2010; Wang & Tchernev, 2012). Of interest, both lines of research stress the growing importance of community, social, and emotional gratifications in the new media environment, sometimes at the expense of cognitive gratifications (Ophir, Nass, Wagner, & Posner, 2009; Song, LaRose, Eastin, & Lin, 2004; Stafford, Royne Stafford, & Shackle, 2004).

From Active Audience to Media Literacy

The interpretive activities of the audience are also central to the research of the user in the new media environment. The term *media literacy* is used to refer to the wider array of audience activities fostered by the new media. Media literacy comprises a set of cultural competencies and social skills, such as play, performance, simulation, appropriation, judgment, and multitasking, all of which are needed for full participation in a new media culture (Jenkins, Purushotma, Clinton, Weigel, & Robison, 2009; Livingstone, 2008). The social-scientific approach to media literacy sees it as a means of protection, aiming to reduce the impact of the media on audiences' beliefs, attitudes, norms, and behaviors (S. H. Jeong, Cho, & Hwang, 2012). A critical/cultural approach views the goal of media literacy as helping people to use media intelligently, to discriminate and evaluate media content, to critically dissect media forms, to investigate media effects and uses, and to construct alternative media (Kellner & Share, 2005; Livingstone, 2008; Potter, 2011).

From Consumers to Prosumers

In the Web 2.0 environment, which is defined by the ability of users to produce content collaboratively, much of what transpires online is generated by the user. Utopian rhetoric surrounding new media technologies often assumes that the greater freedom to produce content holds practical promise for individual freedom, democratic participation, and cultural and human development in general (Benkler, 2006). The convergence of the media environment, however, that is the flow of content across media platforms, the cooperation between multiple media industries, and the migratory behavior of media audiences (Jenkins, 2006), is often considered as a drawback to these opportunities. Sundet and Ytreberg (2009), for example, claimed that the (inter)active audience discourse was adopted by established media institutions so that it could be turned into a tool for their own expansion.

In addition, audience fragmentation, that is, the increased selection of content options provided across a wider array of distribution platforms (Napoli, 2011), is often considered as a danger for a common cultural forum, or worse, as the birthplace of media enclaves and "sphericules" (Gitlin, 1998; Webster & Ksiazek, 2012). The main concern is that selective exposure patterns based on partisan affinity may cause audiences to consume a steady diet of their preferred choices, rather than sampling the diverse range of material usually offered by the mainstream media. Bennet and Iyengar (2008); Hollander (2008); Iyengar and Hahn (2009); and Ksiazek, Malthouse, and Webster (2010) suggested that this steady diet may not only contribute to further polarization of news audiences but also allow them to avoid news altogether.

Thus, the users of the new media era, who engage with the media in diversified ways, are able to critically consume media content and at the same time create it, and are able to beneficially play an active role in their cultural and political environment. At the same time, audiences are still susceptible to the impact of the media on their attitudes and behaviors; restricted as content creators by established media institutions; and prefer to be engaged, media wise, within their own social, communal, and political perimeters. As many turn more and more to new media technologies[1]—the percentage of Americans using the Internet has increased from 14% in 1995 to 81% in 2012[2]—and as interactivity, fragmentation, and convergence continue to develop, the multifaceted character of the audience carry more and more important ramifications for both the private and public spheres. To this end, following Chaffee and Metzger's proposition that the new notion of the audience calls for a reevaluation of theories used in user-centered communication research, we now turn to reevaluate two main such theories— agenda-setting theory and the digital divide.

---

[1] According to Pew research center, the proportion of Americans who read news on a printed page—in newspapers and magazines—continues to decline: in newspapers, from 46% in 2000, to 23% in 2012, and in magazines from 26% in 2000 to 18% in 2012. Radio news has fallen by 10%, from 43% in 2000 to 33% in 2012. Even television seems to suffer: Only about one third (34%) of those younger than 30 say they watched TV news yesterday. In 2006, nearly half of young people (49%) said they watched TV news the prior day. At the same time, the clearest pattern of news audience growth in 2012 came on digital platforms. For example, in 2012, total traffic to the top 25 news sites increased 7.2%; and about one third or more of those ages 18 to 39 regularly see news or news headlines on social networking sites (*In Changing News Landscape, Even Television is Vulnerable: Trends in News Consumption 1991-2012*, 2012).

[2] These data comes from the Pew Research Center's Internet & American Life Project's report "Internet Adoption, 1995–2012: % of American Adults Who Use the Internet, Over Time." Retrieved from: http://pewinternet.org/Static-Pages/Trend-Data-%28Adults%29/Internet-Adoption.aspx.

REEVALUATING THE AGENDA-SETTING THEORY

The agenda-setting theory's core proposition is that the salience of elements on the news agenda influences, in turn, their salience on the public agenda. In the years since McCombs and Shaw's (1972) initial study, these agenda-setting effects have been documented in hundreds of studies on a diversity of issues, using a range of research methods under a wide variety of circumstances. Chaffee and Metzger (2001) argued that "new technologies may give more power to people whose agendas would not normally be reported in the major mass media" (p. 369). As media communication increasingly helps people to locate and contact those who care about similar issues, they concluded, "The key problem for agenda-setting theory will change from 'what issues the media tell people to think about' to 'what issues people tell the media they want to think about.'" Furthermore, they predicted that in the new media environment, measuring the media agenda "will become particularly challenging as available sources of news expand" and that measuring public agenda "will be as equally problematic as people filter and personalize their news using new media technologies."

Over a decade has passed since Chaffee and Metzger made those predictions. Therefore, at this stage we are now able to review the evidence that has emerged to support or refute their predictions—by examining, for example, issues deemed as important by active users, rather than dictated by the traditional media gatekeepers. We also review how the research community has dealt with the methodological challenges and present several theoretical developments.

Agenda Setting in the New Media Environment

The agenda-setting function of the mass media has evolved and continues to do so. Since the initial study, the concept of agenda setting has become more refined and complex (Kosicki, 1993; Roberts, Wanta, & Dzwo, 2002). In 2005, McCombs acknowledged, "Now, the Internet is the new frontier for research" (p. 544). Nowadays, as a result of easy access to media, people can form their own agendas and then find groups with similar agendas. The Internet makes it possible for people all around the globe to find others with similar agendas and collaborate with them (Ragas & Roberts, 2009). Shaw, McCombs, Weaver, and Hamm (1999) proposed that an individual's attachment to social groups might have an impact on media's agenda-setting influence, a term they referred to as "agenda-melding." Agenda-melding focuses on the personal agendas of individuals in terms of their community and group affiliations. Shaw and McCombs (2008) suggested that individuals attach themselves to vertical (traditional) and horizontal (social or interpersonal) media based on their interests. McCombs (2004) argued that agenda-melding is in line with the concept of "need for orientation" and therefore agenda-setting is still relevant, even in the new media environment.

Another claim about the new media era is that the Internet plays an important role in the "reverse agenda-setting" process, in which the public agenda sets the media agenda (McCombs, 2004). Weimann and Brosius (1994; Brosius & Weimann, 1996) suggested a theoretical development in this context by defining the role of opinion leaders as "personal mediators between media and personal agendas" that "collect, diffuse, filter, and promote the flow of information." Combining the classical two-step flow theory (E. Katz & Lazarsfeld, 1955) with the agenda-setting theory, they suggested four possible models (Figure 1).

While observing the phenomenon of blogging as both a form of mass and interpersonal communication, Branum (2001) noted that Brosius and Weimann's description of early recognizers also applies to the actions of the filter-style bloggers, who choose which stories to provide a link for and what comments to make about the stories. Tomaszeski (2006) suggested the following analysis: Bloggers are being sourced by the traditional media, who are taking original content from them and incorporating it into their own messages to the public. The bloggers' input to traditional media places them in the role of mediator between the public agenda and the media agenda (Models 2 and 3). In addition, bloggers' higher visibility to the general public places them in the role of early recognizers whose information flows to the public (Models 1 and 4). Collister (2008) argued that by recognizing the role of opinion leaders in the information flow, Brosius and Weimann's models help to depict the fluid nature of agenda-setting and the inevitable "cross-fertilization" between blogs and traditional media.

Model 1: The Classical Two-Step Flow
Media Agenda → Early Recognizers → Public Agenda
Model 2: The Reverse Two-Step Flow
Public Agenda → Early Recognizers → Media Agenda
Model 3: Initiating the Classical Agenda-Setting Process
Early Recognizers → Media Agenda → Public Agenda
Model 4: Initiating the Reverse Agenda-Setting Process
Early Recognizers → Public Agenda → Media Agenda

FIGURE 1

The Individual's Power

Because traditional media have begun to rely on online blogs in a number of ways that affect the selection and presentation of news stories, blogs are sometimes able to influence what counts as newsworthy (Woodly, 2008). Witness the Clinton–Lewinsky scandal, in which Drudge's use of the Internet to disseminate his scoops symbolized the declining ability of mainstream journalists and political elites to act as gatekeepers, agenda setters, and issue framers. Although the mainstream media managed to recapture control of the political agenda, most of the stories were initially generated through online leaks and rumors (Williams & Delli Carpini, 2004).

Following Chaffee and Metzger's (2001) prediction of "what issues people tell the media they want to think about," Delwiche (2005) compared issues that dominated the agenda of blogs to those deemed most important by journalists and the public during the same period. He found that bloggers were relatively independent and provided alternative topics to those discussed in the media. His conclusion was that blogs have demonstrated their ability to affect the flow of information between traditional journalists and audiences and to bridge those components of the public sphere. Escher (2007) subsequently proposed a new methodology, collecting data from Google News, Google Blogsearch, and Yahoo! Term Extraction and comparing the rank of a story on the blogosphere agenda (number of posts for the story) with the rank of the story on the traditional media agenda (number of articles for the same story). The results presented ranking differences between the two spheres.

Earley (2009) asked whether new media technologies are weakening, strengthening, or transforming the traditional agenda-building process and claimed that the sources evaluated suggested that all three are occurring. By comparing new content on the web (news websites, blogs, and social media) with newspapers, television, and radio, Maier (2010) found that whereas coverage by news websites resembled that of traditional media (almost the same top stories), blogs and social media concentrated on news topics that were sharply distinct from those covered by the mainstream media. After reviewing numerous publications we can conclude that although some researchers found different agenda setting between blogs and traditional media (e.g., Metzgar, 2007; PEJ, 2010; Wallsten, 2007), and others found that the agenda of blogs had almost no influence on traditional media agenda (e.g., Gomez-Rodriguez, Leskovec, & Krause, 2010; Hestres, 2008; McClellan, 2010; Murley & Roberts, 2005), still others found the opposite: that the agenda of blogs did hold some influence on the agenda of traditional media (e.g., Collister, 2008; Cornfield, Carson, Kalis, & Simon, 2005; Lloyd, Kaulgud, & Skiena, 2006; Meraz, 2007, 2009, 2011; Rostovtseva, 2009; Wallsten, 2011; Woodly, 2008).

In an interview, McCombs stated that overall

> the influence is from media to blogs. Occasionally, you'll see spectacular kind of case studies where purely the influence went the other way, but those seem to be the exception rather than the day-to-day rule of what's going on out there on the Internet. (as cited by Silva, 2008, p. 6)

According to Campbell, Gibson, Gunter, and Touri (2009), blogs are less likely to act as the originators of news in first-level agenda setting but instead exert influence through second-level agenda setting. For example, blogs can act as "resuscitators" by following up on stories that the mainstream media either failed to follow up on or considered a low priority, thereby giving them new impetus to reemerge on the mainstream news agenda. Blogs can also act as "reframers" by interrogating, challenging, and making transparent those elements that contribute to the mainstream media's framing of the news. Wojcieszak (2008) suggested, on one hand, a strengthened first-level agenda setting as a result of Internet users turning to major media conglomerates, as well as the focus of some online and offline sources on similar topics. On the other hand, a weakened second-level agenda setting may be attributed to the diversity of the sources online describing the same issue in a different way.[3] Correspondingly, an extensive study of the agenda setting from 1956 to 2004 (Tan & Weaver, 2012) concluded that

> in spite of Chaffee and Metzger's (2001) warning of a diminished agenda-setting power of the mass media, this study did not find that the agenda-setting effect between the "New York Times" and the public has become weaker over time.... One possible reason is the high level of intermedia agenda setting between traditional media and new media. (p. 12)

Another aspect of new media outlets is that of neutralizing the process of "agenda cutting," meaning uncovering news stories that went unreported despite having all the elements required to make them newsworthy (Fahmy, 2010). It is worth noting that during recent protests around the world (e.g., the Arab Spring), activists used social media, blogging, and video sharing to encourage people to protest, and Twitter emerged as a key source for real-time logistical coordination, information, and discussion. Bloggers were found to play an important role in breaking and disseminating the news,

---

[3]First level refers to the impact of media agenda on public agenda, that is, on *what* people think about. Second level refers to the characteristics of the issues as promoted by the media, that is, on *how* people should think about.

and they had higher likelihood of engaging their audience to participate in the revolutions than the mainstream media (Lotan et al., 2011).

Measuring Agenda Setting

In the new media environment, the headlines of online news are rapidly changing and can thus dilute the potential for media agenda setting by narrowing the common perception of what issues are important to the public (Mensing, 2004). Furthermore, in agenda setting there must be a clear delineation between the producers and the consumers of the agenda, for one must influence the other and impart the agenda. The current methodological issues are establishing causality, lag time, measuring objects, and attribute salience (Coleman, McCombs, Shaw, & Weaver, 2009). Berger and Freeman (2011) argued that the time lag cannot exist in the new media because the consumer is acting simultaneously with the producer, and the consumer is also a producer of content and, by extension, an agenda. However, "time lags are tested in numerous ways until the optimal one is found" (Kosicki, 1993, p. 107). Present-day agenda-setting studies can still measure and rank-order the issues (in both traditional and new media), survey the public (Coleman et al., 2009) and use time series analysis to differentiate the agendas (e.g., Lloyd et al., 2006; Watson, 2011). Numerous studies from the previous section (The Individual's Power) emphasize the ability to define who the producers and consumers actually are (even on Twitter, e.g., Wu, Hofman, Mason, & Watts, 2011).

In addition, Coleman and McCombs (2007) looked at the effects of agenda setting on various groups of individuals and concluded,

> Despite evidence that the youngest generation is not exposed to traditional media as frequently as the older generations are, and that the youngest generation uses the Internet significantly more, there is little support for the intuitive idea that the diversity of media will lead to the end of a common public agenda as we have known it. Rather, different media use among the young did not seem to influence the agenda-setting effect much at all. (Coleman & McCombs, 2007, p. 503)

With respect to studies to be undertaken in the future, Takeshita (2005) recommended investigating the web-access patterns of news seekers on the Internet, identifying the "hub" of news sites, and then focusing only on those hub sites. Studies are currently moving toward comparing media sources and using aggregators (search engines) to examine the issue salience in both traditional and new media. Moreover, agendas are being uncovered by focusing on issues that have received the most "traffic" and are thus assumed to reflect common issues for a large number of readers. A new point of view suggests examining the Internet search trend as representative of the public agenda (e.g., Aikat, 2008; Granka, 2009; Y. Jeong, Kim, & Shin, 2008; Scharkow & Vogelgesang, 2011). Weeks and Southwell (2010), who used Google to measure public interest in topics, argued that "Google Trends offers an indicator of an important dimension of public opinion that is not captured perfectly by previous survey work using the 'most important issue' question" (p. 356).

Although agenda-setting theory has been investigated widely in the field of political communication, some attempts have been made to test the theory in other contexts, including business communication, religion, foreign relations, health care, entertainment, and public relations—and all within the new media environment. In one of his recent lectures, McCombs (2012) concluded, "There are a lot of interesting new routes to explore, to fit not just to political coverage, but to a wide verity of news coverage of many topics, and I urge you to follow that road." It seems that "with an expanding media landscape as well as new theoretical domains to explore, the theory of agenda-setting can look forward to at least another 30 years of fruitful exploration in cyberspace" (Coleman et al., 2009, p. 157). Regarding the future: One interesting suggestion is the "Network agenda setting model," the third-level of agenda-setting theory. Guo (2012) found that media agenda networks were significantly correlated with the public agenda networks. This new combination between Social Network Analysis and agenda setting may lead to new and innovative directions for the theory.

REEVALUATING THE DIGITAL DIVIDE

In recent decades, a worldwide debate has focused on the notion of the digital divide, its dimensions and measures. The digital divide is not an entirely new idea: There are certain similarities between the digital divide and the Knowledge Gap hypothesis (Rogers, 2001), based on the original statement, "As the diffusion of mass media information into a social system increases, segments of the population with a higher socio-economic status tend to acquire this information at a faster rate than the lower status segments" (Tichenor, Donohue, & Olien, 1970, p. 159).

In that vein, Chaffee and Metzger (2001) predicted that

> although democratic access to the new media may be true in theory, it is far from what is happening in practice. The problem of the 'digital divide' has received a great deal of attention in scholarly literature and popular press. The fear is that less privileged groups in society will be left behind during

the information revolution because of their impaired economic ability to access new technologies. (p. 377)

The main purpose of the following review is twofold: first, to review how the notion of the digital divide (including related concepts such as access and use) has been reconceptualized among scholars during the past decade; second, to review the empirical evidence documenting the digital divide, the changes in differences among socioeconomic groups and across countries, and the main factors that have emerged to explain the phenomenon.

The Changing Conceptualization of the Digital Divide

In the early stages, the digital divide was defined as the dichotomy that exists between the "information haves" and the "information have-nots," emphasizing the fact that access to and use of the new media was unequal along lines of socioeconomic status and demographic differences. With the digital divide increasing, separating high and low socioeconomic status individuals, privileged and unprivileged groups, and developed and developing countries, information society researchers have increasingly suggested a shift from the concept of "digital divide" to that of "digital inequality," which can refer to differences in access and to inequality among persons with formal access to the Internet (DiMaggio & Hargittai, 2001). Norris (2001) described the digital divide as a multidimensional phenomenon, which including the global digital divide, the social divide, and the democratic divide. Tsatsou (2011) suggested that digital divides are to be viewed as evolving and closely dependent on the sociocultural and decision-making context in which the technology is designed, developed, and consumed. Fuchs (2009) provided a more complex and comprehensive definition for the concept, explaining it as

> unequal patterns of material access to, usage capabilities of, and benefits from computer-based information and communication technologies that are caused by certain stratification processes that produce classes of winners and losers of the information society, and of participation institutions governing ICTs and society. (p. 46)

Changes and developments in defining the digital divide have been accompanied by changing methods and measures used to identify the existence and extent of the divides that exist. Over the years, ways of measuring the digital divide have emerged including the Information Society Index (IDC, 2001), the networked Readiness Index (United Nations Development Program, 2001), the Network Readiness Index (Dutta & Jain, 2004), the

Digital Access Index (International Telecommunications Union, 2005), the Statistical Indicators Benchmarking the Information Society, the Digital Divide Index (Barzilai-Nahon, 2006; Dolnicar, Vehovar, & Sicherl, 2003; Husing & Selhofer, 2004). It should be noted that over the time, new media researchers have suggested more comprehensive and multidimensional digital divide measures: Vehovar, Sicherl, Husing, and Dolnicar (2006, p. 280), for instance, proposed three-level digital divide measurements including log-linear modeling, compound measures, and time-distance methodology.

New Media and New Barriers

A variety of barriers to new media can also contribute to inequality in access and use. DiMaggio and Hargittai (2001) described five dimensions of digital inequality: (a) technical means, such as software, hardware, and connectivity quality; (b) autonomy of use, which refers to the location of access and the freedom to use the medium of one's preferred activities; (c) use patterns, meaning the types of uses of the Internet; (d) social support networks, which refer to the availability of others to whom one can turn for assistance with use, as well as the size of networks to encourage use; and (e) skill, which signifies one's ability to use the medium effectively. Van Dijk and Hacker (2003) added the lack of "mental access," which refers to a lack of elementary digital experience.

For his part, Wilson (2006) argued that there are eight aspects of the digital divide: (a) physical access, (b) financial access, (c) cognitive access, (d) design access, (e) content access, (f) production access, (g) institutional access, and (h) political access. The author went on to connect those eight aspects to six demographic dimensions of the digital divide: gender, geography, income, education, occupation, and ethnicity.

Deichmann and colleagues (2006) also attempted to categorize determinants of the digital divide (applicable both nationally as well as internationally) into three areas: economic factors (level and equality of wealth income), cultural factors (religion and language), and factors associated with the telecommunications infrastructure (ownership, infrastructure, and pricing). Keniston (2004) added four closely interrelated "digital divides": between the rich and poor within every country; between those who speak English or the national language of the country versus those who do not; between rich and poor nations; and between technocrats in knowledge-intensive fields, such as computer science, and other professional groups. Researchers who have studied information communication technologies in developing countries tend to distinguish between economic barriers (the lack of access to information, market, economic opportunities), physical barriers (distance), geographic barriers, political barriers (transparency of governance, access to legal relief, accountability), and social and health barriers (language and literacy, gender issues, health issues, computer literacy).

A Survey of Empirical Evidence: From Access to Use

During the 15 years since Hoffman and Novak (1998) introduced the digital divide between those with and without Internet access, use of the web has risen dramatically. In the United States, the percentage of adults regularly going online has increased form roughly 30% to 80%. Even with this tremendous growth in access, substantial inequalities persist across demographic groups. For example, in contrast to 80% of adults in the general population of the United States who use the Internet, only about 70% of African American and 40% of people older than 65 do so (Goel, Hofman, & Sirer, 2012). Many studies have set out to explore the existence and extent of the digital divide. These studies can be grouped into two categories: studies of the first digital divide and studies of the second digital divide (Attewell, 2001). The concepts of the first digital divide characterized the earlier studies, which argued that the digital divide is a transitory glitch and will be closed in time due to market forces. Selwyn (2004), among others, criticized this optimistic view, saying that although in theory the formal provision of information communication technologies facilities guarantees that all individuals will have physical access to that technology, such access is meaningless unless people actually feel able to make use of the opportunity. Therefore, more and more studies have focused on the so-called second digital divide, suggesting that the emergence of the information society will create new social divisions while it strengthens old ones. Researchers who hold this more pessimistic view claim that groups that are already well networked via traditional forms of information communication technologies will maintain their edge in the digital economy (Sassi, 2005).

Today most studies tackle the second digital divide, rather than the first, whether it is occurring within the same country or between countries, classes, or races. Moreover, new dimensions have been added to the concept of "global digital divide." Ayanso, Cho, and Lertwachara (2010), for example, used a cluster analysis to provide insight into the regional and global digital divide by profiling 192 member states of the United Nations based on their ICT infrastructure. The resulting cluster profiles show two groups of nations, which the researchers label for presentation purposes as ICT leaders and ICT followers. Of the 192 member states, 32 nations were identified as ICT leaders and 146 nations as ICT followers (14 countries were excluded from the cluster analysis due to missing data in at least one of the variables). An examination of the two clusters shows that none of the nations in the region of Africa were identified in the ICT leaders' cluster, whereas 22 European nations, three nations in the Americas, five Asian nations, and two nations in the region of Oceania were identified as ICT leaders.

Pick and Azari (2008) analyzed the influence of socioeconomic, governmental, and accessibility factors on ICT usage, expenditure, and infrastructure in 71 developing and developed countries. The results showed, inter alia, that there are several factors associated with the large digital divide between developing and developed nations, with the technology level more influenced by foreign direct investment and government initiative in developing nations and more associated with the labor force participation of women and educational variables in developed nations. In their study on the digital divide in Africa, Fuchs and Horak (2008) found that the least developed African countries in terms of income, education, and health also have low corresponding access and usage rates. They concluded that the global digital divide means unequal material, usage, skills, benefits, and institutional access to new information and communication technologies by different world regions. In another study, James (2011) divided a sample of developing countries according to whether they have experienced a rise or a fall in the digital divide on the Internet. He discovered that incomes tend to be relatively high in countries where the divide is falling, and vice versa in the case of countries where the divide is rising.

Numerous studies have been conducted to relate the digital divide to differences in race, gender, class, or shortly, between advantaged and disadvantaged groups or individuals. Van Deursen and Van Dijk (2010) examined the differential possession of Internet skills among the Dutch population. Their results strengthen the argument that the original divide between those who do have and those who do not have physical access to new media has led to a second divide, which includes differences in skills for using the Internet. Moreover, the results strongly indicate that a large portion of the population is excluded from actual and effective usage. In exploring the digital divide, Warf (2012) discovered that although penetration rates have grown among all sociodemographic categories, significant differences persist according to age, income, ethnicity, and education level but not gender. Willis and Tranter's (2006) study examining the social barriers to Internet use in Australia over a 5-year period found that although the Internet has become more accessible to all social categories and although further technologies diffusion should widen this accessibility, household income, age, education, and occupational class remain as key dimensions of differential Internet use. Enoch and Soker (2006) studied the effects of social-structural factors, including age, ethnicity, and gender, on Israeli university students' use of web-based instruction. The results showed that despite the great increase in use of Internet and e-mail, a steady and significant usage gap remains in terms of age, gender, and ethnic groups, with nonusers tending to be older, female, and of Sephardic descent. According to the authors' view, this persistent gap, at least to a certain extent, can be viewed as a reflection of these groups' relative position within the stratification structure of Israeli society. Similarly, a study conducted by Schradie (2011), which analyzed data from more than 41,000 American adults surveyed between 2000 and 2008 in the Pew Internet and American Life Project, found that college graduates were 1.5 times more likely than high school graduates to be bloggers, twice as likely to post photos and videos, and 3 times more likely to post an online rating or comment.

Finally, a recent decade-long study, conducted by Rideout et al. (2010) for the Kaiser Family Foundation and reported by the *New York Times* in 2012 (Richtel, 2012), identified an additional disturbing phenomenon: "Despite the educational potential of computers, the reality is that their use for education or meaningful content creation is minuscule compared to their use for pure entertainment." As access to the new media has spread, children in poorer families are spending considerably greater time than children from more well-off families on time-wasting activities (such as games, shows, social networks, etc.). The study lamented that "instead of closing the achievement gap, they're widening the time-wasting gap" (p. 353).

To conclude, our review revealed various definitions of the digital gap, ranging from a simple dichotomy between "information haves" and the "information have-nots" to the more complex and comprehensive definitions describing the unequal patterns of access to and usage of new media. Our review of the empirical evidence unveiled varied measurements of the digital divide in terms of access to and use of the new media. Earlier works identified the digital divide as the gap created between individuals, groups, and countries due to a lack of physical access to the new media infrastructure and proposed that the digital divide would diminish once the new media infrastructure was made available to all potential users. Later works, however, have shifted the focus from access to the new media to the consumer's skills in using those facilities properly, productively, and efficiently. Most empirical results suggest that there is a profound difference in usage of the new media between privileged and unprivileged groups and between developed and underdeveloped countries. Thus, the digital divides reflect the structural inequality in society, both within and between countries.

These emerging trends in the study of the digital divide relate to the propositions made by Chaffee and Metzger: It seems that their fear that the less privileged groups in society would be left behind during the information revolution has become a reality much more in terms of usage but less in terms of access. The relatively free access to new media may undermine the selective nature of mass media production, namely, the role of the gatekeepers. In the conventional media, the institutional gatekeepers could determine who and what are worthy of exposure and publicity. However, in the new media environment, it is enough for a person to have a computer, Internet access, and fundamental proficiency in language and online communication in order to produce content and proliferate it on virtual platforms and social networks. However, the revealed gaps in the usage of the new communication platforms among different social groups may even strengthen the "old" knowledge gap hypothesis by creating and solidifying information gaps across social strata. Thus, although people from a lower socioeconomic position spend much more time on new media compared to people from a high socioeconomic level, they also gain less from this use and do not utilize sophisticated tools such as online information searching (Van Deursen & Van Dijk, 2013; Zillien & Hargittai, 2009).

As to the future: Communication technologies and economic developments may significantly improve the access of unprivileged groups and developing countries to new media platforms. At the same time, the new media environment may become much more sophisticated, demanding higher levels of media literacy in order to fully utilize its potential and opportunities. Thus, Barzilai-Nahon's (2006) argument that "networks and associated technologies are not neutral artifacts but are political and social spaces in their structure as well as in their content levels" (p. 269), may lead us to predict that the new media will continue to reflect the uneven power distribution and the hierarchical social status in any given society groups and within countries. Future research, therefore, should explore how the variety levels of user's media literacy—reproduce, preserve or change the existence and extent of the socioeconomic divisions among individuals, groups, organizations and countries.

POWER SHIFTS

In our current attempt to assess Chaffee and Metzger's predictions on the impact of new media on the notion of mass communication we focus on user-focused aspects. It is important to realize, however, that the user perspective is not the only one, so we believe that there is a need to broaden this review to the media institutions and power reconfiguration perspectives. Chaffee and Metzger argued that if new communication technologies shift power from elite groups to a greater proportion of media users, and particularly if media producers and consumers do become interchangeable, then problems such as media-induced hegemony and democratic access to the media are likely to be less pressing. Furthermore, they predicted that new media will create opportunities for media audiences to challenge the status quo and define their own social reality, thereby rendering ideological control by the elite-owned media anachronistic. Yet they also noted that critical communication theory argues that the history of every technology is toward greater centralized control by groups who are already in power, and thus the Internet is no exception.

Various studies indicated that media ownership concentration is gaining momentum throughout the world even within the new media environment (Caspi, 2012; Hindman, 2009; Noam, 2009). This trend is revealed in the commercial sphere as well. A major implication of the network economy is the shift from the mass-mediated public sphere to a networked public sphere (Benkler, 2006). This shift is based on the increasing freedom that individuals have to participate in the creation and dissemination of information and knowledge and the possibilities that this participation presents for a new public sphere to emerge alongside the commercial mass media market. However, as the fast growth of the digital advertising market implicate,[4] it is easier to speak in the new media environment but harder to be heard. To be heard requires higher volume, which typically means more marketing resources and revenues. As Germano (2009) noted, advertising always played an important role as a major source of media funding, but the recent developments in the media environment mean greater competition for all media institutions, traditional as well as new, over the same volume of advertising. As a result, the advertising industry regularly interferes with the content of both traditional and new media, thus creating media bias in favor of the advertisers (Blascoa & Sobbriob, 2012; Ellman & Germano, 2009).[4] For example, Germano showed that excessive concentration of ownership can lead to substantial bias in areas sensitive to advertisers and that the numbers he obtained as thresholds for the occurrence of substantial bias in equilibrium are potentially alarming. A well-documented example is the coverage of health hazards of anthropogenic climate change (Boykoff & Boykoff, 2004; Oreskes, 2004).[5]

With regard to the assumed growing diversity: A higher number of content providers does not always translate into greater diversity, so the

---

[4] As the Pew Annual Report on American Journalism 2013 noted, the digital advertising market is growing faster than other kinds of advertising. Total digital advertising (including mobile) rose to $37.3 billion in 2012, a 17% increase. News organizations are facing continued competition from other companies for digital ad dollars. Digital advertising, across formats, continues to be dominated by five large companies: Google, Yahoo!, Facebook, Microsoft, and AOL. Within digital, mobile advertising is growing rapidly as well. Although still small, the mobile ad market grew 80% in 2012 (Pew Research, 2012).

[5] Baker (1994), Hamilton (2004), and McChesney (2004) present well-documented accounts of ongoing distortions. For example, Baker (1994) documented the statistical impact of advertising on the coverage of tobacco-related health hazards.

message's concentration does not necessarily change. According to Hindman (2009), search engines, used by the large majority of the online population, serve as powerful gatekeepers that yield a significant autonomous influence in directing traffic on the web and serve also the interests of large commercial players (see also Madsen, 2011). Furthermore, the substantial overlap between Yahoo! and Google's search results seems to reflect winner-take-all linkage patterns. According to Sunstein (2001), the diversity of communication options and range of possible choices online force consumers to filter the information they receive and enable them to immerse themselves in narrowly tailored media environments. The audience, however, will not spin off in all directions, creating endless fragmentation (Webster & Ksiazek, 2011). According to Turow (2012) the customized media environment which people inhabit today reflects "diminished" consumer power. Even though the producers of communication understand that consumers' attention is a crucial commodity in the emerging markets, with some private companies attempting to manipulate consumers and occasionally even engaging in monopolistic practices. Not only ads and discounts, but even news and entertainment are being customized by newly powerful media agencies on the basis of data that people don't know they are collecting and individualized profiles that people don't know they have. The common mass-mediated sphere is being replaced by multiple nonoverlapping spheres catering to particular class identities. Hence, Hindman (2009) suggested that those who had hoped the Internet would expand citizens' access to political information have to contend with two central facts: First, relatively little of what citizens are looking for is political. Second, much of what citizens seek is familiar. In fact, search engines help to keep the attention of the public highly centralized.

In sum, there is evidence supporting Chaffe and Metzger's suggestion that new technologies are shifting power from elite groups to a greater proportion of media users. However, this is only a partial shift. Although media producers can also act as media receivers and vice versa, they are still not interchangeable, and problems such as concentration of media, media-induced hegemony and lack of democratic access to the media still persist even in the new media environment.

CONCLUSION

More than a decade after Chaffe and Metzger first published their predictions, we may now state that although several major communication theories have not lost their relevance, they may need to be readjusted to some degree to reflect changes brought about by the patterns of flow, structure, access, and ownership of new media. Even in this new environment, the original theories reviewed here demonstrate strength and resilience accompanied by flexibility and a certain amount of adjusting. To paraphrase General Douglas MacArthur's famous saying about old soldiers not dying but simply "fading away" (in his address to Congress on April 19, 1951) we suggest that "old communication theories never die; they just readjust."

In conclusion, future attempts to examine the resilience of communication theory should broaden the scope of the theories examined. Here we focused only on several key theories, as highlighted by Chaffee and Metzger. It is our view that future efforts should be directed toward exploring the attributes of new media and their impact on certain theoretical assumptions. If we are determined to reevaluate communication theories regarding production, control, audiences, and effects, then we must also explore the relevant attributes of new media. Eveland (2003) proposed a mix-of-attribute framework for advancing theory, specifically in a quickly evolving communication environment. As Dylko and McClusky (2012) noted,

> To make the mix-of-attribute framework more operationally useful, future studies should proceed by identifying relevant new media attributes, then using quantitative content analyses to document which of these attributes exist in the medium of interest, conclude by relating these new media attribute of new media to communication theories. (p. 269)

Our review shows that although theories may change to accommodate the changes of the new media environment, researchers are still dealing with the "old" issues of power and resistance, and structure and ownership. Delineating the relationship between institutions and individuals, these issues form the bases of both structural functionalism and critical thought in social science. Given the unique role the media play in diverse social, cultural, political, and economic processes, those issues are as relevant to the new media as they were (are) for traditional media. Moreover, the persistence of these issues in the new media era highlights the fact that communication technologies change, as they always did, but they still maintain their roles as important, powerful, and influential social institution. A future challenge will be the search for the factors underlining the resilience (or lack of it) of certain traditional communication theories: What are the features or attributes that predict survival, modification, decline, or sudden death?

REFERENCES

Aikat, D. (2008). *The blending of traditional media and the Internet: Patterns of media agenda setting and web search trends before and after the September 11 attack.* Proceeding of Annual Meeting of the International Communication Association, New York, NY.

Attewell, P. (2001). The first and second digital divides. *Sociology of Education, 74,* 252–259.
Ayanso, A., Cho, D. I., & Lertwachara, K. (2010). The digital divide: Global and regional ICT leaders and followers. *Information Technology for Development, 16,* 304–319.
Baker, C. E. (1994). *Advertising and a democratic press.* Princeton, NJ: Princeton University Press.
Baker, C. E. (2007). *Why ownership matters: Media concentration and democracy.* Cambridge, UK: Cambridge University Press.
Barzilai-Nahon, K. (2006). Gaps and bits: Conceptualizing measurements for digital divide/s. *The Information Society, 22,* 269–278.
Benkler, Y. (2006). *The wealth of networks: How social production transforms markets and freedom.* New Haven, CT: Yale University Press.
Bennett, W. L., & Iyengar, S. (2008). A new era of minimal effects? The changing foundations of political communication. *Journal of Communication, 58*(4), 707–731.
Berger, L. J., & Freeman, M. D. J. (2011). The issue of relevance of agenda-setting theory to the online community. *Meta-Communicate-Chapman University Communication Studies Undergraduate Research Journal, 1*(1), 1–22.
Blascoa, A., & Sobbriob, F. (2012). Competition and commercial media bias. *Telecommunications Policy, 36,* 434–447.
Boykoff, M. T., & Boykoff, J. M. (2004). Balance as bias: Global warming and the US prestige press. *Global Environmental Change, 14,* 125–136.
Branum, J. M. (2001). *The blogging phenomenon—An overview and theoretical consideration* (Final Term Paper). Texas State University, San Marcos.
Brosius, H. B., & Weimann, G. (1996). Who sets the agenda? Agenda-setting as a two-step flow. *Communication Research, 23,* 562–581.
Campbell, V., Gibson, R., Gunter, B., & Touri, M. (2009). News blogs, mainstream news and news agendas. In S. Tunney & G. Monaghan (Eds.), *Web journalism: A new form of citizenship* (pp. 1–25). Eastbourne, UK: Sussex Academic Press.
Caspi, D. (2012). A revised look at online journalism in Israel: Entrenching the old hegemony. In D. Gideon & A. Lev-On (Eds.), *New media, politics and society in Israel* (pp. 341–363). London, UK: Routledge.
Chaffee, S. H., & Metzger, M. J. (2001). The end of mass communication? *Mass Communication and Society, 4,* 365–379.
Coleman, R., & McCombs, M. E. (2007). The young and agenda-less? Exploring age-related differences in agenda setting on the youngest generation, baby boomers and the civic generation. *Journalism & Mass Communication Quarterly, 84,* 495–508.
Coleman, R., McCombs, M. E., Shaw, D., & Weaver, D. (2009). Agenda setting. In K. Wahl-Jorgensen & T. Hanitzsch (Eds.), *The handbook of journalism studies* (pp. 147–160). New York, NY: Taylor & Francis.
Collister, S. (2008). *Network journalism or pain in the RSS? An examination of political bloggers and media agenda-setting in the UK.* Paper submitted for Politics: Web 2.0: An International Conference, Royal Holloway, University of London, England.
Cornfield, M., Carson, J., Kalis, A., & Simon, E. (2005). Buzz, blogs, and beyond: The Internet and the national discourse in the fall of 2004. *Pew Internet & American Life Project.*
Deichmann, J. I., Eshghi, A., Haughton, D., Masnghetti, M., Sayek, S., & Topi, H. (2006). Exploring breakpoints and interaction effects among predictors of the international digital divide. *Journal of Global Information Technology Management, 9*(4), 47–71.
Delwiche, A. (2005). Agenda setting, opinion leadership and the world of web logs. *First Monday, 10*(12).
DiMaggio, P., & Hargittai, E. (2001). From the 'digital divide' to 'digital inequality': Studying internet use as penetration increase. *Center for Arts and Cultural Policy Studies Working Paper.* Princeton, NJ: Princeton University.

Dolnicar, V., Vehovar, V., & Sicherl, P. (2003). *Advanced measuring of the digital divide: Multivariate interactions and digital distance* (Vol. 2004). Slovenia: University of Ljubljana.

Dutta, S., & Jain, A. (2004). *The Network Readiness Index, 2003–2004: Overview and analysis framework, 20*. World Economic Forum.

Dylko, I., & McCluskey, M. (2012). Media effects in an era of rapid technological transformation. *Communication Theory, 22*, 250–278.

Earley, S. (2009). *Agenda building in the new media age* (Class presentation). Elon University, Elon, NC.

Ellman, M., & Germano, F. (2009). What do the papers sell? A model of advertising and media bias. *The Economic Journal, 119*, 680–704.

Enoch, Y., & Soker, Z. (2006). Age, gender, ethnicity and the digital divide: University students' use of web-based instruction. *Open Learning, 21*, 99–110.

Escher, T. (2007). *Bloggers with agenda-developing a methodology to assess whether bloggers rate topics independent from media* (Project Report for "Social Research and the Internet"). Oxford, UK: Oxford Internet Institute, University of Oxford.

Eveland, W. P. (2003). A "mix of attributes" approach to the study of media effects and new communication technologies. *Journal of Communication, 53*, 395–410.

Fahmy, N. A. S. (2010). *Revealing the "agenda-cutting" through Egyptian blogs: An empirical study*. Mass Communication Department, Ain Shams University, Cairo, Egypt.

Fuchs, C. (2009). The role of income inequality in a multivariate cross-national analysis of the digital divide. *Social Science Computer Review, 27*, 41–58.

Fuchs, C., & Horak, E. (2008). Africa and the digital divide. *Telematics and Informatics, 25*, 99–116.

Germano, F. (2009). *On commercial media bias*. Available from http://ssrn.com/abstract=1374241

Gitlin, T. (1998). Public sphere or public sphericules? In J. Curran & T. Liebes (Eds.), *Media, ritual and identity* (pp. 168–175). London, UK: Routledge.

Goel, S., Hofman, J. M., & Sirer, M. I. (2012). Who does what on the web: A large-scale study of browsing behavior browsing behavior at scale. *Proceedings of the International Conference on Weblogs and Social Media*, 130–137.

Gomez-Rodriguez, M., Leskovec, J., & Krause, A. (2010). *Inferring networks of diffusion and influence*. Proceedings of the 16th ACM SIGKDD International Conference on Knowledge Discovery and Data Mining, Washington, DC.

Granka, L. (2009). *Inferring the public agenda from implicit query data*. Paper presented at SIGIR'09, Boston, MA.

Guo, L. (2012). The application of social network analysis in agenda setting research: A methodological exploration. *Journal of Broadcasting & Electronic Media, 56*, 616–631.

Hamilton, J. T. (2004). *All the news that's fit to sell*. Princeton, NJ: Princeton University Press.

Handayani, B. (2011). An examination of media convergence and its implications on mass communication notion. *Communication Spectrum, 1*(2). Available from http://journal.bakrie.ac.id/index.php/Journal_Communication_spectrum/article/view/10

Hestres, L. (2008). *The blogs of war: Online activism, agenda setting and the Iraq war*. Paper presented at the annual meeting of the ISA's 49th Annual Convention, Bridging Multiple Divides, San Francisco, CA.

Hindman, M. (2009). *The myth of digital democracy*. Princeton, NJ: Princeton University Press.

Hoffman, D., & Novak, T. (1998). Bridging the digital divide on the internet. *Science, 80*(5362), 390–391.

Hollander, B. A. (2008). Tuning out or tuning elsewhere? Partisanship, polarization, and media migration from 1998 to 2006. *Journalism & Mass Communication Quarterly, 85*(3), 23–40.

Holmes, D. (2005). "Telecommunity". In *Communication theory: Media, technology and society* (pp. 167–226). London, UK: Sage.

Husing, T., & Selhofer, H. (2004). DIDIX: A digital divide index for measuring inequality in IT diffusion. *IT & Society, 1*(7), 21–38.

IDC. (2001). *The IDC/World Times Information Society Index: The future of the information society*. Framingham, MA: IDC.

International Telecommunication Union. (2005). *Measuring digital opportunity*. Paper presented at the WSIS Thematic Meeting on Multi-Stakeholder Partnerships for Bridging the Digital Divide, Seoul, Republic of Korea.

Iyengar, S., & Hahn, K. (2009). Red media, blue media: Evidence of ideological selectivity in media use. *Journal of Communication, 59*, 19–39.

James, J. (2011). Are changes in the digital divide consistent with global equality or inequality? *The Information Society, 27*, 121–128.

Jenkins, H. (2006). *Convergence culture: Where old and new media collide*. New York, NY: New York University Press.

Jenkins, H., Purushotma, R., Clinton, K., Weigel, M., & Robison, A. (2009). *Confronting the challenges of participatory culture: Media education for the 21st century*. Chicago, IL: MacArthur Foundation.

Jeong, S. H., Cho, H., & Hwang, Y. (2012). Media literacy interventions: A meta-analytic review. *Journal of Communication, 62*, 454–472.

Jeong, Y., Kim, K. H., & Shin, W. (2008). Agenda building function of Internet searches: Measuring the unique contribution of the public agenda on the media agenda. *Proceedings of the annual meeting of the International Communication Association*. New York, NY: International Communication Association (ICA).

Katz, E., & Lazarsfeld, P. F. (1955). *Personal influence: The part played by people in the flow of mass communications*. Glencoe, IL: Free Press.

Katz, J. E., & Rice, R. (2002). *Social consequences of Internet use: Access, involvement, and interaction*. Boston, MA: MIT Press.

Kellner, D., & Share, J. (2005). Toward critical media literacy: Core concepts, debates, organizations and policy. *Discourse: Studies in the Cultural Politics of Education, 26*, 369–386.

Keniston, K. (2004). Introduction: The four digital divides. In K. Keniston & D. Kumar (Eds.), *IT experience in India* (pp. 11–36). Delhi, India: Sage.

Kosicki, G. M. (1993). Problems and opportunities in agenda-setting research. *Journal of Communication, 43*, 100–127.

Ksiazek, T. B., Malthouse, E. C., & Webster, J. G. (2010). News-seekers and avoiders: Exploring patterns across media and the relationship to civic participation. *Journal of Broadcasting & Electronic Media, 54*, 551–568.

LaRose, R., & Eastin, M. S. (2004). A social cognitive theory of Internet uses and gratifications: Toward a new model of media attendance. *Journal of Broadcasting & Electronic Media, 48*, 358–377.

Lievrouw, L., & Livingstone, S. (Eds.). (2006). *Handbook of new media: Social shaping and social consequences of ICTs*. London, UK: Sage.

Lievrouw, L., & Livingstone, S. (Eds.). (2009). *New media. Sage benchmarks in communication*. London, UK: Sage.

Livingstone, S. (2003). *The changing nature of audience: From the mass audience to the interactive media user*. London, UK: LSE research online. Retrieved from http://eprints.lse.ac.uk/417/1/Chapter_in_Valdivia_Blackwell_volume_2003.pdf

Livingstone, S. (2008). Engaging with media—A matter of literacy? *Communication, Culture & Critique, 1*, 51–62.

Lloyd, L., Kaulgud, P., & Skiena, S. (2006, March). *Newspapers vs. blogs: Who gets the scoop?* AAAI Symposium on Computational Approaches to Analyzing Weblogs (AAAI-CAAW 2006), Stanford University, Stanford, CA.

Lorimer, R. (2002). Mass communication: Some redefinitional notes. *Canadian Journal of Communication, 27*, 63–72.

Lotan, G., Graeff, E., Ananny, M., Gaffney, D., Pearce, I., & boyd, d. (2011). The revolutions were tweeted: Information flows during the 2011 Tunisian and Egyptian revolutions. *International Journal of Communication, 5*, 1375–1405.

Madsen, P. (2011, November). *Aggregating agendas: Online news aggregators as agenda setters.* Paper presented at the Public Opinion Frontiers, the 36th Annual Conference of the Midwest Association for Public Opinion Research, Chicago, IL.

Maier, S. (2010). All the news fit to post? Comparing news content on the web to newspapers, television, and radio. *Journalism & Mass Communication Quarterly, 87*, 548–562.

McChesney, R. W. (2004). *The problem of the media: U.S. communication politics in the 21st century.* New York, NY: Monthly Review Press.

McCombs, M. E. (2004). *Setting the agenda: The mass media and public opinion.* Cambridge, UK: Polity Press.

McCombs, M. E. (2005). A look at agenda-setting: Past, present and future. *Journalism Studies, 6*, 543–557.

McCombs, M. E. (2012). *Do the media tell us what to think about? The psychology of agenda setting.* Melvin L. DeFleur Distinguished Lecture, Boston University, Communication Research Center. Retrieved from http://www.bu.edu/buniverse/view/?v=1oODG410H

McCombs, M. E., & Shaw, D. L. (1972). The agenda-setting function of mass media. *Public Opinion Quarterly, 36*, 176–187.

McClellan, N. (2010). *Members of congress respond to the political blogosphere.* Thesis presented to the faculty of the Graduate School, University of Missouri, Columbia, MO.

Meraz, S. (2007). *The networked political blogosphere and mass media: Understanding how agendas are formed, framed, and transferred in the emerging new media environment.* Dissertation Abstracts International Section A: Humanities and Social Science, 68(12–A).

Meraz, S. (2009). Is there an elite hold? Traditional media to social media agenda setting influence in blog networks. *Journal of Computer-Mediated Communication, 14*, 682–707.

Meraz, S. (2011). The fight for 'how to think': Traditional media, social networks, and issue interpretation. *Journalism, 12*, 107–127.

Metzgar, E. (2007, January). *Blogsetting: Traditional media, agenda-setting & the blogosphere.* Paper presented at the annual meeting of the Southern Political Science Association, New Orleans, LA.

Metzger, M. J. (2009). The study of media effects in the era of Internet communication. In R. Nabi & M. B. Oliver (Eds.), *Handbook of media effects* (pp. 561–576). Thousand Oaks, CA: Sage.

Metzger, M. J. (2013). Broadcasting versus narrowcasting: Do mass media exist in the 21st century? In R. Zimmermann & M. Reimann (Eds.), *Oxford handbook of political communication* (pp. 125–141). Oxford, UK: Oxford University Press.

Murley, B., & Roberts, C. (2005). Biting the hand that feeds: Blogs and second-level agenda setting. In *Convergence conference.* Brigham Young University, Provo, UT.

Napoli, P. (2010). Revisiting 'mass communication' and the 'work' of the audience in the new media environment. *Media, Culture & Society, 32*, 505–516.

Napoli, P. (2011). *Audience evolution: New technologies and the transformation of media audiences.* New York, NY: Columbia University Press.

Noam, E. (2009). *Media ownership and concentration in America.* New York, NY: Oxford University Press.

Norris, P. (2001). *Digital divide. Civic engagement, information poverty, and the internet worldwide.* New York, NY: Cambridge University.

Ophir, E., Nass, C., Wagner, A. D., & Posner, M. I. (2009, September 15). Cognitive control in media multitaskers. *Proceedings of the National Academy of Sciences of the United States of America, 106*(37), 15583–15587.

Oreskes, N. (2004). Beyond the ivory tower: The scientific consensus on climate change. *Science, 306,* 1686.

PEJ—Project for Excellence in Journalism. (2010). *New media, old media: How blogs and social media agendas relate and differ from the traditional press.* Retrieved from http://www.journalism.org/sites/journalism.org/files/NMI%20Year%20in%20Review-Final.pdf

Pew Research. (2012). *Digital differences.* Retrieved from http://www.pewinternet.org/2012/04/13/digital-differences/

Pew Research. (2012). In *Changing News Landscape, Even Television is Vulnerable.* Retrieved from http://www.people-press.org/2012/09/27/in-changing-news-landscape-even-television-is-vulnerable.

Pick, J. B., & Azari, R. (2008). Global divide: Influence of socioeconomic, governmental, and accessibility factors on information technology. *Information Technology for Development, 14,* 91–115.

Potter, W. J. (2011). *Media literacy.* Thousand Oaks, CA: Sage.

Ragas, M., & Roberts, M. (2009). Agenda setting and agenda melding in an age of horizontal and vertical media: A new theoretical lens for virtual brand communities. *Journalism & Mass Communication Quarterly, 86,* 45–64.

Richtel, M. (2012, May 29). Wasting time is new divide in digital era. *The New York Times.* Retrieved from http://www.nytimes.com/

Rideout, V. J., Foehr, U. G., & Roberts, D. F. (2010). *Generation M^2: Media in the lives of 8- to 18-year-olds.* Washington, DC: Kaiser Family Foundation. Retrieved from http://www.kff.org/entmedia/upload/8010.pdf

Roberts, M., Wanta, W., & Dzwo, T. (2002). Agenda setting and issue salience online. *Communication Research, 29,* 452–465.

Rogers, E. M. (2001). The digital divide. *Convergence, 7,* 69–111.

Rostovtseva, N. (2009). *Inter-media agenda setting role of the blogosphere: A content analysis of the Reuters photo controversy coverage during the Israel-Lebanon conflict in 2006* (Unpublished thesis). University of North Carolina, Chapel Hill.

Sassi, S. (2005). Cultural differentiation or social segregation? Four approaches to the digital divide. *New Media & Society, 7,* 684–700.

Scharkow, M., & Vogelgesang, J. (2011). Measuring the public agenda using search engine queries. *International Journal of Public Opinion Research, 23,* 104–113.

Schradie, J. (2011). The digital production gap: The digital divide and Web 2.0 collide. *Poetics, 39,* 145–168.

Selwyn, N. (2004). Reconsidering political and popular understanding of the digital divide. *New Media & Society, 6,* 341–362.

Shaw, D., & McCombs, M. E. (2008). *Agenda setting in the new media landscape: Two perspectives and approaches to research.* Paper presented to the Colloquium for Philip Meyer, University of North Carolina, Chapel Hill.

Shaw, D., McCombs, M. E., Weaver, D., & Hamm, B. (1999). Individuals, groups, and agenda melding: A theory of social dissonance. *International Journal of Public Opinion Research, 11,* 2–24.

Silva, J. A. B. (2008). Interview with Maxwell McCombs. *Estudos em Comunicação.* The University of Navarra at Pamplona, Spain. Retrieved from http://www.ec.ubi.pt/ec/04/html/09-Jan_Alyne_Barbosa_e_Silva-Maxwell-McCombs.html#tthFtNtAAB

Song, I., LaRose, R., Eastin, M. S., & Lin, C. (2004). Internet gratification and Internet addiction: On the uses and abuses of new media. *Cyber Psychology & Behavior, 7*(4), 385–395.

Stafford, T. F., Stafford, M. R., & Shackle, L. L. (2004). Determining uses and gratifications for the internet. *Decision Sciences, 35*(2), 259–288.

Sundet, V. S., & Ytreberg, E. (2009). Working notions of active audiences: Further research on the active participant in convergent media Industries. *Convergence: The International Journal of Research into New Media Technologies, 15*, 383–390.

Sunstein, C. R. (2001). *Republic.com.* Princeton, NJ: Princeton University Press.

Takeshita, T. (2005). Current critical problems in agenda-setting research. *International Journal of Public Opinion Research, 18*, 275–296.

Tan, Y., & Weaver, D. H. (2012). Agenda diversity and agenda setting from 1956 to 2004. *Journalism Studies, 14*, 1–17.

Tichenor, P. J., Donohue, G., & Olien, C. (1970). Mass media flow and differential grown in knowledge. *Public Opinion Quarterly, 34*, 159–170.

Tomaszeski, M. S. (2006). *A baseline examination of political bloggers: Who they are, their views on the blogosphere and their influence in agenda-setting via the two-step flow hypothesis* (Unpublished thesis). College of Communication, Florida State University, Tallahassee, FL.

Tsatsou, P. (2011). Digital divide revisited: What is new about divides and their research. *Media, Culture & Society, 33*, 317–331.

Turow, J. (2012). *The daily you: How the new advertising industry defining your identity and your worth.* New Haven, CT: Yale University Press.

United Nations Development Program. (2001). *Human development report 2001.* New York, NY: Oxford University Press.

Van Deursen, A., & Van Dijk, J. (2010). Internet skills and the digital divide. *New Media & Society, 13*, 893–911.

Van Dijk, J., & Hacker, K. (2003). The digital divide as a complex and dynamic phenomenon. *The Information Society, 19*, 315–326.

Vehovar, V., Sicherl, P., Husing, T., & Dolnicar, V. (2006). Methodological challenges of digital divide measurements. *The Information Society, 22*, 279–290.

Wallsten, K. (2007). Agenda setting and the blogosphere: An analysis of the relationship between mainstream media and political blogs. *RPR-Review of Policy Research, 24*, 567–587.

Wallsten, K. (2011). *Beyond agenda setting: The role of political blogs as sources in newspaper coverage of government.* Paper presented at the 44th HICSS—the Annual Hawaii International Conference on System Sciences, Hawaii.

Wang, Z., & Tchernev, J. (2012). The "myth" of media multitasking: Reciprocal dynamics of media multitasking, personal needs, and gratifications. *Journal of Communication, 62*, 493–513.

Warf, B. (2012). Contemporary digital divides in the United States. *Tijdschrift voor economische en sociale geografie.* Oxford, UK: Blackwell.

Watson, B. R. (2011, June). *The agenda-setting effect of "A-List" political blogs: A time-series analysis of presidential approval ratings in 2009.* Paper presented at the Public Opinion Frontiers 36th Annual Conference of the Midwest Association for Public Opinion Research, Chicago, IL.

Webster, J., & Ksiazek, T. B. (2012). The dynamics of audience fragmentation: Public attention in an age of digital media. *Journal of Communication, 62*, 39–56.

Weeks, B., & Southwell, B. (2010). The symbiosis of new coverage and aggregate online search behavior: Obama, rumor, and presidential politics. *Mass Communication and Society, 13*, 341–360.

Weimann, G., & Brosius, H. B. (1994). Is there a two-step flow of agenda-setting? *International Journal of Public Opinion Research, 6*, 323–341.

Wellman, B., & Haythornthwaite, C. (Eds.). (2002). *The Internet in everyday life.* Oxford, UK: Blackwell.

Williams, B. A., & Delli Carpini, M. X. (2004). Monica and Bill all the time and everywhere: The collapse of gatekeeping and agenda setting in the new media environment. *American Behavioral Scientist, 47*, 1208–1230.

Willis, S., & Tranter, B. (2006). Beyond the 'digital divide': Internet diffusion and inequality in Australia. *Journal of Sociology, 42*, 43–58.

Wilson, E. J. (2006). *The information revolution and developing countries*. Cambridge, MA: MIT Press.

Wojcieszak, M. E. (2008). Mainstream critique, critical mainstream and the new media: Reconciliation of mainstream and critical approaches of media effects studies? *International Journal of Communication, 2*, 354–378.

Woodly, D. (2008). New competencies in democratic communication? Blogs, agenda setting and political participation. *Public Choice, 134*, 109–123.

Wu, S., Hofman, J. M., Mason, W. A., & Watts, D. J. (2011, May). *Who says what to whom on Twitter*. Paper presented at the 20th Annual World Wide Web Conference, ACM, Hyderabad, India.

Zillien, N., & Hargittai, E. (2009). Digital distinction: Status-specific Internet users. *Social Science Quarterly, 90*, 274–291.

Shifting Paradigms: Decentering the Discourse of Mass Communication Research

Hanno Hardt
John F. Murray Professor
School of Journalism and Mass Communication,
Department of Communication Studies,
University of Iowa and Communication Studies Department,
Faculty of Social Sciences, University of Ljubljana

This essay addresses the decentering of "mass communication research" as a discursive formation by an alternative cultural discourse that challenges its dominant ideology with a return to communication as an emancipatory practice, guided by the subjective nature of theory, the centrality of human agency, and the permanent critique of social, political, and economic conditions of communication. The challenge coincides with the influence of complex modernist and postmodernist ideas related to notions of culture, ideology, and power, and the increasing relevance of the production of meaning in the study of social formations. Its success is based on the ability to reflect on the role of intellectuals vis-á-vis the instrumental rationality of an administrative or corporate discourse and to reconceptualize the relations of media, communication, and society.

The traditional academic pursuit of communication as an essential social practice with cultural, political, and economic consequences regarding the nature and quality of participation in society has been destabilized by significant theoretical shifts, accompanied by persuasive interdisciplinary claims on the centrality of media and communication for the study of culture and society.

The production of "mass communication" as a specific social subject occurred within the discourse of the social sciences with its particular understanding of communication and the location of media in society. Its popularity produced the formation of "mass communication research" as a specific social scientific practice of generating and circulating knowledge about "mass communication."

This essay addresses the decentering of "mass communication research" as a traditional social scientific enterprise and proposes alternative visions to the spectre of "mass communication" that arise from changing ideological perspectives and the emergence of a socially conscious consideration of communication and media in society. It is a response to the need for self-reflection and for considering the creative potential of change. The latter involves a return to the idea of "communication" as the result of a shifting discourse that produces alternate forms and subjects of knowledge about the nature of communication and media.

The study of "mass communication," particularly after World War II, as an object of an evolving discursive formation (to use Michel Foucault's conceptualization) called "mass communication research," remains identified with the surge of social scientific research practices that characterize the period and dominate attempts to understand media and their effects. Based on work in sociology, social psychology, and psychology, in particular—and, therefore, associated with a traditional institutional apparatus and its disciplinary practices—"mass communication research" is characterized by a strong bias toward quantitative methods and shares the guiding principles of positivism.

Such guiding principles determine thoughts about how communication *really* works as they construct their reality of communication and, ultimately, confirm a social scientific process that promises detached, value-free, and objective observations. The result is a search for a scientifically knowable world—the lived conditions of a media environment—that is the only world that matters as a legitimate terrain of scientific exploration. Whether such a reality is perfectly or imperfectly captured, however, according to the reigning positivistic, or what has been called postpositivistic, theories of the past decades, remains part of a struggle, particularly after the 1970s, over the preservation of a dominant discursive practice that defines the reality of media and communication in terms of invasive technologies and their institutional and collective purposes (or functions). The latter typically cater to specific social, political, and economic interests and provide the context for the rise of "mass communication research" as the source of (social) knowledge and (political) power.

For instance, these interests have been institutionalized by a decisive turn from "communication" to "information" that coincided with the emergence of cybernetics and a scientific or technical explanation of its significance for society. The notion of an information society, in particular, epitomized already existing social scientific canons of context-free generalization and cause-and-effect explanation and celebrated the potential for prediction and control. Better yet, the conceptualization of an information society as a logical consequence of technological developments also removed the uncertainty or ambiguity of the older concept (communication)—problematized and applied during an earlier period of progressive thought by members of the Chicago school—and allowed for a scientific construction of social and cultural uses of media technologies. Such an understanding of communication as information arose and was reinforced through the research practices of the field (of journalism and mass communication) and provided the grounding for a instrumentalist perspective on modern communication processes that became part of the reigning ideology of "mass communication research." The increasing need for identification, definition, and explanation of information phenomena contributed to its success and legitimated its claims as a field of inquiry; it also fostered the ascendancy of the "mass communication" expert with professional ties to commercial and political interests. The resulting links between the production of knowledge and the exercise of power occurred as issues of communication became socially and politically relevant in the context of rising social problems in U.S. society that ranged from illiteracy to violence.

In fact, the presence of "mass communication research" reflected an era of certainty that appeared with the development of a sophisticated social scientific apparatus. It was the outcome of an accelerated postwar development in science and technology and complements the political-military success of the United States in world affairs. Its reliance on the reign of facts revealed an irresistible bias toward the production of tangible social and political information. For instance, the emergence of public opinion polling with its confidence in methodology and faith in prediction reflected the endless possibilities of an applied science that serves the goals of commercial and political interests. It also legitimized the ahistorical and decontextualized nature of such practices, which focus on information rather than knowledge and seek solutions in an immediate response to symptoms rather than in a delayed explanation of complex social behaviors. Such activities were reproduced prominently in the journalism and advertising of the day as manifestations of social or political events. They perpetuated a theory of society whose notions of truth and reality—with the aid of a community of "mass communication" researchers—were imminently discoverable versions of the dominant ideology.

Consequently, "mass communication" as a social phenomenon became a prominent research topic with references to social, cultural, political, and economic practices that embraced the idea of communication as information. At issue were typically questions of compliance with the pronouncements of the reigning social, economic, and political practices—and therefore control of information and information flows couched in terms of media effects—rather than issues of absence or resistance (e.g., what or who is not represented and why?) or historical change. To paraphrase Antonio Gramsci, the hegemonic struggle involves captivating, not capturing, the masses with a media environment that distracts from the real conditions of society. Thus, accessibility of media technologies and standardization of content—or what Theodor Adorno and Max

Horkheimer call the industrialization of culture—are the foundations of an information society that exists with the expenditure of a minimum of communicative efforts or competencies. Their combined effects—important for military and economic purposes during periods of external and internal competition and conflicts—constituted the tangible evidence of production and consumption practices. They provided a measure of "mass communication" in society that speaks to the distribution of power and influence.

Under these conditions, progress in "mass communication research" was the accumulation of knowledge based on perfecting prediction and control of media and information phenomena; it typically occurred under the label of administrative research—to use Paul Lazarsfeld's frequently cited conclusion about contemporary research practices—and preoccupied the "mass communication research" community while providing academic status—including calls for its legitimation as a discipline—and supporting the reproduction of an ideology of "mass communication research" through university-level teaching and research.

Even today, the attempt to understand the notion of media effects and their consequences through experimentation and manipulation (of variables), in particular, reflects a central concern of the field as it continues to relate to social, commercial, and political issues of society. It also constitutes a major preoccupation with methodological issues at the expense of theorizing communication or developing alternative models of media applications.

By the end of the 1970s, the field of "mass communication research" should have been considered a success in the context of competing forces—particularly among traditional university disciplines. However, the social scientific gaze of the observer enforced a regime of decontextualization or randomization that raises questions about the relevance of inquiries whose exclusionary nature provoked the possibility for new paradigms and encouraged critical voices from within the field. Thus, as the result of a theoretical position that produces knowledge by accretion, relies on verification of a priori hypotheses, and seeks a generalizability of its findings, "mass communication research" joined the ranks of a social science tradition whose basic belief structure had come under close scrutiny and outright critique by a growing number of alternative perspectives, even from within the tradition. After all, social scientific constructs, and the idea of "mass communication research" specifically, are still cultural inventions and as such subject to revision and change. Nevertheless, the lingering popularity of "mass communication research" as a legitimate social scientific enterprise continues to help strengthen the institutional claims of the media industry on leadership and control in society and successfully addresses the problem of source credibility while raising the expert status of the "mass communication" researcher.

However, the social and political conditions of communication in the world—beyond the parochialism of U.S. American "mass communication research"—have produced a creative and potentially useful atmosphere of critical introspection, encouraged by emancipatory movements and supported by historically conscious reconsiderations of knowledge about communication. As a discursive shift produces a new understanding of communication, it exposes a contemporary generation of "mass communication" researchers to alternative perspectives on the field by introducing them to a number of useful options to rethink the notion of communication as information. Thus, it is no accident that during the latter part of the 1980s, in particular, refocusing on the "critical" in communication had become widespread as the field looked for new ways of understanding its own history and meeting the challenges to its traditional paradigm.

Accessibility to the more recent cultural discourse in Europe—including a sustained critique of capitalism—also introduces alternative ways of thinking about communication. Its reception by a growing number of theoretically impoverished and politically disillusioned individuals whose academic experience had been confined to working within a "mass communication research" tradition provides the historical context for the adoption of Marxism—and British Cultural Studies, in particular. These new perspectives are particularly effective because they address directly the traditional concerns of U.S. American "mass communication research" related to the role and function of media in society and ranging from questions of participation to issues of democratization. Their different theoretical possibilities, however, contain the potential for a major paradigm shift in the history of the field.

Thus, the previous notion of an information society undergoes an ideological critique when communication is reintroduced as a viable, if complex, concept of human practice. In fact, the idea of communication is related again to agency and the emancipatory struggle of the individual, whereas the political considerations of communication and media encourage practical responses to concrete problems. The result is a discursive shift that provides opportunities for alternative ways of conceptualizing society, the public sphere, and the nature of democratic practice itself, based on an understanding of a historically grounded reality of institutions and practices that can be grasped, interrogated, and reconstructed through a dialectical process. It reflects a materialist–realist position and suggests the importance of material differences in terms of the conditions of communication or the place of the media at a given historical moment.

Furthermore, Marxism and Cultural Studies introduce an ideological dimension to the study of communication; they recognize the importance of power and confirm the significance of human agency for communicative practices. Both insist that the goals of their respective inquiries are the critique and transformation of specific social, political, or economic conditions for the purposes of social and political change, specifically, and emancipation, generally. Thus, they insist on the role of advocacy and are apt to embrace (social or political) activism grounded in the changing nature of historical knowledge and its potential for different explanations of a contemporary way of life.

These considerations are grounded in the belief that communication inquiry is never value-free; in fact, values help shape outcomes and constitute part of a critical theory of media and communication. Under these conditions, the acquisition of knowledge and the emancipatory goals of critical communication studies are defined by the prospects of change and reconstruction as ideas become obsolete and are overruled by new insights and practices. In fact, a critical communication theory and practice renews itself as it confronts different conditions and is propelled into different historical situations.

As a result of these external developments, "mass communication research" has been challenged to realize its supporting role in the dominant power structure and to abandon its secure ideological location. The alternatives suggest a focus on agendas that reflect the activist (and often confrontational) stance of critical communication inquiry. They are based on theoretical constructs that propose that facts cannot be separated from the domain of values, that the relationship of meaning and language to culture is central to constituting reality, that the interpretive nature of culture and communication precludes a fixed or final truth, that the relations between representation and reality are political, that thought is mediated by historically grounded power relations, and that traditional "mass communication research" practices may be oblivious to their role in the reproduction of privilege and oppression in society.

When "mass communication research" comes up against an alternative critical discourse—produced by a convergence of writings identified with the critical theory of Max Horkheimer, Theodor Adorno, Herbert Marcuse, and Erich Fromm, the later work of Jürgen Habermas, the contributions of cultural studies by Raymond Williams and Stuart Hall, and specific references to the works of Louis Althusser, Antonio Gramsci, and Michel Foucault, in particular—it faces a formidable challenge to its traditional position. Because together these writings produce a new and different type of knowledge that focuses on notions of culture, empowers the individual, and addresses the consequences of an industrialization of the mind—to use Hans-Magnus Enzensberger's phrase—to expose relations of power in the process of communication and provide a forceful critique of cultural practices.

Critical communication studies reproduce such theoretical considerations and construct research agendas that reflect the need for alternative readings of communication and media. When postmodernism arrives in the United States amidst such an ongoing critique of "mass communication research" and culture in general, it is met with ambivalence or suspicion, although its arguments help deconstruct the received notion of "mass communication." For example, the work of Jean Baudrillard, whose understanding of media and audiences, which is based on the collapse of the subject into the social and the real into simulacra—results in a radically different understanding of "mass" communication that approximates Adorno's and Horkheimer's totalizing cultural critique. Similar possibilities fascinate and preoccupy Cultural Studies, where postmodernist debates are revisited to acknowledge their substantive critical potential without surrendering control over its own transformative qualities.

Thus, a Marxist tradition open to the critical currents of postmodern social theories promises a postmodernized practice that extends the critique of culture and communication beyond deconstructing the dominant discourse of "mass communication research." Its responsibility in the context of a shifting discourse of communication and media studies is twofold: to identify contradictions and negations located in the objective narratives of empirical "mass communication research" while exposing its ideological nature, and to connect theoretical considerations of communication and media with the specifics of everyday experiences.

The first task involves the review and analysis of the discursive practices of "mass communication research" in its institutional manifestations, including the decontextualized construction of "mass communication" as a social process and the adoption of its definitions across social and political formations. Such a review reveals the discursive practices of "mass communication research" over a considerable period and suggests its limitations as a socially and politically responsive approach to an emancipatory social strategy involving communication and media.

The second task addresses a systematic, historically grounded, and politically informed examination of the nature of contemporary social communication, ranging from issues of access to the means of communication involving all groups in society to questions of domination by specific media interests—including their economic foundations—and notions of alternative systems of communication.

Most significantly, perhaps, both tasks require active participation and suggest social and political commitment to concrete involvement in emancipatory causes that lead to transformations in communication and media with the disclosure of contemporary practices, discourses, and representations of culture. Participation as advocacy of change always occurs in a specific historical and structural framework that helps shape the emerging discourse of critical communication studies.

Paradigm shifts in the context of academic work are the result of complex social, political, and cultural developments that enable ideas to rise and take hold of the imagination of individuals in their own struggle against a dominant professional ideology. The decentering of "mass communication research" occurred under such circumstances—aided by the influence of modernist and postmodernist European ideas related to notions of culture, ideology, and power and the increasing relevance of language (and the production of meaning) in the study of social formations—in addition to a rapidly shifting terrain of communication studies away from narrow conceptualizations of media and toward the inclusive category of culture. Other disciplines, like ethnography or literary studies, also have helped push considerations of communication and media beyond the traditional boundaries of "mass communication research" with creative and innovative analyses that apply a qualitative approach. The resulting practice of theory and research reflects the workings of a critical consciousness on issues related to the privileged and authoritative knowledge of "mass communication research" and contributes to a blending of the humanities and social sciences as a major intellectual project of recent years. Contemporary writings about communication and culture explore these extensions of the field and offer evidence of "mass communication research" as a blurred genre among signs of a more radical break with tradition.

It would be foolish to suggest, however, that decentering "mass communication research" has resulted in terminating universal or general claims to authoritative knowledge of communication and media, and that "mass communication research" in its institutional guise of journalism and mass communication has joined in a sustained critique of media practices or embraced a critical pedagogy for the benefit of future intellectual work. Instead, in a general atmosphere of collaboration between business and education, commercial interests in the production of facts about communication and media in the marketplace increase the political capital of "mass communication research" in the academy and elsewhere.

It is equally clear, however, that "mass communication research" has been challenged by intellectually and ideologically formidable alternatives, and that the process of demystification proceeds with the help of socially and politically conscious examinations of communicative practices and the articulation of emancipatory ideas through an expanding literature that engages the field in a critique of culture and commodification in a democratic society.

More specifically, these opportunities create a space for reshaping the research agenda of a media-centered approach to the study of culture and constructing an emancipatory learning environment for intellectual workers, including journalists, with the goal of strengthening their own professional autonomy in the context of the market-driven practices of intellectual labor.

For instance, a recovery of the history of newswork constitutes a first step in the process of recognizing newsworkers as reified objects in the discourse of commerce and industry and identifying the workplace as a site of economic interests focused on issues of production and profitability rather than public service or social significance. Understanding their position in a system of discourses that constructs the meaning of journalism and describes the boundaries of their own work, newsworkers discover the limits of their participation in the surveillance of society and their loss of control over news and the flow of information.

Likewise, a critical history of "mass communication research" that focuses on the reproduction of the dominant ideology through its production of meanings regarding notions of communication, information, or media may help provide an understanding of the ideological boundaries of academic work and provide a basis for looking at the institutional relations between social-scientific research and social, economic, and political interests in society.

Finally, critical communication studies as an institutional framework may help promote the importance of self-reflection as a first step in a process of reconstructing relations of domination by offering theoretical insights; providing interpretive, qualitative research strategies; and encouraging resistance with the goal of implementing a democratic vision of communication and media. Such a task can only succeed as a socially conscious practice, however, after critical communication studies exposes the relations of power in the production of knowledge and the dissemination of information. Challenging the instrumental rationality of an administrative or corporate discourse reconfirms its own role as an historical agent of change.

Index

Note: Page numbers in *italics* represent tables
Page numbers in **bold** represent figures
Page numbers followed by 'n' refer to notes

Abrahamson, D. 53
academic research: government commissions 103
academic study 143, 145
academics: changing work conditions 135–7
accessibility 73
activation tags 73
active audience theory 41–2, 43; low-level and variable 42–3; newer communication media 52–3
advertising market: digital 172n
Aeropagatica (Milton) 135
Africa: digital divide 169
age of print 103–4
agenda-building 76–8; four step model 77
agenda-cutting 163
agenda-melding 160
agenda-setting theory 71, 72, 73–6, 130, 160, 164, 165; framing 76–9; Internet 164; mass communication theory 149; measuring 164–5; media audience 157; model 84, **85**; process 77; research 76, **76**; salience 73; time lag 164; web access 164
agents of change 10; Arab countries 10; mainstream media 10
aggressive cues 109; males 109
Ajzen, I.: and Fishbein, M. 43
Alexander, J. 10; and Wolfsfeld, G. 12
American Psychological Association (APA): Commission on Youth and Violence 113

analysis modes 133–5
AOL Time Warner 152
Arab countries: agents of change 10
Armstrong, C.B.: and Rubin, A.M. 43
Asch experiment 9
Association for Education in Journalism (AEJ) 98
asynchroneity 49
Atkin, D.: and LaRose, R. 47
attitude accessibility 74
attribution theory 74–5; framing 74–5
audience 159; agenda 80, 86; frames 80, 86; media 147, 157–8; reception theory 153
audience behavior 51; British television 51; Internet 54
audiovisual format features: children viewers 118
Australia: television 30
Azari, R.: and Pick, J.B. 169

Ball-Rokeach, S.J. 102–117
Bassili, J.N. 74
Bauer, R.A. 143
Becker, L.: and McLeod, J.M. 40
before and after exposure model 32
behavior: audience 51, 54; human 57
Behr, R.L.: and Iyengar, S. 78, 79
Bellamy, R.V.: and Walker, J.R. 47
Berelson, B. 42
between-level dimension: framing 80
bloggers 161

INDEX

blogs 162, 163
Blumler, J.G. 40
Bogart, L. 112
Bouwman, H. 30
Branum, J.M. 161
British television: audience behavior 51
broadcast media 17; regulation 145
Bryant, J.: and Zillmann, D. 40
Buchman, D.D.: and Funk, J.B. 47

cable television: national nature 120
Campbell, V.: *et al.* 163
carrier groups: mainstream media 10
case-proving approach: social facts 107
catharsis 109–10
centralized control: media content 142
centralized mass-production: television 19
Chaffee, S.H. 91–101; and Metzger, M.J. 140–54, 156–7, 159, 160, 162, 165, 171, 173
Chamberlain, M.A. 49
Chicago Democratic Party (1968) 108
Chicago school 184
child research: empowered 121, 122
children: cultivation 23; media 118–25; media use 118; media violence 115; universal stages (Piaget) 123; uses and gratifications theory 38; viewers 118
children's television: national policy interest 120; public interest 118, 119; use of 121
Children's Television Act (US, 1990) 119, 120
Christianity 12
church: state 17
circuit switching: Internet 56
co-viewing patterns: parental 23
Cobb, R.W.: and Elder, C. 76
coding: open-ended questions 82
cognitive development research 123
cognitive effects: political communication 71–90
cognitive motivation 40
cognitive processes: rationalization 74
Cohen, B.C. 78
Collister, S. 161
Columbia University: Bureau of Applied Social Research 143
communication technologies: economic developments 171

communicative literature 48
community 92
compression algorithms: telecommunications technology 47
conseffects 40
contemporary media: information transmission 144
content analysis: Dutch television 30
contingent audience orientation 85
control: centralized 142; social paternalistic 103–5
core analytic model 84
Courtright, J.A.: and Perse, E.M. 51
Cowles, D. 54
critical analysis: postulates of science 134
critical communication studies 187
critical theory 151–2
cultivation analysis 16–35; divergences 25–9; international 29–35; methods of 22–3; survey methodology 22; television system 29; television viewing 22–3
cultivation differential: television 21
cultivation process models 24–5, **25**; cultures 24–5
cultivation theory: children 23; concept of 21; demographic variables 23n; direct experience 23–4; diversity of content 150; foreign policy 29; gravitational process 21–2; mass communication theory 150–1; parental co-viewing patterns 23; personal interaction 23; resonance 24; unidirectional flow of influence 23; variations of 23–4
cultural discourse: Europe 186
cultural environment: marketing 17; media 17; state 17
cultural indicator 18; process 16n; storytelling process 16
Cultural Indicator Project: media task force 110; television 20
cultural perspective: Marxism 134
cultural studies: Marxism 186
cultures: cultivation process models 24–5; dominant 24; values 24
curricula: media-related 128–9
Czechoslovakia: demonstrations 11

daily me idea (Negroponte) 149
data collection procedure 92

INDEX

Dearing, J.W.: and Rogers, E.M. 78
December, J. 50
decentering: mass communication 189
DeFeur, M.L. 126–39
deficit males: media violence 115
DeFleur, M.L. 2–3, 126–39
Deichmann, J.I.: *et al.* 167
deliberative democracy 6, 7, 8
deliberative polls 8
demassification 49; mass communication 144; mass messages 49; *New York Times* 49
Demers, D.P.: *et al.* 79
democracy: deliberative 6, 7, 8; discursive 55
demographic controls: pre-exposure orientations 84
demonstrations: Czechoslovakia 11; Germany 11, 12; Romania 11; stage theory 10–11
deprivation theory 42; media strike 42
Dervin, B. 57
developing countries 169
developmental research model 122
Dicken-Garcia, H. 54
differentiation models: media effects 72–3
digital advertising market 172n
digital divide 152, 157, 165–71; Africa 169; changing conceptualization 166–7; concepts 168; determinants 167; eight aspects 167; inequality 167; Internet 169
direct experience: cultivation 23–4
discourse: cultural 186
discursive democracy 55
divergences: cultivation analysis 25–9
diversity: communication 173
Dobos, J. 41, 57
doctoral programs 97n
dominant cultures: mainstreaming 24
Dominick, J.R.: and Wimmer, R.D. 37
Donnerstein, E. 113
Donohew, L.: *et al.* 47
Dunleavy, P.: and Weir, S. 55
Dunn, D.G.: and Perse, E.M. 47, 50
Dutch television: content analysis 30
Dutton, W.H. 48–9

East Germany: new media 9
Eastern Europe 9; stage theory 10

economic developments: communication technologies 171
ego concept 148
Eighmey, J.: and McCord, L. 56
Elder, C.: and Cobb, R.W. 76
electronic revolution: television 18
electronic texts 56
Eliot, T.S. 140–1
Emperor's New Clothes 9
empirical mass communication research 91
empowered child research 121, 122
enclaves: media 159
England: television 30
Enoch, Y.: and Soker, Z. 169–70
environment: mass communication 148
Erie County study: influence theory 130, 131
escapist model 51
essays 1
Europe: cultural discourse 186
events: media 152
experience: communication 57

Feshbach, N.: and Singer, R. 109–10
Fishbein, M. 43
Fishkin, J. 8
Flavell, J.H. 123
foreign policy: cultivation 29
frame-building 81
frame-setting 81
framing 71, 72–6, 80–2; agenda-setting 76–9; attribution 74–5; audience 80, 86; between-level dimension 80; media framing 80, 81; microscopic or psychological approach 75; model 84, **85**; research 80, **81**; typology 80–2; within-level dimension 80
Fry, D.L.: and McCain, T.A. 51
Fuchs, C. 166
functionalism: structural 174
Funk, J.B.: and Buchman, D.D. 47
Funkhouser, G.R. 77, 83, 84

Gallup, G.: career recognition 99; data collection procedure 92; early career 93; and Nafziger, R. 91–101; sampling method (1940s) 96–7; Vietnam War 99
Garramone, G. 51
Garrison, B. 56

INDEX

Gerbner, G. 16–35
German demonstrations 11, 12
Germano, F. 172
Germany: demonstrations 11, 12
Gerson, W. 38
global digital divide 168
government: academic research commissions 103; open-book 54
Gramsci, A. 184
gratification: media 40
gravitational process: cultivation 21–2

Ha, L.: and James, E.L. 48
Hallin, D.: and Mancini, P. 8
Hamm, B.J.: and Shaw, D.L. 149
Hardt, H. 182–90
Hawkins, R.P.: and Pingree, S. 29–30
heavy viewers: television 23, 27, 29; US programs 31
Heeter, C. 48, 52
Heider, F. 74–5
Hindman, M. 173
Horkheimer, M. 185
Huesmann, L.R. 112
Humanities Abstracts 120
humans: behavior 57; storytelling process 16
hydraulic model 110
hydraulic patterns 82
hypermedia 53
hypertext markup language (HTML) 56
hypertext technology 56
hypertextuality 56

ICT: UN infrastructure 168; usage 169
independent contribution: television viewing 21
industrial revolution 17
industrialization 142; of culture 185; storytelling process 17–18
infant cognitive ability 123
influence: unidirectional flow 23
influence theory: Erie County study 130, 131; selective and limited 129
information: cascade 11; have nots 170; haves 170
information processing: memory-based model 73–4; post-exposure orientation 86
information society 183; notion of 186; United States 127

Information Society Index 166
information transmission: contemporary media 144
Innis, H. 11
innovation theory 130
integration lack: programmatic approach 133
interactive media 54
interactivity 48–9; five dimensions 48
Internet 53, 54, 144, 147, 151–2; addiction and newer communication media 53; agenda setting 164; audience concept 54; circuit switching 56; digital divide 169; hypertextuality 56; multimedia 55; packet switching 56; talk 54; uses and gratifications theory 53–7
Introduction to Journalism Research (Nafziger and Wilkerson) 97
Islam 12
Iyengar, S. 75, 79, 81; and Behr, R.L. 78, 79; and Kinder, D.R. 80, 87

Jacobs, R. 47
James, M.L.: *et al.* 47
James, J. 169
Johnson, L.B. 105–6
Journalism Quarterly 92
judgments: and perceptions 75

Kang, J.G.: and Morgan, M. 30
Katz, E. 2, 6–15
Keniston, K. 167
Kennedy, Senator J.F.K. 106
Khomeini revolution (1979) 12
Kinder, D.R.: and Iyengar, S. 74, 80, 87
King, M.L. 105–6
Klapper, J.T. 38, 39
Korea: television 30
Kosicki, G.M.: and Pan, Z. 74

landmark researchers 1
Lang, G.E.: and Lang, K. 77
LaRose, R.: and Atkin, D. 47
Lazarfeld, P.F. 185; and Merton, R.K. 7–8
learning 148; mass communication 148; probability (violent act) 109
Legitimation of Violence, The (Ball-Rokeach) 115
Levy, M.R.: and Windahl, S. 41
lifestyle types 47

INDEX

light viewers: television 23, 29
Lin, C.A. 47
Lind, R.A. 52
Lohmann, S. 11, 12
long-run effect: media 7

McCain, T.A.: and Fry, D.L. 51
McCombs, M.F. 160, 163, 165; and Coleman, R.164; *et al.* 72, 83; and Shaw, D.L. 78, 79, 160, 161
McCord, L.: and Eighmey, J. 56
McLeod, J.M.: and Becker, L. 40; *et al.* 84, 85, 86
McQuail, D. 76
magic bullet theory 129
Maier, S. 162
mainstream media 10; agents of change 10; carrier groups 10
mainstreaming 24–5; dominant cultures 24
males: aggressive cues 109
Mancini, P.: and Hallin, D. 8
marketing: cultural environment 17
Marxism 188; cultural perspective 134; cultural studies 186
mass communication: academic study 143, 145; definition 140, 141; end of 140–54; process and effects 126–39; study 183
mass communication theory: agenda-setting 149; critical theory 1512; cultivation 150–1; end of 149–52
mass media 2, 74, 152; levels of importance 83; rise of 142; scholars 50; stage theory 11; theoretical productivity 131
mass messages: demassification 49
mass mobilization 9
mass production: centralized 19
Massey, K.B. 57
media: children 118–25; combinations 6; cultural environment 17; events 152; framing 80, 81; institutions 141; mainstream 10; mobile 3; new 8–9, 12, 144, 151, 159; planners 57; politics 8; social problem 145; of space 11; stage theory 11; systems 31; of time 11, *see also* mass media
media audience 147, 157–8; agenda-setting theory 157
media broadcasting 145; US advertisers 17

media communication: summary of differences 147, *148*; user motivation 148
media content: centralized control 142
media effect: antisocial 104; differentiation models 72–3; long-run 7; notion of 185; research 37; studies 147
media enclaves: sphercules 159
media gratification: primary social origins (Blumler) 40
media industries 50–1; labour force 128
media influences: scientific study 129
media labor force: growth of 127–8
media producers 152
media schools: programs 143; vocational skills 143
media strike: deprivation theory 42
media task force: Cultural Indicator Project 110; report findings 110; research-related activities 108–9; violence 106–8, 108–11
media theory: development 129
media use: children 118
media violence 102–17; children 115; deficit males 115; normal males 115; politics of studying 105; regulation 112–14
media-related curricula: growth of 128–9; professional programs 128; US higher learning institutions 128; World War II 128
memory tags 73
memory-based model: information processing 73–4
Mendelsohn, H. 38
Mengistu, G.: *et al.* 155–81
message system database: television 20n
messages: mass 49
Metzger, M.J.: and Chaffee, S.H. 140–54, 165, 171, 173
microscopic or psychological approach: framing 75
Minnesota Star and Tribune 97
mix-of-attribute framework 174
mobile media 3
mobilization: mass 9; stage theory 10–11
modeling theory 130
moral panic 37
Morgan, M. 27; and Kang, J.G. 30
multimedia 55
multitaskers: users 157–60

INDEX

Nafziger, R.: Association for Education in Journalism (AEJ) 98; career trajectory 97; community 92; early career 93; and Gallup, G. 91–101; golden years 98–9; *Minnesota Star and Tribune* 97; war and innovation 94–6
narcotizing dysfunction 7–8
national policy interest: children's television 120
National Television Violence Study 119–20
Negroponte, N. 149
Nelson, T.H. 48
Netherlands 30
network agenda-setting model 165
new media: characteristics 144; East Germany 9; examples 8–9; inside and outside 9; proliferation 12; resonance 151; window shopping 9
new media era: users 159
New York Times 49
newer communication media 53; active audience 52–3; hypermedia 53; Internet addiction 53; uses and gratifications theory 52–3; Web 53
Newhagen, J.: and Rafaeli, S. 55, 58
Nickelodeon 119
non-white bad guy 110
normal adults/males: violence 104
Norris, P. 166

online blogs 162
open-book government 54
open-ended questions: coding 82
opinion leaders 161
Oren, R.: *et al.* 155–81
oxymoron 141

packet switching 56
Palmgreen, P.: and Rayburn, J.D. 39–40, 43
Pan, Z.: and Kosicki, G.M. 74
parental co-viewing patterns 23
parsimony: vs precision 72–3
paternalistic social control 103–5
Payne Fund Studies 37, 129, 130–1
Pearson, D. 105, 107
perceptions: and judgments 75; of television violence 24
Perse, E.M.: and Courtright, J.A. 51; and Dunn, D.G. 47

personal interaction 23
Pew Annual Report: American Journalism (2013) 172n
Pew Internet and American Life Project 170
Pew research center 159n
Piaget, J. 123
Pick, J.B.: and Azari, R. 169
Pingree, S.: and Hawkins, R.P. 29–30
planners: media 57
Playing with Power in Movies, Television and Video Games (Kinder) 122
pluralistic ignorance 9
Pokemon 118, 124
police brutality 9
political communication: cognitive effects 71–90
political context factors 107–8
political self-designation: television viewing *28*, **28**
political views: television 27
politics 7; media 8; semantic 103; of studying media violence 105
polls: deliberative 8
Pool, I.D. 57
Pornography and Obscenity Commission 112
post-exposure orientation: information processing 86
power: individuals 162; redistribution of 145; and violence 102
pre-exposure orientations: demographic controls 84
precision: vs parsimony 72–3
predisposition: notion of 32
Price, V.: *et al.* 82
primary frameworks 75
priming 71, 72–6, 80; model 84, **85**
producers: media 152
production 183; mass 19
professional programs: media-related curricula 128
profit maximization 142
programmatic approach 132–3; lack of integration 133
programs: media schools 143
proliferation: new media 12
public 18; definition 7
public deliberation 7
public interest: children's television 118, 119

INDEX

public opinion 7
Putnam, R. 7

qualitative methodologies 57–8
qualitative research 138, 143
quantitative research 138

Rafaeli, S. 53; and Newhagen, J. 55, 58
rationalization: cognitive processes 74
Rayburn, J.D.: and Palmgreen, P. 43
reality: conceptions of 20
reciprocal effects development model 112
regulation: broadcast media 145; media violence 112–14
report findings: media task force 110
research 136–7, 183, 184, 185, 187, 188; child 121, 122; framing 84, **85**; qualitative 138, 143; quantitative 138
research-related activities: media task force 108–9
researchers: landmark 1
resonance: cultivation 24; new media 151; television 24
Rice, R.E.: and Williams, F. 56
Rideout, V.J.: *et al.* 170
ritualized viewing 42
Rogers, E. 50; and Dearing, J.W. 78
Romania 11
Rosengren, K.E. 39
Rothschild, N. 27
Rubin, A.M. 40, 41, 42, 44, 51; and Armstrong, C.B. 43
Ruggiero, T.E. 36–70

salience: agenda-setting and priming 73; individual level 79
Sandbothe, M. 56
Scheufele, D.A. 71–90
schools: media 143
Schradie, J. 170
science: postulates of 134
selective exposure pattern 159
semantic politics: violence 103
Sesame Street 121, 122
Shaw, D.L.: *et al.* 160; and Hamm, B.J. 149; and McCombs, M.F. 78, 79, 160
Sherif, M. 75
Simon, A.: and Iyengar, S. 80
Singer, R.: and Feshbach, N. 109–10
social action: violence 102

social control: paternalistic 103–5
social facts: case-proving approach 107
social movements 9; stage theory 10
Social Science Abstracts 120
social sciences: shifting agenda 132
societal problem 141–2
society: television 18–22
Soker, Z.: and Enoch, Y. 169–70
Sold Separately (Kinder and Seiter) 122
Sophisticated Poll Watchers Guide (Gallup) 97
sphercules 159
stage theory 10–11
state: church 17; cultural environment 17
storytelling process: cultural indicator 16; humans 16; industrialization 17–18
structural functionalism 174
Sundar, S.S. 53
Sunstein, C.R. 173
Surgeon General's Report (US, 1972) 112
survey methodology: cultivation analysis 22
Swanson, D.L. 44

Tarde, G. 6, 7, 8
task force: media 106–11
teaching and research essays: overview 3–4
technological developments: television 19
telecommunications technology 46–8; compression algorithms 47
Teletubbies 124
television 32; Australia 30; cable 120; centralized mass-production 19; children's 118, 119, 120, 121; comparison to other media 19; conceptions of reality 20; cultivation concept 21; cultivation differential 21; Cultural Indicators Project 20; Dutch (Netherlands) 30; dynamic process 21; electronic revolution 18; England 30; Korea 30; message system database 20n; perceptions of violence 24; political views 27; resonance 24; Soviet 31; systems 29; technological developments 19; United States 19, 29–30, 31, 119; version of world 22; violence 110

INDEX

Television and Child Development (Van Evra) 120
television viewing 24, 39–40; cultivation analysis 22–3; heavy 23, 27, 29; independent contribution 21; light 23, 29; political self-designation 27, *28*
tenure offers 137
texts: electronic 56
tiered communication system 54
traditional academic pursuit 182
traditional definitions: mass communication 141
Tranter, B.: and Willis, S. 169
Tregerman, M.M.: *et al.* 155–81
Tsatsou, P. 166
Turow, T. 152
twentieth century: theories 2

undergraduate enrolment 137
unidirectional flow of influence 23
United Nations (UN): ICT infrastructure 168
United States of America (USA): Children's Television Act (1990) 119, 120; children's TV programs 119; higher learning institutions, media-related curricula 128; home television 19; information society 127; media broadcasting advertisers 17; Motion Picture Research Council 37; Surgeon General's Report (1972) 112; television 19, 29–30, 31, 119; Violence Commission 102–17
urban riots 10
urbanization 142
user motivation: media communication 148
users: multitaskers 157–60; new media era 159
Uses and Gratifications at the Crossroads (Windahl) 40
uses and gratifications theory 36–70, 130; building 45–6; children 38; communicative literature 48; criticisms 38, 44–5; critics 39; cutting edge theory 60–1; flaws 45; human behavior 57; interactivity 48–9; Internet 53–7; mass media scholars 50; models 50; newer communication media 52–3; qualitative methodologies 57–8; research (1950–60s) 38–9; research (1970s) 39–40; research (1980–90s) 40–1; structural models 52; telecommunications technology 46–8; theoretical synopsis 58–9; twenty first century 61–2; Web 50

values: cultures 24
variables: temporal order 79
VCR 47
Vietnam War 99
viewers: children 118; heavy 23, 27, 29, 31; light 23, 29
viewing 24, 51; motivations 51; ritualized 42; television 21, 22–3, 24, 27, *28*, 29, 39–40
views: political 27
violence: different worlds 111; media 102–17; media task force 106–8, 108–11; non-white bad guy 110; normal adults 104; and power 102; semantic politics 103; social action 102; television 110; white good guy 110
Violence Commission (US) 102–17
violent act: learning probability 109
vocational skills 143

Walker, P. 137
Wanta, W.: and Wu, Y. 84–5
war and innovation 94–6
War of the Worlds (Wells) 37
Warf, B. 169
Wartella, E. 118–25
Weaver, D.H. 54; *et al.* 71
Web 50, 53; access 164; content 147
Weber, M. 102
website 147
Wei, R. 1–5
weighted media use 86
Weimann, G.: *et al.* 155–81
Weiss-Blatt, N.: *et al.* 155–81
Weir, S.: and Dunleavy, P. 54, 55
white good guy: violence 110
Williams, F.: *et al.* 49
Willis, S.: and Tranter, B. 169
Wilson, E.J. 167
Wimmer, R.D.: and Dominick, J.R. 37
Windahl, S. 40, 41, 44; and Levy, M.R. 41
window shopping: new media 9

INDEX

within-level dimension: framing 80
Wober, J.M. 30
Wolfsfeld, G. 10; and Alexander, J. 12
working conditions: academics 135–7
World Summit on Children and Television (Melbourne, 1995) 120

World War II (1939–45) 128, 129
Wu, Y.: and Wanta, W. 84–5

Young, K. 53

Zillmann, D.: and Bryant, J. 40